Great Northern Bushplanes

by Robert S. Grant

ISBN 0-88839-400-4
Copyright © 1997 Robert S. Grant

Cataloging in Publication Data
   Grant, Robert S.
   Great northern bushplanes

   Includes bibliographical references.

   ISBN 0-88839-400-4

1. Transport planes—Canada, Northern. 2. Bush flying—
Canada, Northern. 3. Bush pilots—Canada—Anecdotes. I. Title.
TL711.B88G72 1997 629.13'0971 C97-910521-8

Printed in Canada—Jasper

Editing: Colin Lamont
Production: Sharon Boglari and Nancy Miller
Cover Painting: Cher

Published simultaneously in Canada and the United States by

HANCOCK HOUSE PUBLISHERS LTD.
19313 Zero Avenue, Surrey, B.C. V4P 1M7
(604)538-1114 Fax (604) 538-2262
HANCOCK HOUSE PUBLISHERS
1431 Harrison Avenue, Blaine, WA 98230-5005
(604) 538-1114 Fax (604) 538-2262
email address: *sales@hancockhouse.com*

Contents

Dedication

To my wife, Linda, and my daughter, Rhonda, for their unbelievable patience. They transcribed, filed, edited and typed while dealing with my total absorption in a microcosm of pencils, paper, books and tapes.

Also to Hugh Whittington of the long-gone Canadian Aviation *magazine, the editor who made me work so damn hard.*

Introduction

After my first book *BUSH FLYING: The Romance of the North* went into the bookstores, I was surprised that so few people knew of the airplanes that helped open the northland. Once the decision to write about these amazing flying machines had been made, it seemed the best way to describe them would be with the words of men and women who flew and worked on them. The selection of airplanes to feature in *Great Northern Bushplanes* became the primary task. In some cases, especially with pioneering types long vanished from Canada's air trails, decisions came easily. It didn't seem to matter where I looked a Bellanca landed here, a Noorduyn Norseman carried this or a Junkers delivered that. These workhorses certainly played important parts in wilderness transportation.

The more modern types went on the list mainly because they brought back personal memories. As a pilot earning a living with several aviation companies across Canada, I recalled the pug-nosed Beavers, boxy FBA-2Cs and sleek Cessnas which carried me through highly exciting or scary times. Others, like twin-tailed Beechcraft or gull-winged Stinson SR-9s, I saw in action either during my days as an awestruck kid on a lakeside dock or in later life, when someone let me have a shot at the controls while writing for aviation magazines. Many of them, like the battered Bellancas and dimpled Fairchild Huskies, I heard described with reverence whenever veteran pilots clinked their glasses together in dimly lighted flight shacks or darkened corners of northern bars.

Some types received little or no mention, but their absence does not imply they were unimportant in Canada's transportation picture. The movement of nearly any airplane influenced the lives of Canadians in some way. Even a few minutes in flimsy Cessna or Piper trainers counted as novices took the first steps to becoming professional pilots.

While researching and interviewing, I always kept in mind that people fly and maintain airplanes. As readers explore *Great Northern Bushplanes*, I hope they understand my sincere efforts to get into the minds of these authentic Canadian heros.

Hopefully, readers will feel sweat upon their palms as shallow shorelines and high trees appear through oil-splattered windshields. Like the men and women named here, they will also experience the all-encompassing satisfaction when skill or luck allows them to fly another day.

Many people cooperated in this book and showed an abundance of patience while answering my questions, drawing upon their memories and dipping into work-stained logbooks. Too numerous to mention, every one of them contributed greatly in this attempt to honor the mechanical marvels which enabled Canada's northern pilots to explore our wilderness.

Canadian Registrations

Canadian airplane registrations may sometimes confuse the reader. Much like automobile license plates, they were initially applied in 1920 and consisted of five-letter groupings. The first affixed to a Canadian airplane used G-as a prefix followed by CA and two more letters, e.g. G-CAAA, a Curtiss JN-4. The Air Board in Ottawa also decided that military aircraft should carry letters beginning with G-CY, e.g. G-CYAA, which was an Avro 504K.

In 1928, federal authorities allotted CF- markings beginning with CF-AAA, a de Havilland DH.60 Moth. When that series became exhausted by the mid-1970s, a new block beginning with C-G came into use.

Loads and Weights

While researching and interviewing, conflicting reports and opinions of weight, airspeeds, fuel consumptions and other details kept turning up. When quoting hands-on personnel such as pilots and mechanics, their experiences sometimes contradicted each other. To illustrate performance, it was decided to table payload with full gasoline tanks. Northern air services rarely top their tanks but using the comparison provides a reasonable yardstick.

1   The First Bushplanes

Fabric Freighters and Corrugated Clunkers

On August 10, 1840, a hot air balloon ascended slowly from the center of Saint John, New Brunswick, and drifted northward. Louis Anslem Lauriat, described by the *New Brunswick Courier* as an "intrepid aeronaut," floated his *Star of the East* across the chimney tops and touched the soot-covered gas bag down 21 mi. (34 km) from the city. A self-proclaimed professor of chemistry and aerostatic exhibitions, Lauriat had reached a height of 7,200 ft. (2,160 m) and became the first person to complete a manned flight in Canada.

Lauriat also qualified as the first "pilot" who tried to earn his living with an aeronautical device in Canada. Unable to interest investors in the possibilities of air travel, the discouraged professor slipped south to Massachusetts by steamer and never returned.

Canadian aviation carried on without Lauriat and on February 23, 1909, J. A. D. McCurdy's 49 ft. (15 m) Silver Dart biplane flew from snow-covered Bras d'Or Lake at Baddeck, Nova Scotia. This event marked the first flight of a heavier-than-air machine in the British Empire.

Over the next two decades, Canadian commercial aviation became a reality through barnstorming, mail flights, newspaper delivery and other such practical uses. Having mastered survival in the air, a few hardy, ex-World War I pilots ventured into the uncharted "North" with fabric-covered, open cockpit Curtiss HS-2L flying boats, Curtiss JN-4s and Avro 504s.

Clad in fleece-lined pants, leather coats and moosehide mitts, the new aviator breed searched for forest fires and mapped vast, sparsely populated and immense tracts of wilderness. Peering through bug-splattered windshields, pilots and mechanics established patterns for flying different from aviation elsewhere. Relentlessly, they pushed their flimsy craft through smoke, turbulence and unpredictable weather, sparking legends of the Canadian genius for adaptability and resourcefulness.

Curtiss HS-2L

The Curtiss HS-2L became one of the most widely known airplanes in Canada. Flown on both Atlantic and Pacific coasts, these "water-cooled noise makers" were originally developed for submarine warfare. By the time they entered civilian service, the "H-Boats" were tired conglomerations of wood, piano wire and fabric not expected to last long as they thumped into lakes and roared away at maximum power takeoffs. In fact, federal aviation authorities tried to discourage the Ontario government from purchasing the jaded HS-2Ls in a letter to Minister of Lands & Forests James W. Lyons on January 28, 1924.

"...only fair to your department however to point out that in our opinion, the purchase of this particular type of boat at this time is of doubtful wisdom...cannot be called efficient aircraft...and are now obsolescent," wrote G. J. Desbarats, deputy minister for the Department of National Defense (DND) which monitored aviation activities.

Disregarding Desbarats' advice, officials went ahead and created the Ontario Provincial Air Service (OPAS) in 1924. The OPAS became the nation's largest civil HS-2L operator.

To the average backcountry native, prospector or trapper, the H-Boat came across as extremely impressive. Northerners were astounded at the 74 ft., 1 in. (22 m) wing span and what one writer described as a "squirrel cage" of wires between the upper and lower mainplanes. Powered by low compression twelve-cylinder

400-h.p. Liberty engines, they cruised between 60–75 mph (97–121 km/h) although one wit claimed their most noticeable airspeed was straight down.

Classed as "moody," the Liberties weighed several hundred pounds and were supported by wooden struts behind and above the pilots. Inside their thin metal jackets, they carried twelve gallons of water which sometimes spurted out to scald the crew and passengers. Ex-forestry observer James Acton Bartlett who rode the front cockpit during fire patrols in 1927, recalled that H-Boat pilots felt they could survive any accident. In an emergency, they told him, the engine would break loose, go forward over their heads and land in his cockpit—not theirs. The preflight safety briefing did nothing to put Bartlett at ease.

"I was told that when a crash was imminent, I should wait 'til the last moment, and then dive overboard into the lake into which we were presumably crashing," he said.

Comforts aloft were meager. Flight attendants did not exist and food consisted of lard, flour, bacon and oatmeal from a knapsack opened very cautiously in flight. The nearest sit-down comfort station could only be found in the vast forests below.

"A milk bottle served as a washroom and before my first flight, I was cautioned NOT to empty it in flight," Bartlett said. "It seems that the two men behind me did not wish to be anointed with urine so the bottle was dumped and rinsed after we were down on the lake."

Takeoff runs became lengthier as water soaked into mahogany hulls and increased total weight. Chewing their way slowly into the sky, the huge H-Boats barely cleared the shorelines. Pilots had no choice but to become experts in their profession. Always thrilling to watch, takeoffs seemed to last forever before an HS-2L reached the "on-the-step" or planing position. Frustrated pilots often needed assistance from whatever unfortunate soul happened to be on board. On the initial portion of the run, a mechanic or passenger stood up and jumped rhythmically in time to the airplane's movements.

For all its inherent faults, the H-Boat landed easily. On final approach, front cockpit passengers were expected to step backwards across 18 in. (46 cm) of deck and into another cockpit—all this without the benefit of grab bars, railings or rope. With extra weight now rearward, the nose came up easily before touchdown.

Forced landings became the pilots' forte. In OPAS service during a twelve-month period, thirty-three failures occurred with twelve operational Curtiss HS-2Ls and most resulted from overworked Liberties. One went down ten times, another eight, and almost all suffered the dreaded sudden silence of power losses. Instead of the legal 100 hours before compulsory overhaul, figures showed that the troublesome Liberties rarely lasted past ninety-five hours.

Curtiss HS-2Ls, which did not meet their ends on hilltops or wilderness shorelines, gradually deteriorated as mahogany, pine and spruce rotted beneath weathered, dope-covered fabric. Many logbook notations bluntly stated: "Written off through fair wear and tear."

Not until 1935 did Canada's aviation industry produce an airplane specially designed for hinterland flying. Before then, German-built Junkers, Dutch Fokkers and American Fairchilds dominated the market. Some came directly from factories with "incomparable cabin coach-work" dressed in silk roller shades and containing fully equipped lavatories. Canada's bush airline owners quickly relegated such superfluous amenities to the upper rafters of the nearest tool shed.

Junkers

One of the most practical bushplanes turned out to be a German-designed, unstreamlined low-wing monoplane assembled from corrugated metal in Dessau, Germany. The Junkers caught the public eye in March 1921 when Imperial Oil sent two 175-h.p. JL-6 versions named "Rene" and "Vic" down the MacKenzie River toward Norman Wells for the first flights into the Northwest Territories. Before long, missionaries and Natives began coming into regular contact with airplanes from civilization, covering in a few hours what previously needed weeks by canoe or dog team.

After the "Rene" and "Vic" flights, entrepreneurs and airline owners thought the Junkers would be an ideal money maker. Commercial Fisheries & Transport Ltd. of Montreal, for example, planned using an eight-passenger model powered by a 310-h.p. six-cylinder Junkers L-5 engine to haul sturgeon from lakes near Senneterre, Quebec. However, the company declared bankruptcy before its Junkers entered service.

In July, 1928, Western Canada Airways of Winnipeg ordered a Junkers W 34 or air-cooled model (W 33s were liquid cooled) from Junkers Corporation of America in New York for $19,500. With dark blue fuselage and "high visibility" yellow wings, it carried the Canadian registration CF-ABK and began freighting on May 14, 1929. Unlike other types, the cabin and cockpit stayed dry if the airplane broke through the ice; the lengthy multi-spar wings stopped the Junkers from sinking to the bottom of the lake. Docks or trees did not puncture the metal covering easily and helpers found the roomy interior easy to load.

By the time Canada's last Junkers W 34 went on display in Ottawa's National Aviation Museum on September 17, 1962, nearly 100 had been built and eleven flown in Canada, the majority with Canadian Airways, successor to Western Canada Airways.

Incredibly durable, the Junkers nevertheless suffered minor "snags," or defects. One complaint stemmed from fasteners used on engine covers and gasoline tanks. At Fort McMurray, Alberta, bush pilot Walter Gilbert landed hastily after his front side panels blew away during takeoff. Other pilots ridiculed the weak ski undercarriages. One Junkers went through ten ball-joint fitting breakages in twelve months. On April 1, 1933, Art Schade heard something snap.

"I can give no reasons for this to break but have noted on occasions that it was not a hard bump but there seems to be a certain angle just as the machine is at the point of taking off," he reported. "And if you touch the skis on a lump of snow or a little rise in the snow, it will break."

During a career from 1924 until 1932, Curtiss HS-2L C-GAOA flew a total of 2,509 hours with seven different pilots. Written off through "fair wear and tear," the Ontario Provincial Air Service (OPAS) spent $19,961.56 in overhauls and material.

Photo: Ont. Dept. of Lands & Forests

In 1932, OPAS director Roy Maxwell admitted "...molecular fatigue has evidenced itself this year..." in the Curtiss HS-2L Liberty engines. Pilot Tom Woodside recalled a 142 mi. (229 km) trip from Sudbury to Sault Ste. Marie, which took six hours and one stop. Both pilot and engineer/observer were obliged to chew wads of gum in case the water-cooled radiator needed plugging.

Photo: Ont. Dept. of Lands & Forests

First flown on Sept. 18, 1913, the British Avro 504 became a popular trainer. Believed to be with the Canadian Air Force, G-CYDA may have been one of thirty-five "N" models. A 180-h.p. Armstrong Siddeley Lynx provided an 85-mph (137 km/h) cruise on wheels and a 255 mi. (411 km) range. The first Canadian-built seaplane version flew on July 2, 1925. *Photo: Ont. Dept. of Lands & Forests*

Junkers W-34 CF-ABK, at Winnipeg, arrived in Canada in 1929 for Western Canada Airways. Ordered as a standard freight/photo machine, it had a quadrant throttle instead of the typical push-pull type. *Photo: Richardson Archives/Winnipeg*

As seaplanes, the Junkers W 33/34 line did especially well compared to the Curtiss HS-2Ls. In May, 1933, CF-ARI and CF-AMZ had their Junkers floats exchanged for Canadian-built Edo JD 7080s. At takeoff weights of 6,600 lb. (2,970 kg), these "ships" needed thirty-five seconds to get into the air and another seventy-five seconds to reach 1,000 ft. (300 m) from Lac du Bonnet, Manitoba. With 410-h.p. Pratt & Whitney Wasp, Jr. engines, they cruised at 95 mph (253 km/h) and weighed approximately 4,048 lb. (1,822 kg) without fuel, oil or pilot.

One Junkers went down in northern British Columbia near McDonnet Lake. Both wings sliced several jackpine and the left broke off after uprooting a spruce 2 1/2 ft. (0.75 m) in diameter at the butt. The right "spiked" a tree. When the Junkers slammed into the ground in a level attitude, another spruce severed the tail.

"We thought it might interest you to know what your planes can stand under such conditions," wrote a Bell-Irving Insurance Agencies representative. "The durability of the metal wings and the construction of the machine aided by the contact with the trees, undoubtedly saved the lives of the pilot, engineer and two passengers."

Most of Canada's current bush air services prohibit flight in outside air temperatures lower than -40°F (-40°C). However, their predecessors had little choice except to dedicate themselves to "getting on with the job" under appalling cold weather conditions. Sometimes, they received frightening surprises.

On January 20, 1935, Con Farrell took off from Fort McMurray, Alberta, in Junkers W 34 CF-AMZ with 650 lb. (293 kg) of freight and no passengers. Air temperatures steadied at -54°F (-48°C) and a blanket of ice fog obscured the runway to a height of twenty feet. Mechanic F. Hartley occupied the front right seat.

"After a short run, the aircraft left the ground with one wing slightly low but on attempting to level the wings, he (Farrell) stated he found the aileron control locked," wrote civil aviation district inspector H. C. Ingram. "He thereupon cut the motor and landed and almost immediately noticed Fairchild CF-ATZ standing in his path."

Farrell could not avoid the Fairchild. After the collision, a quick inspection revealed that a forgotten aileron locking pin had jammed the controls. The officious Inspector Ingram felt no sympathy for the terrified crew. He recommended that: "...both should be censured for failing to ensure that the aileron controls were not in working order."

Encouraged by profits earned by the smaller Junkers, Canadian Airways president James A. Richardson went on to purchase the largest single-engine airplane ever to fly in North America—a record which still stands. Called a Ju 52, it made an initial Canadian flight on November 28, 1931, at Montreal under the control of pilot Alex Schneider.

Nicknamed the "Flying Boxcar" by the public, the monstrous craft needed only seventeen seconds in a 25-mph (40 km/h) wind to take off fully loaded. Powered by a 685-h.p. BMW water-cooled engine, its wingspan measured slightly over 95 ft. (29 m). Registered CF-ARM, the Junkers' size and roomy cabin practically guaranteed that any bulk hauling work in Canada came to Canadian Airways.

In January 1932, mechanics placed CF-ARM on 1,200 lb. (540 kg), 16 ft. (5 m) skis. The maximum allowable gross weight at the moment of takeoff became 16,755 lb. (7,540 kg) and the empty weight totalled 9,724 lb. (4,376 kg) which left room for 7,031 lb (3,164 kg) for pilot, gasoline, survival equipment and actual payload. Average cruise speed turned out to be a leisurely 88 mph (142 km/h) One observer noted: "The machine appears to be fanning itself in." Pilots reported landing speeds between 47–60 mph (76–97 km/h).

Canadian Airways manager Victor M. Drury voiced doubts about the multi-ton Ju 52's ability to handle the north's ice-covered lakes. Until then, few airplanes larger than the W 33s or W 34s had flown in winter. However, the Boxcar soon landed on the ice regularly without breaking through but reports rolled into Winnipeg head office as kinks developed.

Almost immediately, the plywood covers on each ski proved too sensitive to landing and taxiing shocks until they were replaced with metal. Undercarriage parts snapped on hard-packed, ice-hummocked lakes. The critical junction where axle, shock struts and radius rods met became a constant headache and resulted in an accident at Cold Lake, Alberta.

"The first breakage was on the right side and occurred as soon as the aircraft commenced to move; apparently one side of the undercarriage moved ahead of the other," said superintendent of maintenance Thomas W. Siers. "The second breakage was on the left hand side and must have occurred just as the aircraft was leaving the ground, for a distinct crack was heard..."

Pilot W. J. Buchanan landed but the left side collapsed after running a short distance. Repairs were made and the Ju 52 went back to work shuttling freight from various points in Canada. On one occasion, the BMW engine shook badly and stopped but the pilot landed safely. Top level management began calling CF-ARM a "white elephant" although they admitted performance was "eminently satisfactory" whenever it could be kept operational.

In spite of the potential, the Flying Boxcar spent 297 days grounded during one year of operation. Management realized it was only a matter of time before a serious accident occurred. Up to this point, only the skills of the company's "aeropilots" and mechanics kept CF-ARM from becoming a tangled mess of twisted metal. On January 17, 1936, Winnipeg hangar crews ran up a newly installed 825-h.p. Rolls Royce Buzzard III MS engine and the Ju 52 returned to the bush after a quick test flight over the city.

Canadian Airways' original faith in the gigantic Junkers finally paid off. As the freighter began living up to expectations, the company searched for another. Unfortunately, assembly lines in Germany had switched to the three engine Ju 52/3m model and Ju 52s were no longer in production. By 1943, CF-ARM'S Buzzard engine had flown out its allotted flying hours and needed a costly major overhaul. Parts and a replacement powerplant were unavailable in wartime so CF-ARM disappeared from inventory. A final note in its history appeared in a Winnipeg newspaper which stated: "Veteran Plane Scrapped."

Fairchild

In 1923, American Sherman M. Fairchild founded the Fairchild Aerial Surveys (of Canada) Ltd. in response to requests from the Laurentide Paper Company for photographic surveys in Quebec. In spite of severe cold, Fairchild's pilots used several open cockpit biplanes including a Standard J-1. These bone-chilling flights marked the first time a Canadian air service had worked year round.

While watching chief pilot Kenneth F. Saunders fly a rare ski-equipped type called a Huff-Daland Petrel, Sherman Fairchild noticed how terribly his pilots suffered from the cold. Concerned, he decided to build a more practical high-wing, strut-braced monoplane with a heated cabin. The first production order came on November 15, 1926, and before long, the "Fairchild Cabin" or FC series proved itself. Late aviation historian Kenneth M. Molson wrote that the Fairchilds played a leading role in opening the northland from the standpoint of numbers and longevity.

The Fairchilds were smaller and lighter than the summer-only Curtiss HS-2Ls. More interesting from a potential buyer's point of view, one pilot could do the job and the FC-2 cruised 10 mph (16 km/h) faster. This design resulted in drastic shifts in the thinking of northern operators. By 1932, no more unwieldy H-Boats flew in Canada.

Although the Fairchild line improved through customer demand, not everyone could be satisfied. When Western Canada Airways purchased Fokkers instead of Fairchild FC-2s, Saunders was quite perturbed since he had been corresponding steadily with the company and expected sales. He asked for an explanation of February 23, 1928.

"When drifts occurred, the Fairchild undercarriage would not stand up to the bumping. The Fairchild does not load as easily nor trim as easily as the Fokker," came the reply. "The majority of our pilots prefer to be outside rather than inside of the cabin as is the case with the Fairchild. It seems to be the view of our boys that taken all in all the Fokker is a more rugged machine for our work."

Believed to be the last Junkers W-34 to enter Canada, CF-ATF flew with four Canadian air services until delivery to Ottawa's National Aviation Museum on September 17, 1962.   *Photo: Western Canada Aviation Museum*

Delivery of Dessau-built Ju 52 CF-ARM took place in November, 1931, at Montreal. On the initial Canadian flight, Alex Schneider needed seventeen seconds in a 25-mph (40 km/h) wind to take off on wheels with a 7,490 lb. (3,371 kg) disposable load. Soon, CF-ARM was converted to skis and began moving Hudson's Bay Company freight for Canadian Airways.   *Photo: Richardson Archives\Winnipeg*

The Fairchild FC-2 came with folding wings for easier storage. Powered by a Wright J-5 Whirlwind engine, G-CAIU flew with Prospector's Airways in Haileybury, Ontario, on May 5, 1928, and remained with the company until 1936.

Photo: Ont. Dept. of Lands & Forests

The first project undertaken by Fairchild's Canadian division was the Fairchild 71C. Besides a combined window-emergency ceiling exit, 71Cs like CF-OAP at Sault Ste. Marie had improved cabin heating, seats and slightly redesigned engine cowling. Only eleven were built until production ceased in 1935.

Photo: Ontario Bushplane Heritage

One customer who seemed interested in the "Seventy-One" (basically an enlarged FC-2) was the OPAS. Fairchild's Farmingdale, N.Y. head office despatched a 71B to Sault Ste. Marie for demonstrations. OPAS director Roy Maxwell stood by patiently with a stopwatch and noted the "undeniably very slow" cruising and top speeds. However, the possibilities as an aerial photography platform caught his attention.

"Its climb to the necessary photographic ceiling was as desired...I might add that I would have no hesitancy whatsoever in recommending that the Department make purchase of a machine of this type," Maxwell wrote to the manufacturer on October 28, 1930.

Almost immediately, Fairchild Aircraft assistant secretary-treasurer R. B. Irvine compiled a price list. A rebuilt model with only 325 hours flying on the airframe listed at $15,000. With yellow wings and blue fuselage, it had an electric hand inertia starter and metal-clad interior. The sale nearly fell through when federal-provincial spending was drastically cut, leaving practically nothing for new equipment, replacements or repairs.

After lengthy negotiations, a pay-as-you-fly hourly arrangement worked well for both sides. On June 17, 1932, bush pilot Romeo Vachon delivered a Canadian-built Fairchild 71C registered CF-ATB to Sault Ste. Marie from Longueuil near Montreal. Maxwell changed the lettering to CF-OAM, in accordance with OPAS policy of requesting CF-O blocks from the DND for provincially-owned airplanes. Soon, another 71C was delivered as a demonstrator by Fairchild vice-president Ernest Robinson and general manager Hubert Pasmore.

Both 71s arrived in Sault Ste. Marie with Fairchild-built seaplane floats. The OPAS switched to Canadian-made Edo flotation gear because of a standardization policy for its immense fleet of de Havilland Moths, Hamiltons and other bushplanes. The streamlining and lighter weight added further dimensions to performance.

"The floats have more buoyancy, thus lifting the craft higher from the water. The propeller does not thrash so much in a swell.

The undercarriage is more rigid," said pilot Fred Dawson at Port Arthur. "The bow struts do not weave which, with the previous undercarriage, always gave the pilot some concern in high seas. The aircraft has a tendency to leave the water and does not require the amount of pull on the controls to get her off as with previous gear."

While the OPAS operated Fairchilds nearly troublefree, Canadian Airways' pilots experienced several alarming engine stoppages. A 71 registered CF-AAX crashed near Greenville, Maine, on a mail run from Saint John, N.B., to Montreal.

The report stated that pilots preferred draining gasoline tanks until the engine coughed before switching over. However, the 71 developed an unnerving tendency to stop when they retarded the throttle. In CF-AAX's case, it spluttered and would not regain power, forcing the aircraft into trees less than 2 mi. (3.2 km) from a Canadian Pacific Railway line.

This was the fourth stoppage in Canadian Airways' Fairchilds. A complete dismantling of the carburetor at Pratt & Whitney's Longueuil plant ruled out sediments or water in the fuel system. Eventually, mechanics concluded that the failures occurred because of air locks in the gasoline lines. To prevent further problems, operating manager A. F. Ingram ordered pilots not to drain tanks before switching to a full one.

Other types of forced landings continued. An overworked cabin heater caught fire and created some excitement in a Fairchild FC-2W2 flying from Moisie near Sept Iles on September 10, 1932. With 1000 lb. (450 kg) of freight and passengers, E. Morris landed safely in spite of flame and smoke, and patched the fabric. Still, his customers were not satisfied. Jean Levesque demanded and received compensation for goods burned including 5 lb. (2.3 kg) of pepper, 3 lb. (1.4 kg) wool yarn, yeast cakes, "one *tabliette papier a ecrire* (writing pad) and six *mouchoirs* (handkerchiefs)."

Aviation historians point out that more air freighting took place in Canada during the 1930s than the rest of the world. Air transport's future looked so promising, Fairchild decided to investigate the development of larger bushplanes.

In the early summer of 1935, test pilot Alex Schneider flew the first Fairchild 82. Powered by a 550-h.p. Pratt & Whitney engine and heavier than predecessor Fairchild 71s, it used the same wing structure. The company introduced side-by-side cockpit seating and received approval for a gross weight of 6,325 lb. (2,846 kg). Besides a 170 lb. (77 kg) pilot, 80 lb. (36 kg) of oil and 100 gal. (455 l) of fuel, the seaplane version carried a 1,465 lb. (659 kg) revenue load for 490 mi. (789 km). Some pilots wrested even better performance:

"I have taken off 1,700 lb. (765 kg) and wing tanks on a very hot muggy day with ease in twenty seconds," testified a Prospectors' Airways pilot at Senneterre, Quebec, in August 1935. "It lands well with full load as you claim at 50 mph (81 km/h) and if it has any bad habits aerodynamically, I have yet to find them."

Fairchild's 82s had several features devised solely for bush flying. Large 42 in. x 39 in. (107 cm x 99 cm) doors allowed bulkier items into the 180 cu. ft. (5.4 m^3) cargo space. A sliding roof hatch above the "control compartment," i.e., cockpit, allowed quick access to the wing for refueling and served as an escape exit. Special belly fittings held a canoe and wings folded for easier storage. A July 1, 1936, list quoted a special price of $20,294 for a wheeled model with a rebuilt engine.

The Fairchild 82 carried dynamite, ball bearings, lime sacks, canoes or anything that fit or could be made to fit inside or outside. Charles R. Robinson, who began his flying career in 1928, remembered the airplane as his favorite. It carried up to eleven people and cruised at 115 mph (185 km/h) with the overheating engine located no more than 12 in. (30 cm) from the pilot's feet. Working with the 82 demanded special techniques.

"We couldn't drop the flaps, of course, because we didn't have any. The thing to do would be to lift one float out of the water and that worked pretty good," Robinson said. "There wasn't much windshield but we had a good side view, not like today's (de Havilland) Otter which is pretty blind. Some guys detested the thing but I thought the 82 was a mighty good airplane."

Distances between outposts, nursing stations and hospitals often necessitated long mercy flights. During a freight run in 1938, Robinson "bucked" snowstorms for ninety minutes with his Starratt Airways & Transportation Ltd. Fairchild 82 CF-AXG from Hudson, Ontario, to the mining community of Pickle Lake. Grounded by the weather for his return flight, he drained his engine oil for the night and checked into the Pickle Lake Hotel.

Just as Robinson settled into his room, a medical nurse wanted to transfer an emergency stretcher case to Sioux Lookout, a distance of 102 mi. (164 km). He returned to the frozen lake, replaced the oil and rewarmed the engine as a truck arrived beside the idling Fairchild 82. A bulkhead between his seat and the freight compartment had been installed to prevent hay, lime and other debris from drifting into the cockpit during bumpy weather. Unable to see behind him, Robinson waited patiently, his engine ticking over as unseen attendants loaded the patient and, he presumed, a nurse.

"It's pretty crummy outside with snow blowing to beat the band when somebody opens my door and tells me to go," he said. "So I went. It was getting dark and I was down to a couple hundred feet and a couple times, it looked like I'd have to land.

"I lined up a few times when I thought I spotted a trapper's cabin or an Indian settlement but didn't know for sure where I was so went south when I suddenly smelled coal smoke and there was a bloody train going underneath me. We got to Sioux Lookout and I stayed in the cockpit while they took the stretcher out."

Later, still shaking from his close brush with what aviation historian Frank Ellis described as the "great white wilderness," Robinson walked to nearby Clarke's Cafe. As he tried to calm himself, a Starratt Airways agent announced that his stretcher case had given birth to twins.

"I said: 'Who had twins?' He said: 'The woman.' I said: 'What woman?' He said: 'The woman you brought in from Pickle.' And I said: 'Good God, what about the nurse?' And he said: 'There was no nurse.' The woman had been by herself. I thought it was some guy who'd fallen down a mineshaft."

The Fairchild Aircraft Co. solicited testimonials for potential customers. Starratt Airways & Transportation Ltd. of Hudson, Ontario, which owned several Fairchild 82As, wrote: "I must admit frankly that the machine has a most satisfactory performance as a seaplane. If the succeeding machines have equal performance less the petty maintenance troubles that we have had to contend with in our machine, there is every chance that they will be real revenue makers."

Photo: Charles R. Robinson

Fokker Super Universals like G-CASK at Labine Camp, Echo Bay, Northwest Territories, depended on a hand crank near the left side windscreen for starting. The pilot or mechanic could reach it through an opened hatch. Fifteen Canadian Vickers-built "Supers" and thirteen U.S. models carried Canadian registrations.

Photo: Manitoba Archives/Winnipeg

Originally flown by the Royal Canadian Air Force, Bellanca CH-300 Pacemaker CF-BFB was said to have structural strength 12 percent more than U.S. Department of Commerce requirements. With "incomparable cabin coach-work," large baggage compartment, wide opening doors, and two-spar wood wings, the type fitted well into Canadian bush flying. This one lasted until 1938 after striking a ditch at Sophie Lake, Saskatchewan. *Photo: Manitoba Archives/Winnipeg*

No nails were used in the Bellanca CH-300 Pacemaker's two-spar wood wings; only glue. The gasoline tanks were of welded aluminum and covered by birch plywood. The 300-h.p. Wright Whirlwind could be started with a hand inertia device in the cockpit. *Photo: J. M. Park/Chapleau, Ont.*

The Fairchild 82's welded steel tube, fabric-covered fuselage and wood wing construction built around spruce box spars and ribs was considered a strong design. Although the basic uncovered airframe appeared flimsy, its strength and shock absorbing qualities saved many pilots. Robinson learned how well his favorite 82 provided protection for those who rode inside.

Starratt Airways' Fairchilds routinely carried up to five drums of fuel oil from Gold Pines, 53 mi. (85 km) northwest, to the Jackson-Manion Gold Mine and returned with empties. The round trip usually took an hour and twenty-five minutes. On one occasion, mine officials asked Robinson to take back a 500 lb. (225 kg) electric motor. When no one arrived with his load, he left with an empty freight compartment hoping to reach home before darkness. Passing over the lake's shoreline, his engine quit.

As Robinson glided over the mine manager's house, a woman shaking a rug saw the silent red and yellow Fairchild. Seconds later, Robinson plunged nose down into a stand of mixed poplar and jackpine trees. Emerging with only a few scratches from the shattered freighter, he sat on a stump.

"Finally, I heard someone coming through the bush and here's this woman that I'd seen shaking the mat on her back step. She didn't see me, so I says 'hello' and she fainted," Robinson said. "And two guys I'd seen working on the roof of a mine building came and saw her lying in the leaves, so they put her on the stretcher, took off and left me sitting there."

The Fairchild 82 was appreciated for more than economics and solid structure. Tall aircrew with the British Yukon Navigation Company of Vancouver liked the spacious cockpit and control arrangement.

"Pilot advises that there are no inconveniences in flying from the left-hand side. In fact, he finds it to advantage to sit in the middle straddling the stick, and as he is tall enough to do so conveniently, he uses the two outside (rudder) pedals—the pilot's left and the copilot's right," said a testimonial letter on January 16, 1936.

Fokker

The 82s often performed in company with another line of airplanes similar in size and layout. Dutch-born Anthony H. G. Fokker founded a branch of his European company in 1924 at Hasbrouck Heights, New Jersey, 6 mi. (10 km) from New York City. One of his first Canadian sales was the open-cockpit, 200-h.p. Wright Whirlwind-powered Standard Universal with a 2,110 lb. (950 kg) empty weight which carried a 1,200 lb. (540 kg) payload with full 78 gal. (355 l) fuel tanks.

Passengers in this strut-braced monoplane rode comfortably in an enclosed cabin. A 1928 sales specifications sheet claimed a 98 mph cruise, a $14,200 minimum price and the pitch that it needed only forty minutes to climb to 10,000 ft. (3,000 m)—useless information since bush pilots rarely flew so high. On snow or water, the Standard Universals performed satisfactorily in adventures like the 1929 Hudson Strait Expedition from Wakeham Bay in northern Quebec or the world's first major Arctic airlift from Cache Lake, Manitoba, to Churchill on Hudson Bay. One pilot who logged hundreds of hours on type found the seaplane version exceptionally underfloated. Taxiing downwind on breezy days had to be done carefully and slowly or the airplane dipped its brass-tipped wooden propeller into the water.

The later 410-h.p. Pratt & Whitney Wasp Fokker Super Universals acquired reputations for increased speed and stability. This six-passenger seaplane weighed 2,750 lb. (1,238 kg), had 48 more cu. ft. (1.44 m^3) of cargo space and carried a payload 28 mph (45 km/h) faster than the lighter Standard Universal. The American parent company produced eighty and, of these, Canadian air services imported thirteen. In 1929, Canadian Vickers in Montreal built another fifteen. They sold for $19,340 at a time when a Chrysler-built Plymouth Roadster with rumble seat cost $860, and butter sold for forty cents a pound in northern Ontario.

Like the Fairchild 82, fabric-covered steel tubing trusses made up the Fokker fuselage and tail section. The main differences could be seen in the enormous strut-free, one-piece 50 ft., 7 in. (15 m) wing. Covered with birch sheeting, repairs became extremely time-consuming and in storage, the three-ply veneers turned to useless organic matter.

Fokker customers acquired many extras in the factory price, salesmen quickly pointed out. These included safety belts for the pilot and one propeller. Luxuries like toilet accessories or electrical wiring in the wing were optional. The Super and the Standard cockpit featured "non-magnetic controls."

"We were proud to fly them. We started off in a little Gipsy Moth, then moved into Fox Moths and then, by God, they gave us this great big Fokker," recalled Douglas Cameron who flew the type in Manitoba and Ontario. "To me, it was quite a thrill, even if most of our work was hauling oats and hay for horses in the mines."

Bellanca

Pilots expected reliability and ruggedness; they also had an eye for proper curves and streamlining. For this reason, they enjoyed the distinctive appearance of the Bellanca series with airfoil-shaped lift-struts which improved aerodynamic efficiency and lessened drag. Produced for the "discriminating" by Bellanca Aircraft Corporation of New Castle, Delaware, they were simple, economical and presented an attractive picture to bush airlines.

The first "airplane with a pedigree" came to Canada in May, 1929, and Montreal-based Canadian Vickers assembled several under license. When the last one went out of service in 1944, at least seventeen had carried Canadian registration. The 300-h.p. Wright Whirlwind Pacemaker version climbed at 650 ft. (195 m) per min. with a 4,800 lb. (2,160 kg) total weight. As a seaplane, it cruised at 110 mph (177 km/h) with two-thirds throttle for 770 mi. (1,240 km).

"Equipped with twin metal floats, the Pacemaker seaplane has been found to be free from the feeling of loginess usually associated with pontoon-equipped ships," said a Bellanca sales brochure. "Its performance and maneuverability on floats have been the delight of all pilots who have flown the ship so equipped."

Bellancas and their pilots became well known. The public began expecting airmail as their natural right and bush organizations showed themselves happy to comply. Commercial Airways of Edmonton used three ski-equipped Bellanca CH-300 Pacemakers and a Lockheed Vega to open the Slave River-Mackenzie River mail route between Fort McMurray, Alberta, and Aklavik, Northwest Territories. On December 10, 1929, one of Canada's most publicized flights began when W. R. May and Idris Glyn-Roberts left "the Fort" and tracked "down north" to Aklavik with a pair of mail-stuffed Bellancas.

This trip marked the first Canadian airmail contract beyond the Arctic Circle. Despite air temperatures as low as -60°F (-51°C), the Pacemakers functioned perfectly along the mighty MacKenzie's naked cliffs and muddy banks. Later, seaplane versions proved their worth by overflying the Beaufort Sea to Herschel Island on the Alaska/Canada border. May went on with Bellancas to Great Bear Lake and later became one of the first white men to penetrate the legendary Headless Valley of the Yukon.

Canadian Airways, Canada's largest seaplane operator, also believed in Bellancas and compared the 420-h.p. Junkers with the 330-h.p. Bellanca. In nearly all respects, the high wing Bellanca seaplane stood out as a far better buy. Hourly fuel consumption averaged 13 gal. (59 l) less with a 19 mph (31 km/h) increase in cruising speed, in spite of the Junkers W 33/34's smaller cabin.

Canadian Airways liked the Bellanca line enough to bid on four Pacemakers declared surplus by the Royal Canadian Air Force (RCAF). District superintendent Romeo Vachon discovered they needed complete refabrication and paint but luckily, he found no rust in the fuselage tubing. The lot sold for $16,400 in March, 1937, and after costly rebuilding, the ex-RCAF Bellancas turned out to be excellent buys considering that, normally, such "...a machine would be in the neighborhood of $20,000 to $25,000."

Bellanca 31-55 Senior Skyrocket CF-DCH, first flown on skis at Edmonton on February 28, 1946, had shorter ailerons than American models. The wings had Port Oxford cedar spars with plywood and spruce ribs. The struts were assembled from metal spars and ribs, and were fabric-covered. Side and rear bush seats were factory options. *Photo: Western Canada Aviation Museum/Winnipeg*

The gigantic 13-passenger Bellanca Aircruiser had a 65 ft. (20 m) wing span. Pilot Harry Swanson, Sioux Lookout, Ontario, remembered that the "Flying W"—so called because of its unusual wing struts—had to be landed carefully on both floats. "If you landed on one, you'd never hold it because it'd swing in a huge circle," he said. Wheel/skis were produced by the Alberta Boat Company and carried approval for 11,700 lb. (5,265 kg). *Photo: National Aviation Museum*

In civilian colors, the Bellancas hauled fish and cost Canadian Airways only thirty-three cents per mile instead of the Fokker Super Universals' forty cents per mile with similar loads. Bellancas occasionally flew the company's international air route between Pembina, North Dakota, and Winnipeg. Others specialized in the same high-altitude photo work they excelled at in the RCAF.

On Canada's eastern side, exploration companies, dogged by short seasons and total isolation, demanded reliable airplanes. Two Bellancas of Newfoundland Skyways explored Labrador's rugged interior. Camps at Lake Ashuanipi, 200 mi. (322 km) north of present day Sept Isles, Quebec, and North West River, 114 mi. (184 km) inland from Cartwright, Labrador, served as operational bases.

"The Bellancas cruised at 105 mph (169 km/h) and with maximum fuel load would have a payload of 1,000 lb. (450 kg) and an endurance of four hours. About fifty percent of our flights were for the purpose of transporting fuel and oil and laying down caches in the bush," said chief pilot Tim Sims in Larry Milberry's *Aviation in Canada.* "Canoes, sometimes two at a time, were tied to the floats. In this condition, the takeoff distance was not greatly affected but the rate of climb was drastically reduced."

After World War II, it became clear that new bushplanes would be needed to carry on in remote regions. Authorities in New Castle granted rights to Northwest Industries in Edmonton to build the Bellanca 31-55 Senior Skyrocket. Designed to fill a vacuum left by the war years in the equipment of northern operators, it used a 550-h.p. Pratt & Whitney Wasp engine for power. Stanley R. McMillan made the first flight on February 28, 1946, in ski-equipped CF-DCH.

Unlike Pacemakers, Skyrockets came equipped with flaps and removable bush seats. Almost immediately, pilots discovered that lowering wing flaps damaged the doors when unloading. As a result, most models had their flaps locked up. Salesmen, including Northwest's president Leigh Brintnell, pushed their product whenever and wherever they could.

"I would like to tell you that I am not making Bellancas from a sales standpoint but because of my own operating experience," he wrote to OPAS director George E. Ponsford who had succeeded Maxwell in 1935. "I am firmly convinced that the Skyrockets are the best bush airplane of its kind and that I can make a contribution to the development of northern Canada.

"The price of the Skyrocket, subject to approval by the Director of Aircraft is $31,000 FOB from Edmonton on wheels less engine. The engines for these planes will probably average about $3,000 each."

The OPAS did not consider Brintnell's proposal nor did the Bellanca Skyrocket live up to factory expectations. Only 13 Canadian versions were built when production ceased in 1949. Serious competition came from hundreds of surplus Noorduyn Norsemen dumped on the market by the RCAF and USAAF. Air services also rushed to modify small, twin-engine ex-trainers such as Avro Ansons and Cessna T-50 Cranes into fish freighters or passenger transports.

Although similar to Norsemen in terms of performance, built-in disadvantages made the factory-fresh Senior Skyrockets unpopular. The cockpit lacked doors and consequently, pilots crawled through the rear side entrance over freight and passengers—not easy for seaplanes on windy days. The 152 imp. gal. (692 l) in the wings gave excellent range but the huge tanks lacked baffles to prevent gasoline sloshing. In a banked attitude, the engine sometimes stopped; quite disconcerting while sideslipping between needle-sharp jackpine into narrow bays.

"Important, particularly in turns, avoid side slips and skids to the left when the left-hand fuel tank is being used," read a placard near the pilot's seat. "Avoid side slips and skids to the right when the right hand fuel tank is being used."

If anyone overlooked these helpful hints, the engine "spit and quit," said pilot Don McClellan, who flew CF-DCH for Ontario-based Mattagami Skyways during the early 1960s. He remembered, too, that the Skyrocket's float attachments were so far forward, it porpoised easily on takeoff. Another pilot spluttered that "...flying a Skyrocket was like flying your own coffin."

Conclusion

Like the Skyrockets, most wilderness airplanes developed quirks. Some gained reputations for shedding wings in flight. Another became nose heavy with passengers placed near the front. One notorious breed suffered abrupt high speed "stalls" or loss of wing lift without warning. The usually stable Junkers Ju 52 sometimes swung out of control on takeoff unless both pilot and mechanic jumped on the rudder pedals.

In spite of these peculiarities and well-publicized incidents and accidents, the traveling public accepted bushplanes. Movement of any kind of goods or passengers became routine as pilots and mechanics improvised patience, poles and tin snips to stay aloft.

2   Noorduyn Norseman

Nobody Stays Clean

Behind the pilot, several parka-clad Cree Indian trappers and their families winced at the overpowering engine noise as he slowly eased the throttle forward. The Noorduyn Norseman bushplane did not move; its wooden skis were frozen solidly to the snow-covered lake surface. Wilfred Wright of Pikangikum Air Services in northern Ontario pulled the red fuel-mixture knob backwards and stopped the engine.

Wright stepped outside into subzero cold and rocked the wing struts to loosen the ice's grip. Throwing the well-chewed, stub of his cigarette into the snow, he climbed back into the airplane and restarted the 600-h.p. engine.

Finally, the Norseman slid noisily across the ice. It bored on, shaking and slamming from drift to drift as frozen beaver carcasses rattled along the airplane's plywood floor toward the tail. As jackpine and spruce became colorless blurs on each side of the oil-streaked windshield panels, Wright yanked the control wheel back and the heavily loaded craft labored over a conifer-covered shoreline.

An hour later, Wright circled Namiwan Lake, a winter-locked pond 12 mi. (19 km) east of the Ontario/Manitoba border, and landed to unload. After the ice melted from the lake, he would return with the Norseman mounted on aluminum floats to carry furs south to civilization. At the moment, underlying slush and deep snow held him prisoner once again. After slamming controls from side to side with the engine shattering the stillness, Wright eventually managed to struggle airborne.

Few airplanes can absorb such brutal punishment and fewer still have contributed as much to developing Canada's north as the Noorduyn Norseman. Conceived in the mind of Dutch-born Robert Bernard Cornelis Noorduyn, the "Wooden Wonder," as some pilots called the pug-nosed freighter, made a first flight on November 14, 1935. Test pilot W. J. McDonough took off from the St. Lawrence River in twenty-three seconds and landed twenty minutes later.

"One is able to say with confidence that the Noorduyn Norseman Convertible Seaplane represents a distinct advance in aircraft construction," reported McDonough.

Later, RCAF pilot Sq. Ldr. John Henry Tudhope flew the prototype on skis at Rockcliffe Aerodrome near Ottawa. He, too, wrote favorably of the only Canadian airplane designed expressly for bush flying and concluded by saying: "...the aircraft does not appear to have any undesirable characteristics."

Assigned registration CF-AYO, the first Norseman went almost immediately to a Rouyn, Quebec, bush airline called Dominion Skyways Ltd. The new owners quickly learned that the 420-h.p. Wright Whirlwind engine was underpowered. Carrying core boxes, lumber or other materials needed by exploration parties, road-building crews and freighting companies proved far more difficult than test flights with empty airplanes.

Noorduyn had warned his customers. During the design phase, he suggested the more powerful Pratt & Whitney engine but the heavier powerplant needed a higher grade of fuel. Operators were already inclined to the Wright and its use of lower grade 80 octane and stocked their warehouses accordingly.

Noorduyn, after discussions with Dominion Skyways president Peter Troup, carried out several modifications to CF-AYO at spring break-up. Noorduyn decided to upgrade later Norsemen to the 550–600-h.p. Pratt & Whitney R-1340 Wasp. Flown on November 5, 1936, the updated model proved popular. In calm air without head winds to add extra lift, a fully loaded "Mark IV" could take off from a lake in twenty-two seconds.

Earlier Mark II and Mark III production and test versions took four seconds longer. To a pilot faced with the euphoric realization that he has suddenly run out of space and faces a granite cliff, these few seconds represented a considerable improvement.

Initially offered at a base price of $23,500, the Noorduyn Norseman was gradually accepted by the bush flying community. As civil airlines placed orders, the Noorduyn trademark became synonymous with backwoods bush flying.

The aviation press covered the airplane whenever possible, something Robert Noorduyn encouraged. When the thirteenth model left the factory for Skylines Express, a party of journalists and photographers climbed in for a scheduled daily run from Montreal to the gold mines of Kirkland Lake, Ontario. "Loud in their praise of both the Norseman and the organization of the operator," a trade paper reported. This seemed an unusual remark since today's Norseman pilots agree that those aboard must have been airsick. The flight took more than seven hours and in June, 1937, few bushplanes flew in smooth air above the clouds.

Even the nonflying public noticed the Norseman. Intentionally designed with eye appeal, early models left the factory with at least six coats of high-gloss finish and well faired fuselage lines. Compared to the boxy Junkers and Fokkers, the Norseman turned out to be a favorite. One writer dubbed it a "crowd pleaser."

Not everyone believed Canada's "home-grown" bushplane would be a winner. Ontario government officials voiced criticism of its suitability for short-duration, low-level work. They also expressed concerns with the supercharged Pratt & Whitney Wasp since their flights rarely went above 2,500 ft. (750 m).

"It has always been my impression that frequent takeoffs and landings would be a very severe test on a supercharged engine," noted one individual.

Canadian Pratt & Whitney Aircraft Company Ltd. at Longueuil, Quebec, assured Ontario's watchdogs that the "S3H1" version of their engine was capable. They cautioned, however, that users should never exceed the published limitations. The mechanics and pilots must have listened, for they eventually operated a fleet of fourteen bright yellow Noorduyn Norsemen from 1944 until 1952.

The Norseman's role in the northland was assured because of an exceptional ability to absorb punishment. When damaged, the airframe could be repaired easily with whatever materials came to hand. Stories abound about how pilots taxied into trees or clipped wings while landing. To repair ripped fabric, they chopped holes in the ice, filled pails with water and threw them on the airplane where the liquid instantly froze. Using branches or moosehide mitts, they smoothed out the rough surfaces and flew home.

During World War II, Noorduyn increased production and sold Norsemen to several military air arms with the largest order to the United States Army Air Force (USAAF). Ironically, when hostilities ended in 1945, Noorduyn found himself competing with his own product after armed forces everywhere declared their airplanes surplus. Although the company added fifty-three improved models called Mark Vs to the line, ex-war trainers and transports could be purchased for a fraction of new prices. Few struggling air services could afford the cash for factory-fresh transports.

Many UC-64s, or American versions, recrossed the border to Canada and were modified to civilian standards by removing wartime hardware. One item mentioned in an operating instructions handbook was a radio destroyer push button. A footnote cautioned: "...bodily contact with the receiver should be avoided at the time of destruction." Other items superfluous to the world of bush flying included navigator tables, cabin fuel tanks and parachute flares.

Bush pilots accustomed to cramped Fairchilds, Fokkers and Junkers craved the Noorduyn Norseman. Nearly every hinterland air service kept at least one or two at work. Canadian Pacific, for example, used twenty-one from bases across the country. The pug-nosed, short and stubby silhouette became even more recognized when government organizations like the RCMP enforced the law in the remotest communities. In Saskatchewan, Norsemen acted as aerial ambulances and in Newfoundland, they carried mail to the shallow shores of Labrador.

One highly experienced pilot claimed that anyone who flew the Noorduyn Norseman hated it for the first hundred hours. He went on to say that after 200 hours, they started to like it. When the 400th hour went into the logbook, "You're in love!" he said.

Most men and women assigned to Norsemen came away with an overwhelming impression of size and the "no nonsense-just right" design. To pilots and mechanics familiar with types such as diminutive de Havilland two-seat Moth biplanes, "Canada's Own," as Noorduyn comptroller Lorne M. Coughtry called the yet unflown design back in 1935, came across as awesome.

"The first fifty hours in it terrified the bejesus out of me. At first, every landing and takeoff was a terrifying experience," recalled pilot/mechanic Hartley Weston of Merville, B.C. "Hang on and grit your teeth was all it was but after the terrifying times, we had a pretty good understanding of each other."

By the time the last production Norseman completed a test flight at Cartierville, Quebec, on December 17, 1959, 903 had been built. Although Mark IVs and Vs remained on the Canadian register, the majority of working Norsemen were Mark VIs or converted UC-64s adapted almost exclusively to seaplane floats or skis.

The Norseman had a fabric-covered, all-wood wing with a span of 51 ft., 6 in. (15.5 m) and a length of 32 ft. (10 m) The factory graciously provided a hand crank to start the engine when the normal electrics did not work. The cockpit came with fluorescent lights on adjustable swivel joints.

Best of all, at least in some airplanes, a plastic unheated relief tube could be reached by a desperate pilot whose seat was adjustable. "To move seat, the pilot relieves it of his full weight," an instructional manual said. Pre-war civilian models also came with a 12-gauge shotgun and special made broad-bladed paddle. Other cabin furnishings were spartan as pilot Con Farrell of Canadian Airways noted: "I do not think the present streetcar type or bush seats for the Noorduyn are very satisfactory as if one person gets sick the rest of the passengers get the benefit of it and the result is that you end up with a plane load of ill people. This has happened to me already."

A shortage of doors forced pilots to scramble over baggage and passengers in many bushplane types; the versatile Norseman came with four large openings, including one on each side of the cockpit. Detachable freight doors permitted easy loading of awkward items such as the ubiquitous fuel drums, plywood sheets and diesel generators. What could not be crammed into the 150 cu. ft. (4.5 m3) interior, ingenious loaders tied outside. Fuel oil tanks or lengths of timber could be fastened to the float struts or special racks.

Few Norsemen retained their high-gloss factory finishes in the real world. Many carried 18 ft. (5.4 m) wooden freighter canoes strapped to their struts. While lashing these cumbersome objects in place, it was common to puncture the fabric. A patch of tape quickly allowed the airplane to get airborne. As engine hours increased, constant vibration loosened fittings, windshield panels and door handles. Oil leaks streaked almost every external part.

"The Norseman slides through the air with all the oil on it," said pilot Gerald Bell of Red Lake, Ontario. "You do a walkaround preflight inspection crawling along the float spreader bars and all the bracing wires are dripping and the belly's smooth. You just get covered with it. Nobody stays clean flying a Norseman."

Pilots spoke in wonder of the Norseman's unparalleled ability to "lift a good snort" or heavy load. On floats, for example, a Mark V model registered CF-BHT weighed 4,985 lb. (2,243 kg) empty. With pilot, survival equipment, oil and half-filled gasoline tanks, it had room for another 1,855 lb. (835 kg) of freight or passengers before reaching maximum allowable takeoff weight of 7,540 lb. (3,393 kg). A Fokker Super Universal with the same fuel could carry only 1,310 lb. (590 kg).

One skiplane pilot carried wall-to-wall slabs of beef from Thompson to Churchill. Loaded to maximum weight, the tail ski could barely unstick from the ice on the takeoff run. Nevertheless, he wrenched the airplane into the air but quickly realized his freight had been placed too far rearward for correct balance. As the nose came up, he slammed the controls forward and "...ran out of places to push that wheel.

Test pilot W. J. McDonough spoke highly of CF-AYO's great strength "at the most vulnerable points of the structure," particularly in wing and undercarriage trusses. His opinion has been vindicated; the Norseman achieved a reputation as being able to absorb exceptional punishment on wheels, skis and floats.   *Photo: J. F. Sears*

Norseman CF-OBI was delivered to the Ontario Provincial Air Service (OPAS) at Sault Ste. Marie on July 7, 1945. After a series of owners including Transair, which later became Canadian Airlines Ltd., it sank through ice at Foxe Channel on January 1, 1951. Sales brochures claimed the Mark V burned 26 imp. gal. (118 l) of 80/87 gasoline per hour at 5,000 ft. (1,500 m).   *Photo: F. Shortt/National Aviation Museum*

"So anyway, it was just a matter of dropping a wing," he said casually. "Left wing, as a matter of fact, just dropped it a bit, then a touch of rudder to kick the tail up and presto! It was level!"

Flying overweight became a common practice because pilots often preferred to avoid a second trip. One Noorduyn sales brochure even hinted at this with brief mention of "tonnage beyond its normal stated capacity." In the north where federal inspectors rarely ventured and where time and money ruled the airways, pilots set their own limits. Robert Noorduyn pointed out to a potential customer that the US Army in Alaska habitually took off at a gross weight of 9,000 lb. (4,050 kg). "No wonder they mildly intimated that they would like some larger floats," he remarked.

When asked about overloads, almost every pilot requested anonymity. One carried Native children from wilderness settlements to residential schools. He described loads of 1,800–2,000 lb. (810–900 kg) but could not remember how many "heads" he flew. At 40–60 lb. (18–27 kg) per child, his Norseman would have had standing room only. Operating manuals stressed that only ten passengers were legal under any circumstances.

Another described a visit to Cumberland House, Saskatchewan, in the late 1960s. Expecting to fly out a crowd of hung-over survivors of an all night drinking party, he filled every inch of space inside his Norseman with men, women and children. Before leaving the muddy shoreline, he used a paddle to stop other potential customers from coming aboard and sinking his ship.

After a particularly long takeoff down the winding North Saskatchewan River, he set course for Prince Albert, 155 mi. (250 km) southwest. En route, he noticed a slight swing to the left but attributed it to the Norseman's advanced years. After landing, he discovered an unwanted passenger clinging to the outside ladder. Miraculously, the now-sober individual had kept his grip upon the slippery rungs without plummeting to his death. The unsympathetic, business-like pilot charged him full fare.

A retired airline jet captain claimed to have carried seventeen fire fighters from a large northern Ontario lake during his bush flying days. Each man with equipment weighed approximately 200 lb. (90 kg) which put the possible load at 3,400 lb. (1,530 kg).

Another Norseman "driver," as pilots are euphemistically called, remembered dozens of fish hauls. In remote lakes, commercial fishermen chartered float and ski airplanes to move their catches to markets. The "tub" (a plastic or wooden box weighing approximately 100–110 lb. (45–50 kg) of fish and chipped ice) became the standard measure of aircraft performance. Normally, ten tubs sufficed for a fully fuelled Norseman but some airplanes were known to carry twenty on short trips.

"You could get off most times never knowing which mile the aircraft was actually going to break water," said a pilot who flew Manitoba fish hauls. "In winter, it was a matter of knowing how many hard-packed snowdrifts to bounce off."

Norsemen takeoffs under most circumstances required what was described as a "touch of finesse." Water technique consisted of working the control wheel back and forth until the airplane reached a balance point and skimmed across the lake accelerating second by second to the crucial "on the step" position. If the pilot held the wheel too far rearward, the float heels created excessive drag. If too forward, he porpoised out of control. By watching the white water mark move back toward the center of the floats, the pilot knew when his airplane would fly. Sometimes with a heavy "jag" or load, becoming airborne could be difficult.

"When the airplane wouldn't come up on the step, it was a matter of 36 in. (91 cm) of boost (a measure of engine output) and slamming around in a big circle until we hit our own wake," said Keith Olson, an ex-bush pilot who moved on to Air Canada Boeing 747s. "Of course, we'd be way down the lake and the poor old engine was really roasting but it never let anybody down from running too hot."

One of the strangest suggestions to improve Norseman performance came from Ontario's legislative buildings when a deputy minister passed on a proposal concerning "Auxiliary Takeoff Units." Rocket propulsion offered a possibility, agreed OPAS director George Ponsford, and a flood of correspondence began.

The Aerojet Engineering Corporation in Pasadena, California, claimed that a JATO or Jet Assisted Take Off (actually a rocket) bottle could reduce a run by as much as twenty seconds and shorten takeoff length from 2,600 ft. to 500 ft. (780 m–150 m). However, each rocket weighed over 430 lb. (194 kg) and would diminish payload. Without a wind tunnel program, the flame path from the bottle could not be predicted and it was obvious the fabric fuselage would catch fire.

"The Norseman is about the most unsuitable airplane anyone would think of as an external structure would have to be built on to it to take the tremendous thrust of the jets," said Robert Noorduyn. "The great drag of such a structure would be carried around throughout the ensuing flight, cutting down the speed and climb."

Aerojet candidly admitted the project would be costly, too heavy and impractical. They suggested instead that the OPAS consider three-blade propellers as replacements for the standard "two-blader" type for increased performance. Ponsford heeded their advice. Figures showed that a forty-seven-second takeoff run dropped to thirty-seven seconds with a loaded airplane. Pilot Carl Crossley volunteered that he could "...still hardly realize my good fortune," after the new propeller went into service.

Every spring, mechanics removed the Norseman's wooden skis and converted the airplane back to seaplane configuration. Usually, they worked under a lakeside A-frame but some bush airlines went through "change-over" at airports without suitable lakes nearby. In this case, they used a multiwheeled dolly or oversized cart on which they carefully lowered the lightened Norseman for what pilots described as the "hairiest takeoffs." The powerful engine made the procedure tricky because the dolly sometimes swung out of control.

"It tended to torque to the left on you, eh?" recalled Hartley Weston. "You had both feet on the opposite rudder to keep straight and poured the coal to it. 'Christ, c'mon, c'mon, bitch, go for Christ's sake,' you'd say. You went thundering down the runway with this thing screaming away, airspeed slowly building. 'C'mon, c'mon.' It'd finally get up and go around 60 mph (97 km/h)."

At "freeze-up," when lakes hardened, pilots returned their seaplanes to wherever the skis happened to be. Landings on grassy areas with airplane floats were common but pilot Allan R. Williams of Edmonton found himself weathered in at Reindeer

Lake, Saskatchewan, unable to return to Lynn Lake, Manitoba, for changeover. When he finally left, temperatures had dropped enough to freeze his intended landing area. With no other choice or idea of what to expect, he prepared to land a float-equipped Norseman CF-DRD on the ice-covered lake.

"I gently approached the ice surface at about 90 mph (154 km/h), carrying plenty of power so as to allow for about a 100 ft. (30 m) per min. descent," he said. "After a fairly long and very flat trajectory, I was gratified to hear the keels of my floats come into gentle contact with the surface."

As Williams' forward speed dropped to 5 mph (8 km/h), the ice began splintering. Large flat sections tilted outward to left and right as CF-DRD settled into the hole. His progress to the shoreline mimicked the action of an ice breaker. The Norseman's weight forced the ice to submerge and "...a million shards of ice floated to the surface in my wake."

Norsemen were stable in level flight and calm air but on gusty days, they required plenty of "stick handling" and a heavy hand on the controls to keep the nose pointed toward some faraway reference point. In winter, standard equipment included a wool blanket across the pilot's knees and a map to insert in the sliding window so it would not rattle open.

Noorduyn designed a heater under the pilot's seat with outlets along the cabin walls for passenger comfort. One man admitted the device produced a slight temperature rise and "...people used to declare that they could tell the difference when it was on." Keith Olson called his Norseman's heater the "Northwind" because "...that's all we ever got out of it."

Summer flying brought the opposite problem. Some air services removed heaters to increase payload. Still, everybody suffered and complained. In hot weather, pilot and front seat passenger nearly succumbed from heatstroke. One chief pilot said the interior was "...just too damn hot for comfort!" Another—Gerald Bell—described it well in 1992: "You fly with the windows open, sweating, your feet burn on the rudders; then you get in the thing in early spring or late fall with the ice and snow and you freeze in there," he said. "You get your big mukluks on, your wool socks, stamping your feet to keep them warm—there's no happy medium."

Canada's Norsemen survived not only because of durability and reliability but because bush pilots, when caught with few tools and no hangars, became resourceful. Keith Olson, working out of central Manitoba, used his imagination during a frantic commercial fish haul: "As I taxied toward a dock at Cross Lake (50 mi. [81 km] north of Norway House, Manitoba), the Indians were all pointing to the airplane and I figured we must be on fire or something but couldn't tell if anything was wrong. So I pulled around and docked facing away from shore and got out to have a look."

To Olson's dismay, too many loads of decomposing fish scraps and pounding water during full power takeoffs had rotted the belly fabric and it simply fell away in flight. He had a choice of either flying to his base, waiting for help or improvising. Knowing his employer encouraged self-sufficiency, Olson unloaded his fish and flew as slowly as possible to Wabowden, 52 mi. (84 km) south of Thompson.

"We went up to the Bay (Hudson's Bay Company) and bought a cotton sheet with pink stripes that looked more like a barber pole than a bed sheet," he said. "By the end of the day, we'd sewn the thing on and slapped a couple coats of dope on and it looked quite nice."

Olson's ingenuity allowed him to return to the serious business of fish hauling. His boss was pleased and so were the customers. As for the bed sheet, it stayed on the Norseman's belly for months.

Canada's Own depended on an engine-driven fuel pump to keep a constant flow of gasoline from two 50 imp. gal. (228 l) welded aluminum wing cells. All Mark VI models left Cartierville with an extra belly tank installed below the cabin floor. With the Pratt & Whitney R-1340 Wasp burning 26–35 imp. gal. (118–159 l) of red 80/87 gasoline per hour, some Norsemen could fly 1,200 mi. (1,932 km). Each wing tank had a primitive but reliable direct reading glass tube protruding from the bottom of each cell. The pilot only needed to glance outside to read his quantity.

Lamb Airways, a charter company headquartered in The Pas, Manitoba, prized the Norseman's long range capabilities. The settlements they serviced, such as Rankin Inlet, Chesterfield Inlet, Eskimo Point and many others on Hudson Bay's west coast, were far from gasoline depots. Arctic winter hazards included temperatures cold enough to cause instant frostbite, as well as short daylight hours, featureless terrain and constant storms.

Each season, federal or territorial governments contracted northern airlines to fly teachers to and from Eskimo settlements north of the 60th parallel. Operators fortunate enough to win these lucrative contracts needed airplanes capable of flying long distances. The Norseman fit the criteria. One pilot found himself scheduled to move a load of teachers and their annual supplies from Churchill to Baker Lake, Northwest Territories.

The itinerary called for a direct 400 mi. (644 km) run from Churchill above the ice of Hudson Bay and inland across an area famous for "whiteout" where pilots lose the ability to discern between sky and snow-covered surfaces on overcast days. Not surprised at the weather—ice crystals, blowing snow and low cloud—he expected to be five hours en route. Unable to map read, the trip was a "...matter of just bogging along," waiting for his radio receiver to home on Baker Lake's low frequency navigation beacon.

After four hours in the gust-battered Norseman, the pilot never received so much as a "tweet" from Baker Lake on his radio and decided to find the Hudson Bay coast for safety's sake. Luckily, he overflew Eskimo Point, 162 mi. (261 km) north of Churchill, and then pushed on northwards to a village on a collection of islands called Whale Cove. His passengers changed their minds and requested him to fly another 60 mi. (97 km) to Rankin Inlet. Anxious to please, he carried on and landed.

"We were in the air six hours and fifty-five minutes which is a good haul, but it showed the practicality of flying that type of airplane," the pilot casually concluded.

Perpetual winds rushing across thousands of miles of what novelist Herman Melville termed "dumb blankness" hardens Arctic snow into cementlike consistency. Tracked vehicles have been known to cross gigantic drifts and barely leave a mark. Skis, often wooden ones designed at the Noorduyn factory, absorbed brutal blows as the airplane decelerated after touching down. Finding smooth areas took plenty of patience and a willingness on the part of customers to walk a few miles if necessary.

Although the aviation center of Churchill had advantages like hangars, electrical plug-ins and gasoline supplies, landing skiplanes at the seaport community could be tricky. With only one runway cleared and packed, pilots had to use it regardless of wind direction. Worse, skiplanes had little control on ice-covered surfaces and required some "fancy dancing" on the controls to keep straight. Keith Olson handled the situation the way he had been taught by "high timers" or veteran pilots: "When you landed in there, you used a blast of power to straighten it out and then if it turned sideways, another blast and by the time you got to the turnoff (for the terminal building), the airplane was slowed down. Luckily, the Norseman had a big rudder on it and you could blow the tail around pretty quick."

Norseman landing gear, in spite of a spindly legged appearance, carried an unbelievable inherent strength. Nelson Scutt, a maintenance engineer with Arctic Wings, an air service which specialized in flying north of the tree line, remembered watching Noorduyn Norsemen "hell damners" slide out of control after landing: "I seen them things go skitterin' sideways and sideways and sideways and you'd figure the first snow bank's gonna take the gear off but we never lost one."

A Royal Canadian Air Force Norseman seaplane flown by 413 Squadron left Yellowknife, Northwest Territories, for Flin Flon, Manitoba, in April, 1950. On arrival, it was pitch dark and neither pilot or crewman had been to Flin Flon. They descended to 300 ft. (90 m) over the water and switched on the landing lights. The resultant glare dazzled both men. The shaken pilot said: "The hell with this," closed the throttle, pulled the nose up and stalled the wings.

The Norseman hit with a tremendous crash, splattering water over the wings and windshield. When the noise and shuddering stopped, it remained level on the lake and did not sink. The crewman quickly stepped outside with a flashlight to assess the damage but found the belly unwrinkled. They taxied rapidly to shore with all doors open ready to evacuate if necessary. Few airplanes could survive such a blow.

Experienced pilots usually agreed the Norseman could be gentle to fly at cruise altitude on calm days. Sometimes, however, it produced unexpected surprises, regardless of how cautious or skilled the pilots.

Ronald MacDonald, chief pilot for Severn Enterprises Ltd. in northern Ontario, relaxed on an eighty-four mile flight from Sioux Lookout to a lake near Savant Lake in July 1954. Inside, he carried three passengers and assorted camping gear. Outside, on the right, he and mechanic Alfred Noakes had securely fastened a 17 ft. (5 m) wooden canoe. While approaching Hamilton Lake, MacDonald finished his standard prelanding procedures and brought the throttle slowly to idle. He reached overhead to select the flaps and then, without warning, the Norseman abruptly pointed almost straight down.

"My altitude at this time was approximately 200 ft. (60 m) above terrain and on the edge of the lake. I knew something was wrong and opened the throttle full bore and full fine pitch on the propeller," he said.

As the airplane pitched down, two passengers screamed that the canoe had shifted and was coming loose. MacDonald's Norseman slammed into Hamilton Lake in a level position and bounced back into the air. Under "somewhat abnormal conditions," he managed to hang on and fly a precarious oval pattern around the lake. MacDonald needed both hands to keep the control wheel fully back to remain level.

While positioning for a last chance landing, MacDonald kept the throttle wide open and cautiously edged closer to the surface. The canoe acted like an elevator control and threatened to slam the airplane nose first into the lake. In his career, MacDonald had carried at least fifty canoes on a Norseman and never encountered such a critical and terrifying situation.

"I actually touched the water utilizing 38 in. (97 cm) of boost and full 2,300 rpm," he said. "The aircraft touched nicely and I would estimate ran on the step for approximately one quarter of a mile. I then eased back very slowly on the throttle and shortly after, the aircraft, without warning, flipped over on its back."

Unbelievably, everyone survived. Later, accident investigators discovered that a fitting on the external load rack had broken and allowed the canoe to swing outward.

Under normal situations, Norsemen aficionados considered landings relatively easy in seaplane configuration. With engine lever throttled back enough to keep the propeller turning slowly, most pilots used an 85 mph (137 km/h) glide. They rarely flew at night and when they did, the results were sometimes tragic. Two young brothers witnessed a fatal accident at Red Lake, Ontario, during the early 1950s.

Hearing a Norseman approaching the darkened community, they could barely see the wing tip navigation lights. Both boys quickly jumped into a canoe and paddled toward some boathouses to watch the landing. The pilot throttled his engine back, obviously planning to use the town's lights for landing reference.

"All of a sudden we heard this kind of snap, bang, crack like something's hitting something very hard, then this ungodly roar, the engine came on full bore and you could hear it screaming. He just popped up over the church and it seemed like he was hanging on in the moonlight and we could see him gradually turn and start to fall backwards before it hit the water just about vertical."

After the Norseman slammed into the water, foam spread outward and boiled and bubbled up from the engine's heat. The fish haul had been scheduled as its last before fall freeze-up—the pilot died on impact.

Among the floating iridescent silver trout, the boys watched a brown boot wobbling in the wavelets with the laces dangling and catching the moonlight. It contained the pilot's foot.

Some pilots, if they had to make a night water landing, used the exhaust system as a primitive echo sounder—a trick known to a few bush flying veterans. On approach, the pilot adjusted the nose to a slightly up attitude and listened. Before long, he heard the engine noise reverberating from the water below the belly and eased his throttle in to control descent until he felt the welcome kiss of liquid on his floats. The method worked only in long narrow bodies of water.

Although many veterans thought the Norseman easy to land, it seemed like a handful to anyone spoiled by finger-tip control airplanes. One aviation journalist/pilot found himself at the controls of a Norseman above Lac Seul, 70 mi. (113 km) northeast of Kenora, Ontario. The company pilot had generously switched seats with the journalist. Approaching a seaplane base, they could see stump-studded Lac Seul narrowing toward the town of Ear Falls. On final with excessive speed, the journalist eased the throttle back and slowed for landing. As a cluster of dead jackpine trees passed under the floats, he waited. Accustomed to de Havilland Beavers and Otters, he leveled off too low in a nose down attitude—the last position a Norseman should be in when near the surface. They touched the lake gently. For an instant, nothing happened. Without warning, the floats dug in.

"I instinctively hauled the control wheel back but not before the staggering airplane again struck the water with a terrific whack, vibrating the airframe enough to make the cross braces on the windshield disappear in a blur," the journalist said. "It leapt out of the water roaring at full power and slammed back down again. After several more lessening leaps, we found ourselves taxiing right side up with tiny rivulets of water dribbling down the airplane."

The stalwart Norseman survived but the flustered company pilot needed several days to steady his shaking hands.

Through the years, incidents far more severe than the one on Lac Seul have claimed Norsemen. Others, dragged behind a hangar, rotted out of sight when expensive major overhauls came due and specialists in fabric sewing and woodworking could not be found. Nevertheless, many still fly in backwoods areas where airstrips have not marred the land.

Today, there is no lake, tract of muskeg, stretch of barrens or mountain top that has not been overflown by a Norseman. Many men and women, unable to describe Canada's first true bushplane, lapse into respectful silence as they strive to tell the tale of the wood-winged wonder.

3 Stinson Gull Wings

Elegance in the Bush

With feet dangling in a patch of weeds beside a wooden dock, a pair of young Dogrib brothers watched the two-blade propeller turn over several times. Seconds later, bluish white exhaust smoke doodled backwards and vanished quickly in the crisp morning air at Yellowknife, Northwest Territories.

The boys' parents rode inside the Stinson SR-9 seaplane. Registered CF-OAW and owned by Ptarmigan Airways, the pilot completed an engine warm up, lowered the wing flaps and applied takeoff power. The floats soon left the surface of Yellowknife Bay. As the boys stared, the airplane made a gentle right turn toward Rae-Edzo, 59 mi. (95 km) northwest.

Canada's introduction to Stinsons came about because a remarkable young woman went aloft in a hot air balloon over Kansas City, Kansas, in 1911. Intrigued with this brief brush in aviation, Katherine Stinson sold a piano for $200 and by July 13, 1912, had soloed an airplane. Her reputation as a daring aviatrix quickly spread and within four years, she began carrying passengers from small towns on the Canadian prairies.

Katherine Stinson's family shared her enthusiasm and formed the Stinson Aeroplane Company in Dayton, Ohio, during the 1920s. Katherine dropped out of aviation in 1918 because of exhaustion and tuberculosis but her brother Edward continued.

In 1926, ignoring experts who believed airplanes could not be flown without open cockpits, Edward designed the revolutionary Detroiter with fully enclosed cabin. Immediately successful, it became the first commercial Stinson bushplane in Canada after crossing the border on December 11, 1926. That year, the company's name changed to the Stinson Aircraft Corporation and a family of airplanes followed.

Stinsons quickly broke records. One took off from Harbour Grace, Newfoundland, and eighteen days later, the "Pride of Detroit" landed near Tokyo, Japan, after flying 12,295 mi. (19,795 km) across the Atlantic Ocean, Europe and Asia. Another flew nearly thirty nonstop hours over water until a broken oil line forced it down south of the Azores. The world's endurance record fell to another Stinson when two pilots stayed aloft for 553 hours and forty-one minutes. As its products won awards and attracted customers worldwide, the Stinson Aircraft Corporation built an 80,000 sq. ft. (7,200 m^2) factory at Wayne, Michigan.

In 1931, Brooks Airways of Prince Albert, Saskatchewan, imported a model called the Stinson SM-8A. Powered by a 125-h.p. Lycoming R-680 radial engine, it landed at 45 mph (72 km/h) and used Edo P-3300 floats for charters and joy rides in Prince Albert National Park. The SM-8A burned 10 U.S. gal. (46 l) of gasoline per hour and sold for $5,575 on wheels. Less than a year after its order date, CF-AQH burned in a nose hangar fire.

The "straight wing" Stinsons, as historians called the early series flown by Brooks Airways, was replaced early in 1936 by the SR-7. This new type broke sharply with tradition with a completely new wing design. The "Gull Wings" or "Reliants" gave the four-seat SR-7 a distinctive birdlike appearance. In plan form, the trailing edge tapered sharply forward nearly to a point at the tip while the front remained straight. Factory brochures claimed the novel aerodynamic approach made each new Stinson a "masterpiece of styling and elegance."

At the time, salesmen compared airplanes with automobiles and extolled their "motorcar width" seats and other carlike amenities. They lifted the solid look of familiar surroundings into the air. Even automobile type "regulators" or roll down window handles added to the flying car illusion. When customers expected more luster and luxury, Canadian Airways trotted out their

Stinsons instead of spartan Fokkers, Fairchilds and Junkers freighters.

Powered by a 260-h.p. Lycoming R-680-B5 radial engine, a Canadian Airways' SR-8CM weighed 2,345 lb. (1,055 kg) empty on wheels and swung an 8 ft., 6 in. (2.4 m) Hamilton controllable propeller. In their prime, the SR-8CMs were considered good performers relative to comparable size bushplanes. General superintendent C. H. (Punch) Dickins reported that CF-AZV could takeoff in thirty seconds in spite of glassy water, 99°F (37°C) heat and a full load. The secret, he said, could be found in the setting of the horizontal stabilizer by a crank above the pilot's head.

The Stinson company had introduced flaps or "speed arresters" in 1934 but pilots were slow to appreciate the advantages of these low speed/high lift devices. In the SR-8's case, engine vacuum pressure activated the flaps and could be controlled by a valve on the instrument panel. Salesmen pointed out that flaps operated on the same principle as the "...operation of brakes and gear shifting mechanism in trucks and passenger cars."

Flaps, said factory service manager Arthur Thompson, changed the airplane's gliding angle to a pronounced nose down attitude. On the takeoff, he suggested placing stabilizer trim in a nose heavy position and, after a 200 ft. (60 m) run, the pilot should depress a lever, push his control wheel forward and then sharply back. Thompson warned that the Stinson Aircraft Corporation could not guarantee results nor accept responsibility for whatever happened.

Canadian Airways' pilots took off by selecting flaps down at 60 mph (97 km/h) to jump the airplane 30 ft. (9 m) into the air. After becoming airborne, they increased airspeed slowly and eased the flaps up while gaining height. Winnipeg's general traffic manager V. H. Patriarche believed the method carried some risk, especially in bumpy air.

"The present full down position of the flaps introduces so much braking effect that their use on takeoffs, while perfectly feasible if care is used, does not appear to me to be altogether safe," he said.

As hours on the Lycoming engines increased, Canadian Airways experienced many mechanical problems. Piston failures, cylinder distortion and almost daily spark plug changes hampered revenue flying. One factory representative altered the carburetors to provide a richer fuel mixture but this helped little, if at all, and engines kept malfunctioning.

"No operating company in the world can afford to purchase so many new parts for the short period of time these engines have been in operation," wrote Canadian Airways maintenance manager Tommy W. Siers on November 17, 1936.

Later, mechanics concluded that pilots had handled the Lycomings incorrectly. Dickins suggested idling for no more than three minutes whenever possible. As soon as an engine accepted full throttle and oil pressure met minimums, the airplane was ready for takeoff. He added that all taxiing should be carried out "on the step" position to give the engine time to adjust to surface temperatures and reduce propeller wear. Dickins thought that the Stinson SR-8CM really was "...low-powered and very sensitive and will not respond to heavy-handed methods."

"It's not good policy to 'pump' this aircraft on to the step; rather coax it and better results will be obtained," he said. "Breaking of float suction can be helped greatly by gently swaying the aircraft with the rudder. Under this procedure, aircraft will rock itself onto the step and start to run free."

By 1937, the Reliants had built enviable sales records. Further development brought out the memorable five-seat Stinson SR-9 with special "class" in its sleek shape. Customers had a choice of engines but most Canadian SR-9s used the Pratt & Whitney R-985 Wasp Jr. which produced 450-h.p. at a takeoff rpm of 2,300. An outstanding feature turned out to be a molded two-piece windshield blending artfully with the cockpit lines. Previous Stinsons used flat glass drag-inducing panels. In one year, Stinson sold more than 200 SR-9s.

Bush airlines appreciated the reliability and performance of the Pratt & Whitney R-985s compared to the sensitive Lycomings.

Exploration companies like McIntyre-Porcupine Mines used CF-BIM for carrying geologists and field staff into prospective backcountry mineral sites. Business-suited executives enjoyed speedy air travel from their Toronto headquarters to meet with clients or examine drill core. Another mining company called Territories Exploration based CF-BEA in Toronto but lost it 45 mi. (72 km) south of Gordon Lake, Northwest Territories, when sparks from a bush fire ignited the fabric.

At 4,010 lb. (1,805 kg) on Edo Wb 5030 floats including pilot, survival equipment and half the maximum 102 U.S. gal. (464 l) of gasoline in the wing tanks, a Stinson SR-9F version carried a 1,020 lb. (459 kg) payload at nearly 135 mph (217 km/h). With proper technique, pilots could land as slow as 63 mph (101 km/h). In 1937, SR-9s sold for $18,000 as a wheelplane. Bush airlines had the option of adding extra doors, metallized freight interiors and floats.

Although Stinsons were flown Canada-wide, Ontario became the province which saw more of these elegant classics than anywhere in the country. As early as 1936, director George Ponsford attended three meetings with Stinson president B. D. Deweese and engineer-in-charge Robert W. Ayer concerning the adaptation of Gull Wing Reliants to Ontario's needs. Ponsford knew the airplane—his pilots could hardly avoid them as commercial flying companies used them throughout the north.

While Ponsford contemplated Stinsons, Ayer paid an informal visit to Canada. While tramping the forests on a moose hunt with his civil service hosts, he hinted strongly that their antiquated Moths, Vedettes and other obsolete types should be replaced with something faster. When Ayer left, he had learned much about the Canadian way of doing business. Besides a possible Gull Wing order, he discovered that bringing moose flesh by rail to the United States proved more difficult than selling seaplanes.

"By the time we got through with pulling moose meat out of the water cooler and putting it under the radiator, then removing it to the men's washroom, the Negro porter nearly had a serious case of nervous breakdown," Ayer wrote later.

On June 27, 1937, Ayer acknowledged that the Stinson Aircraft Corporation felt "...tickled pink to read that the comptroller has approved your appropriation for new equipment." His company would, he continued, bend every effort to prove the suitability of Stinson Reliants in northern Ontario. Ponsford, a cautious, dedicated man, intended to obtain the best value for the taxpayer's dollar.

Ponsford wanted his Stinsons "Canadianized." Much of the correspondence between OPAS headquarters in Sault Ste. Marie and Wayne, Michigan, concerned winter operations. Until then, the OPAS manufactured skis inhouse but discontinued these costly wintertime projects because of time constraints. Ponsford settled on Elliott Brothers skis built in Sioux Lookout.

Float selection became another time-consuming matter. At first, Ponsford expected to equip his SR-9s with license-built Edos from MacDonald Brothers in Winnipeg. Their quote of $3,600 was far more than Canadian Vickers' in Montreal. Unfortunately, for Vickers, licensing their floats on SR-9s was impossible without costly stress analysis and flight testing.

Eventually, the OPAS decided on the Edos. Ponsford recommended installing front and diagonal float struts to enable experimentation with various settings. He claimed that every manufacturer's specifications ultimately needed changing to reach peak takeoff performance.

Ponsford, knowing his approval might mean lucrative quantity orders for Stinsons, pressed every advantage. Standard SR-9s sold with built-in, throw-over type control wheels which detracted 20 lb. (9 kg) from the payload. This awkward feature made training difficult when pilots gathered for customary spring checkouts on Sault Ste. Marie's St. Mary's River. Ponsford besieged the Stinson plant with telephone calls and lengthy letters.

"For instructional purposes, I do not like the throw-over wheel, as it does not give the pilot-in-charge of the aircraft an opportunity to correct any mistakes which may be made by the pupil," he argued.

Well-built freighters, Stinson SR-9Fs, like CF-BGS, were constructed from 4130 plate and steel tubing with wood formers and fabric-covering. The rear seat held three passengers and the cabin area was heavily insulated and sound proofed. Sadly, Stinson SR-9 was lost near Chapleau, Ontario, in the summer of 1961.

Photo: via Panis Productions, Red Lake, Ontario

Imported in 1937 as an executive ship, SR-9F CF-BGJ went on to wear Ontario Provincial Air Service (OPAS) yellow until becoming a fish freighter in Ontario and Manitoba. In 1964, an engine fire in flight destroyed the airplane.

Photo: Ont. Dept. of Lands & Forests

Stinson's sales department gave in and supplied a light, single-control column with a removable second wheel at no extra cost.

Ponsford expected the Stinsons to continue the aerial photography roles of the slower Vickers Vedettes but a photographer noticed that proposed camera locations would not be adaptable. With lenses positioned in the forward cabin floor, floats and cross bracing wires obstructed fields of view.

"Unless the camera can be put well through the floor, it does not seem possible the camera hole can be placed between the two spreader bars as the space between the floats does not give sufficient clearance," wrote Deputy Minister of Forestry C. R. Mills.

On February 24, 1937, Ponsford wired his parliamentary superiors that the manufacturers had altered the design. Now, the Stinsons could handle certain camera makes "very nicely." Modifications included a customized view finder which did not interfere with the 8 in. (21 cm) focal length. This time, the OPAS did not escape—the extra hole and special engineering cost another $84.

Many bush airplanes needed hand starting and others depended on crank-activated inertia systems coupled to a clutch turned by hand. This apparatus added unnecessary weight so the OPAS decided on the "Type M Coffman" starter sold by Federal Laboratories in Pennsylvania for $450 each. A cartridge resembling an ordinary shotgun shell and fired by a trigger created gases to turn the engine over.

Without heavier batteries, booster magnetos and assorted wiring, the Stinson's gross weight came out as 70 lb. (32 kg) less. As frightening as cartridge starts may have been to passengers or any wildlife that happened to be nearby, they extended engine life since pilots needed less fuel to prime the cylinders. The OPAS received a credit for the factory electric starters.

"With the Coffman starter, you have positive starting which will function in ten to fifteen degrees colder temperature than other methods," said Federal's president J. W. Young. "It enables the pilot to successfully start his own ship without assistance of ground force. This frequently is very helpful when taking off after a forced landing."

Ponsford soon regretted his decision. Cartridge prices soared dramatically and field reports showed many defective shells and mismatched sizes. Sometimes, cartridges did not ignite—a condition intolerable in lake areas with high trees, rocky shorelines and fast-running rivers. It had been a costly error; the OPAS claimed the dubious honor of being the first Canadian civil organization to use Coffmans. Ponsford reverted to the industry-wide direct drive starters.

A sales contract between the Province of Ontario and the Stinson Aircraft Corporation contained several riders on performance, delivery and weights differing slightly from factory specifications. On floats, cruise speed had to be at least 147 mph (237 km/h) with a 1,540 lb. (693 kg) useful load at a 4,800 lb. (2,160 kg) gross weight. The agreement also called for a 65-mph landing speed and a 17,500 ft. (5,250 m) service ceiling.

"The ships shall take off in calm air and fresh water and attain an altitude of 70 ft. (21 m) within a distance of one-half mile under conditions of 90°F (32°C) and 95 percent humidity and from a standing start," the document read. "Engine operation must be kept within limits at all times but throttling back immediately after clearing the obstacle is permitted to accomplish this."

Although the specified speeds were probably never attained, two Stinson SR-9FMs registered CF-OAV and CF-OAW became the property of the Ontario Government on July 2 and July 20, 1937. Without wheels, tires, tubes, brakes or wheel pants, they cost $34,159.44 with another $5,800 for Edo Wb 5030 floats. Powered by the popular 450-h.p. Pratt & Whitney R-985, each had a brilliant yellow paint scheme on the wings and an aluminum-colored fuselage. An upholstered, sound-proofed cabin with leather trim and adjustable front seats was a giant step from the OPAS's open cockpit heydays.

Stinson sold several more SR-9s to the OPAS and one SR-10F with Edo 59-5250 later joined the fleet. Historian Joseph P. Juptner said it was "nigh onto impossible to make something that was already good, any better," but flush-mounted cabin doors on the SR-10F reduced drag. Payload was similar although the wing tanks held 26 U.S. gal. (118 l) less than the SR-9. It also used the Pratt & Whitney R-985 but reverted to a flat panel windshield because factory engineers decided the SR-9's gracefully curved windshield created too much distortion. The "Ten" became one of the final Reliants and stayed in production until 1941.

Classed as "semi-transports" by Ponsford, the Stinsons proved their worth. On fire patrols, they carried two men with water pumps, hose and other equipment. More costly to operate than Moths, the faster Stinsons' ability to transport a complete fire-fighting unit offset the monetary disadvantages. By 1940, OPAS accountants calculated a cost of $54.04 per hour including overhead, fuel, depreciation and salaries.

"There is little doubt that this policy has resulted in our being able to hold to small proportions many fires that would ordinarily reach major proportions," boasted Ponsford. "This is a particular type of ship that we find most useful."

Ontario's Stinsons did not always fly clean, light loads. Assigned to Algonquin Park, north of Toronto, on garbage runs, their opulent interiors often contained festering, maggot-laden camp debris. Worse, external loads from the park's short lakes frightened many pilots. Conservation officers, animal surveyors or anyone with the enviable task of managing forests and wildlife became part of the daily loads, winter and summer.

At one point, a Stinson carried a de Havilland Moth fuselage. Another on a fire support mission made ninety-five flights, boarded 118 fire fighters and moved almost 140,000 lb. (63,000 kg) of equipment including six canoes in four days. No question, said one observer, the Pratt & Whitney engine changed the Stinson from the "fastest boat on the lake" to an efficient freighter and people-mover.

In Temagami, 207 mi. (333 km) north of Toronto, one of the most important developments in forest fire suppression history took place when pilot Carl Crossley devised a scheme in which he proposed aerial water dropping. Assigned to SR-9FM CF-OAY, he experimented by filling a cabin tank with 40 imp. gal. (182 l) of water and discharging it through a 3.5 in. (9 cm) pipe in the floor.

"It was proposed to use a pressure pick-up scoop at taxi speed for filling the tank but all experiments and tests to effect this have failed so far," Crossley wrote. "For the air tests, this pipe was fitted with pump hose connections at the lower end and the tank filled with a fire pump."

The water load left the Stinson in thirteen seconds after release with a lever beside the pilot seat but broke instantly into small droplets. After watching three test flights, observers pronounced aerial suppression feasible only if another dropping method could be found. Crossley's experiments proved to be the first of many leading the Ontario government into the forefront of aerial fire fighting. Today, Ontario's pilots fly a fleet of multiengine Canadair CL-215 air tankers capable of dropping a massive 1,200 gal. (5,460 l) punch in less than a second.

In the first years of service, all went well with OPAS Stinsons until 1937 when the aviation industry received a shock after a wing separated from a Norwegian Reliant at Oslo. Quickly, Stinson representatives persuaded Canadian authorities that the incident was an isolated one and their products still stood out as the safest on the market. Investigators decided that the problem resulted from a fractured lift strut fitting.

While in Sioux Lookout, visiting Stinson mechanics carried out strengthening modifications to CF-OAV. After this, Ponsford informed his superiors that the SR-9EM lost by Norway's Wideroe Flyveselskap had been subjected to undue strain in shipping, assembling or overloading and "...the Stinson people were completely exonerated."

Unfortunately, an SR-9 belonging to General Airways went down near Sioux Lookout. After this tragedy, Canadian aviation inspectors ordered strengtheners installed on all Stinsons registered in Canada. Each Reliant was grounded until a qualified mechanic certified its airworthiness. No more structural failures occurred and the OPAS carried on.

John Underwood in his *The Stinsons, a Pictorial History*, said the Stinsons dramatically conveyed an impression of "regal loftiness." No one denied that the Gull Wings were beautiful to look at and a pleasure to fly but like aging divorcees, they required frequent, costly maintenance. Spark plugs, for example, rarely lasted and needed replacement at least every twenty hours flying time.

"From experience, we have found it necessary to dismantle and thoroughly clean both electrode and shell and to reset to .012," complained OPAS mechanic W. G.Chapman of the spark plugs. "The causes of failure are excessive heating of the magnetos and the building up of lead from the gasoline."

The OPAS attributed short plug life to the Stinson's close-fitting engine cowling which did not cool the magnetos properly. Air passing over cylinder fins escaped easily and pooled warm air behind the magnetos. The factory agreed on a modification to help lower temperatures and allow easier access to the back of the Pratt & Whitney. Until then, field staff had dreaded inspections, since it meant a two-man, day-long undertaking to remove the cowlings.

During winter, typical Northern Ontario temperatures necessitated plumbers' blow pots for engine preheating. This procedure resulted in impaired lubrication and premature propeller bushing replacement. The fault was thought to be uneven heat distribution in the engine.

"We are further of the opinion that much of this heat is directed through the front of the nose cowl," said Ponsford. "In so doing, a great deal of the heat is naturally applied to the propeller hub. The grease in the hub and in the blades is reduced to a condition where it flows very readily."

When the propeller rotated, centrifugal force threw the softened lubricant from the hub. Ponsford suggested applying a "half gun full of grease" into each blade before flight. His idea must have worked for no further records of complaints exist. Another method of retaining heat involved wrapping heavy insulating material and asbestos around all lines to prevent solidified oil.

One design fault gave pilot Arthur E. Burtt a terrible fright while flying CF-BGM from a forest ranger station to Fort Frances near International Falls, Minnesota. A strong odor of burning rubber permeated the cockpit and seconds later, flames and heavy smoke forced him down on a lake. After bringing the fire under control with a Pyrene fire extinguisher, he tried to find the cause.

Burtt removed inspection covers but found nothing. After a short wait to settle his nerves, he decided to take off. Again, smoke and flames forced him back. After drifting on Beaverhouse Lake, he paddled to a cabin and waited two days for a mechanic. A closer look revealed an oil-impregnated felt packing ring which had contacted an exhaust pipe. The fire had followed the airflow to the cockpit through a small inspection door near Burtt's feet.

Ponsford issued a notice to all pilots and mechanics to inspect their engine packings. No more fires occurred.

Other than occasional engine failures and the destruction of CF-OAZ after pilot error at Biscotasing on August 23, 1943, OPAS Stinsons established excellent safety records. Only one was involved in a fatal accident. On May 27, 1948, James Westaway could not climb CF-OAV over a stand of trees on the Severn River, 70 mi. (113 km) north of Toronto. Two passengers escaped but Westaway drowned.

During World War II, the OPAS's opportunities to buy new aircraft were curtailed. The United States Army had the authority to commandeer any Pratt & Whitney-powered airplanes they could find. In 1944, Ponsford bought his last SR-9—McIntyre-Porcupine Mines' CF-BIM. Previously flown by noted pilot/author A. G. K. "Gath" Edward, it contained Canada's first ADF or automatic direction finder and Canada's first constant speed propeller.

Ponsford continued planning ahead to keep his fleet in the forefront of forestry aviation. Sadly, he realized his beautiful Reliants would soon be technically obsolete. The Noorduyn Norseman caught his eye but at a cost of $40,000 each, he hesitated investing government money and again contacted Stinson Aircraft Corporation.

"We have found the Wasp-powered Reliant that you manufactured for northern conditions to be very well suited to our needs...," he wrote. "On the other hand, we can use something with a higher payload, if your company contemplates something along these lines."

Stinson showed no further interest. Nothing, it seemed, would be available to match the SR-9s. Ponsford had little choice but to look further into the Noorduyn Norseman. Eventually, fifteen of these pug-nosed freighters carried the colors of Ontario's Yellow Birds. The Stinson fleet began going on sale in 1948.

Commercial bush air services across Canada snapped them up. Chukuni Airways in Red Lake bought CF-OBB and Inter-Provincial Air Services in Windsor handed over $6,000 for CF-BIM. Green Airways in Red Lake operated CF-BGN to help build a foundling airline into the multi-airplane fleet it is today. These ex-OPAS Stinsons served their new owners well by hauling everything from frozen fish to overheated "turkeys" or tourists. The last known SR-9 to operate commercially in Canada was CF-BGM which went down near Temagami in 1977, killing both men aboard.

By the time Gull Wings reached their postwar peak in the forties and fifties, many pilots had become accustomed to the sterling performance of the de Havilland Beaver. Like Norseman pilots, would-be aviators found themselves afflicted with the notion that Stinsons would not perform. Nevertheless, a special breed existed which had eyes only for SR-9s. These few began their bush flying careers on Cessna 180s and smaller types with horizontally opposed automobilelike engines and looked forward to the Pratt & Whitney radials with awe. Some skeptics had warned about a peculiar tendency of the Stinsons to become "nose-diggers."

"The SR-9 was a little bit heavy on the front end and you really had to watch the thing, especially on glassy water where you could really stub your toes," said Mike McCluskey in Campbell River, British Columbia. "In the air, you couldn't let it fly too slow because of those little tapered wing tips or it dropped a wing quick on you if you weren't careful."

"Stubbing the toes" or digging the fronts of the floats on landing could be avoided with a nose up approach. McCluskey

One of the first Stinsons SM-8As in Canada, CF-AQH lasted only eight months with Brooks Airways in Prince Albert, Saskatchewan, before destruction by fire in a nose hangar during December, 1931.   *Photo: National Aviation Museum*

pointed out that the floats were mounted in such a manner that the fronts drooped slightly downward.

"So in order to land, you had to have the nose quite high and if you didn't, that's why they dug," he explained. "It'd throw water right up over the windshield and wings and scare you to death. Once you got onto the fact it'd dive for the bottom of the lake if you didn't have that nose sticking straight up when you land, it was all right."

Although licensed for five seats, SR-9s, like many of their fabric-covered, bush-country sisters, often carried far more than legal loads. One pilot took seven men from a lumber camp and another hauled three, their equipment and a boat strapped to the outside.

"I could never use cruise power because it would sink on me so we had to follow all the valleys and all the lakes all the way back because the weather was closing in and the guys wanted out," he said.

Another pilot said that it never seemed to make a difference how much had been crammed into the cabin, the airplane would fly. A takeoff run, however, lasted for miles and speed was critical.

"Best way was to yank it off and you had to be careful when you did that because, of course, it's just about an eighth of a mile above the stall, you know," a pilot said. "If you waited for a Stinson to get into the air by itself, you'd be out of water pretty soon."

Takeoffs from small lakes could be shortened by step turning around a shoreline and slamming on full throttle the instant the nose pointed into wind. An SR-9 carried nearly the same load as a Beaver but "...needed at least three turns around the average northern Ontario lake before getting into the air," said the late Robert Gareh of Lakeland Airways in Temagami in 1992.

Flaps caused many frustrating moments in SR-9s. One with Orillia Air Services in Ontario had its vacuum system changed to electric. The operator quickly used up his supply of motors so reconverted to hydraulic.

"One flap would come down all the way and the other maybe a couple inches," said Stan Nichols in North Bay. "Once you got the airplane speeded up, they'd equalize with the air pressure under the wings. It looked funny and everybody used to holler and scream but as soon as you got up to 25 or 30 mph (40 or 48 km/h), they were okay and when you landed, no problem—they'd come down evenly."

Whatever technique used, the "poor man's Beaver," as Gareh called it, did well with tourist-oriented enterprises like Lakeland Airways. Gareh's CF-BGM generally stayed within an eighty mile radius of his home base. He considered the airplane ahead of its time because of inherent strength, streamlining and speed.

That thing would climb, boy, I'll tell you," he said. "It'd go up at 1,000 ft. (300 m), 1,500 ft. (450 m) per min. and of course, it was a very fast airplane too. On floats, the cruise was roughly between 120–125 mph (193–201 km/h)."

Another experienced pilot remembered carrying outpost camp equipment like four-burner propane stoves roped to the floats. He also staggered aloft with complete cottage walls with windows still in place. One man, unable to fit a player piano inside his SR-10, wrapped it in plastic sheeting and tied the package between the left float and wing strut. Boats snugged on the float spreader bars became routine except they were awkward to manipulate. "You had to stand in the water; it was a helluva time," Nichols added.

Throttle position during takeoff was one of the most puzzling features of the Pratt & Whitney Reliants. In de Havilland Beavers, for instance, pilots never pushed a throttle "to the wall" as they did on the lighter Cessna line. In the SR-9s and SR-10s, however, Mike McCluskey pointed out that pilots "...just open the tap and push it to the fire wall and away you go." Experienced with at least 600 hours on type, he never blew any "jugs" (cylinders) during his career.

"In the winter, I'm sure you'd blow the tops right off at forty below but not at sea level on summer days," McCluskey explained. "A lot of it might have been because those cylinders had been reworked so goddamn many times and honed out and put back on again."

The Stinson airframe was built of welded 4130 plate and steel tubing. Wings had an alloy steel main spar beam, dural metal rear spar and ribs covered by fabric. One writer claimed the Gull Wings were "practically indestructible and plowed through rough air like an ocean liner." Stan Nichols compared them to the "proverbial brick" and aviation aficionado Justin Major in Toronto said they were as solid as a railway bridge.

Not all Reliants were fabric-covered. An SR-10 registered CF-HVP had been converted to metallized wings which continually cracked. The owner, disgusted with seeing profits eaten up in maintenance, decided to change back to fabric. Other special order models came from the factory with extra doors. In fact, CF-HVP's huge cargo entrance on the cabin's left rear side proved excellent for freighting 45 imp. gal. (205 l) drums. "We hauled about nine empty or three full ones," remarked Nichols.

Alan R. Williams learned the hard way that Pratt & Whitney engines occasionally malfunctioned. He flew CF-BGS for Parsons Airways Northern from Flin Flon, 430 mi. (692 km) northwest of Winnipeg. Many of his duties entailed supplying exploration camps deep in Manitoba's fly-infested bush country. On one occasion, the pests became so irritating that a group of line cutters clearing brush for claim staking could no longer work outdoors. Williams answered their plaintive call for "rescue" with CF-BGS.

Williams flew east of Flin Flon to File Lake where he loaded passengers in all seats and crammed the cabin to the ceiling with their equipment. After a long glassy water takeoff run, the SR-9 barely climbed higher than 1,200 ft. (360 m) before cylinder head and oil temperatures moved into the red danger zone. Forced to throttle back, Williams began losing height.

"My right hand had not yet come to rest on the propeller pitch and throttle controls when a sharp metallic sound made us all forget the high temperature and mosquitos. The sound was followed almost immediately by black oil on the windscreen," said Williams.

When Williams opened the left window, the oil immediately smeared his eyes. Two passengers quickly wrapped a towel around his head so he could see forward in spite of the 115 mph (185 km/h) wind blasting into the cockpit. Unable to find a suitable size lake, he turned left. The engine still idled at minimum power and produced a small amount of thrust but every instrument red-lined and oil gurgled out and down the Stinson's side. A small pond barely visible through ribbons of coffee-colored oil slithering up the windshield took shape ahead.

As the Stinson approached, a successful forced landing seemed out of the question. Williams estimated he was less than 20 ft. (6 m) above the sharp spruce tops when the engine seized completely. Only 175 ft. (53 m) from the shallow, island-studded lake, he'd almost made it. In a nose heavy airplane with a tendency to dig in, Williams knew he was in serious trouble.

"The trees disappeared from view and immediately I felt the control column spring back toward my chest and then relax once again," he said. "The elevator had brushed the tree tops at the water's edge."

Williams came to a gentle stop less than an airplane length from a rock island. He knew Stinsons did not normally land and stop in such short distances. Everyone escaped unhurt and the beautiful Reliant CF-BGS did not have a scratch.

In later years, Williams discussed his near miss with another pilot who remarked that the glide ratio of a stopped engine SR-9 was "zero plus." The pilot added that "...throwing out a greased anvil and passing it on the way down" aptly described the descent rate. This SR-9 characteristic made Williams' achievement even more remarkable.

Gull Wing Stinsons no longer have a place in the commercial world. In spite of being the "ultimate in elegance," as historian John Underwood called them, the Stinsons had come to the end of the line. The complicated structure would be too expensive to produce in modern, fast-paced factories. Besides, admitted one aficionado, roll-down windows and leather-trimmed upholstery had no place beside the plastic stamped out metal panels of today's commercial airplanes.

The distinctive shape which caught the traveling public's attention can still be seen at aviation meets and fly-ins. Museums, too, have restored several. In any case, these graceful classics will always occupy a conspicuous place in Canadian aviation history.

4   Beech 18

Twin Engine Wonderboat

The ten-year-old boy stood quietly on the sandy shoreline of the Kebsquasheshing River in northern Ontario. As water lapped his shabby running shoes, he heard voices. At the weathered, wooden dock of Theriault Air Services, he saw them.

Turkeys.

Not birds, but men who came to Chapleau from a faraway country where the streets were paved with gold—American tourists.

It was not the invaders from the south that captivated the child. Two dock helpers were loading a twin-engine seaplane, one so huge it dwarfed a yellow-and-black Cessna 180 resting nearby. Its sleek twin tails and bullet shape looked out of place in a land where thundering Noorduyn Norsemen shattered the stillness nearly every summer morning. Even at his age, the boy recognized the classic Beechcraft 18.

The Beechcraft 18 had existed long before the boy watched the silver monoplane take off. The concept of streamlined, low drag airplanes originated when Walter and Olive Ann Beech founded the Beech Aircraft Company in April, 1932, in the aviation-minded community of Wichita, Kansas. Several months later, their revolutionary fabric-covered Model 17R "Staggerwing" biplane swept across the wheat fields. As orders picked up, Walter Beech and his design team began considering a low wing mini-liner orientated toward business and charter markets.

By November 1935, the "Model 18" began taking shape on the factory floor. After months of improvements, redesign and government paperwork, the 18A rolled out as a small, all-metal twin with seating for eight and powered by 320-h.p. Wright R-760-E-2 engines. Trans World Airlines pilot James N. Peyton made the maiden flight on January 5, 1937. Within a month, the first Beech 18, registered NG15810, appeared on the cover of February's *Aero Digest* in company with a Staggerwing. The magazine's no-nonsense description of the new twin's structure made it sound like it came from a foundry: "The center section differs from conventional construction details in that it includes a single, heat-treated steel tube spar which is fitted into the fuselage to provide a convenient structure to carry engine, landing gear and wing stresses. Outer wing panels are of simplified design. Excessive bending stresses are carried by a heat-treated welded tube monospar which bolts to the center section beam...spliced to a dural girder."

The "Twin Beechcraft," or plain "Beech" or "Twin Beech," as it became known, was not welcomed instantly in an era when biplanes were still much in favor. The prototype went to the air-minded Ethyl Corporation in the United States but the factory built only six Model 18s during the first production year. As they became accepted for unmatched durability and dependability, sales increased.

Customers liked the sound-proofed interiors and choice of six cabin seats or four overstuffed chairs or two chairs and a couch in the cabin. A molded safety glass windshield and wiper appealed to pilots, and efficient hot air ducts kept everyone comfortable in the coldest weather. However, the published 55 mph (89 km/h) landing speed undoubtedly did more than any feature to attract Canadian buyers.

Montreal-based Aircraft Industries of Canada became Canadian agents. On April 20, 1937, pilot Romeo Vachon accepted an invitation to attend a Beechcraft 18 demonstration at St. Hubert Airport near Montreal. An experienced Canadian Airways pilot and mechanic, Vachon reported favorably on general Beech workmanship. Impressed with rivetting throughout the airframe, he did criticize the engine cowlings as not particularly strong. The undercarriage, he added, was designed only to handle wheels. For ski flying, new landing gear would have to be developed. Vachon reported to general manager George Anson Thompson in Winnipeg: "The aileron control is very sensitive. A light touch will put the machine in a practically vertical bank, and by shutting the motor inside the bank, it is possible to re-right the machine, in fact, send it in the opposite bank by merely pressing with your little finger on the wheel, and it will respond so fast that the passengers in the cabin have to hold down to something."

Vachon lauded Beechcraft stability by comparing it to a "wedge." He believed exceptional takeoff and climb performance made it acceptable for VFR flying. In fact, demonstration pilot Don Martin needed only an eight-second takeoff with eight aboard and half fuel. In cruise, Vachon noted 185 mph (298 km/h). For instrument flying, however, control oversensitivity impaired handling in cloud.

Vachon showed special interest in blue prints portraying a Model 18 on seaplane floats. Nevertheless, the lack of a track record in the bush deterred Canadian Airways from ordering a Beechcraft until May, 1940. Aircraft Industries of Canada quoted $78,877.74 for a package with Edo 7170 floats and special ski legs and forks.

Starratt Airways and Transportation of Hudson, a few minutes west of Sioux Lookout, Ontario, became the first Canadian Beechcraft owner when CF-BGY cleared customs on December 15, 1937. In the field, the bright blue paint scheme made the Model 18A the smartest airplane in bush country. In truth, the Wright R-750-E-2 engines lacked sufficient power. Charles R. Robinson remembered clearly that CF-BGY could barely drag its Edo 7170 floats off northern Ontario's lakes.

Empty, seaplane CF-BGY weighed 4,742 lb. (2,134 kg) and could carry 966 lb. (435 kg) of fuel in its 133 imp. gal. (605 l) wing tanks. Most Hudson area trips rarely lasted longer than two hours. Consequently, payloads with pilot, half fuel and equipment (anchor and survival packages) averaged 1,698 lb. (764 kg) with a legal maximum takeoff weight of 7,170 lb. (3,227 kg). With these figures in mind, Starratt Airways considered CF-BGY a money maker until 1941.

On January 7 of that year, operations manager Dale Sidney Atkinson learned that pilot A. W. Starratt had not returned to Hudson after leaving Red Lake. In spite of intermittent snow squalls and approaching darkness, Atkinson began an air search. Unsuccessful in finding CF-BGY, he stayed overnight at Gold Pines, 35 mi. (56 km) southeast of Red Lake. Next morning, he discovered something which "...appeared to be a very small flame or a large glowing amber" in the snow on Bruce Lake, 16 mi. (26 km) from Gold Pines. The Twin Beech had smashed into the ice after Starratt was overcome by carbon monoxide poisoning.

The Hudson's Bay Company had also joined the exclusive club of Canadian Beech 18 owners. Pilots Paul Davoud and Duncan D. McLaren flew CF-BMI direct from the factory to Winnipeg in April, 1939, and then to Edmonton for float installation. The pale gray Model 18 was an ideal communications vehicle for visiting trading posts. One expedition took Davoud and Hudson's Bay management staff down the MacKenzie River, over to Yellowknife and Uranium City and then to Norway House before returning to Winnipeg. Such work in open-water seasons became routine.

Winter trips with CF-BMI were more difficult, especially with the *National Geographic* 97 mi. (156 km) = 1 in. (2.54 cm) maps used to navigate. During a flight to central British Columbia, short daylight hours forced Davoud into several stops. Both wings needed cumbersome canvas covers to prevent frost forming overnight. Each morning, one man patrolled with a fire extinguisher as blanket-covered plumbers' blow pots under each engine blasted heat upwards into the propeller and cylinders.

The Company used CF-BMI until September 5, 1941. After landing at Richmond Gulf on the east coast of Hudson Bay, the Beechcraft suffered float damage and parts were flown in for repairs. Overnight, a 50 mph (81 km/h) gale created waves large enough to tilt the Beech's wing tip into the rollers and CF-BMI went to the bottom. In twenty-eight months of Hudson's Bay

Company service, it had covered almost a hundred thousand miles to nearly every fur trade district in Canada.

Wartime shortages hindered the search for a replacement but the manufacturer, renamed Beech Aircraft Corporation, located another with slightly more powerful 330-h.p. Jacobs L-6 engines. Originally owned by a Mr. Clenison of Middletown, New York, 70 mi. (113 km) north of New York City, it carried United States registration N18578.

Pilot Duncan D. McLaren and mechanic Jerry Buchan drew the assignment of bringing the Beechcraft to Canada in mid-November, 1941. After a three-day wait—which included their first experience with television at Clenison's home—they flew N18578 to Roosevelt Field, Long Island. There, they arranged an export certificate of airworthiness and a hangar crew painted the new lettering CF-BVM on the wings and fuselage. An unexpected military event in Hawaii upset plans for the flight to Winnipeg.

"On the afternoon of Sunday, December 7, 1941, I was laying on my bed in my room at Roosevelt Inn, listening to the radio when the program was interrupted and the attack on Pearl Harbor by the Japanese was announced," recalled McLaren.

Not yet aware that all export licenses were cancelled, they left Long Island and arrived at Burlington, Vermont, under a 500 ft. (150 m) ceiling and reduced visibility in snow showers. A customs agent immediately impounded CF-BVM. A month later, the flight continued after Canadian and American officials agreed on the proper paperwork. McLaren and Buchan overnighted at Kapuskasing, Ontario, and looked forward to a pleasant, relaxed journey the following morning.

Less than an hour after leaving Kapuskasing, oil began running out of the front section of CF-BVM's left engine, entered the tubing and continued into the heating system.

"Before I could cut off the heat or shut down the engine, the cockpit was filled with smoke so thick I lost sight of the instrument panel," said McLaren. "I managed to press my face against the side cockpit window and kept from stalling or diving by maintaining a downwind angle of the wing tip relative to the horizon."

With one engine shut off, McLaren and Buchan turned for Pagwa, an emergency airstrip which had been part of the Trans-Canada Airlines system during the 1930s. Facilities there were primitive but McLaren knew that tractor-towed rollers were available to pack the runway. McLaren expected to be down for quick repairs and off again within a short time.

On final approach, McLaren instructed Buchan to lower the landing gear. With the handle in the "down" position, nothing happened. Applying throttle to the good engine, they executed a missed approach procedure and circled the airport. While working to lower the wheels, a hand crank broke in McLaren's hand. He had no other choice except a belly landing.

"As I started to flare, I selected the flaps to the 'up' position hoping they would retract in time to avoid any damage to them. At the last second before touch down, I cut the electrical master switch. The windmilling propellers both went glub-glub as they curled back around the cowlings and we stopped. There was no fire."

Luckily, the soft snow surface minimized damage. McLaren continued to Winnipeg by CNR train while his partner remained behind to do the repairs. Less than a month later, McLaren was surprised to receive a telegram informing him that CF-BVM no longer existed.

Extracts from the minutes of a Hudson's Bay Company meeting attributed the loss to fire caused by the effects of sunlight on a magnetic compass. The company's association with Beechcraft ended forever. After World War II, the Bay acquired a Noorduyn Norseman to replenish remote trading posts.

Several Beechcraft continued flying with Prairie Airways of Moose Jaw, Saskatchewan, as well as Starratt Airways in Ontario and Canadian Airways in Manitoba. Wherever they flew, the "Wichita Wobblers," as aviation historian Chuck Sloat called them, stood up to the rigors of northern conditions. One landed on snow-covered muskeg and knocked a wing tip off on a stump. The pilot and mechanic hammered out a new part from a fuel drum and stove bolts and kept working.

Refinements in design continued. By 1939, the 450-h.p. Pratt & Whitney R-985 engine became the standard powerplant. During World War II, Beech produced 5,230 Model 18s of various designations and production peaked at twelve per day.

The RCAF purchased its first in 1941. By war's end, the Beech "Expeditor" had trained pilots, navigators, and radar officers by the hundreds. Figures showed 9,388 Beechcraft 18s built in thirty-three years—the longest production run of any airplane in history.

Thirty-two variations of the Twin Beechcraft flew in nations around the world but Canada presented the severest challenges. Back country air services needed freighters to handle short lakes and heavy loads where few airstrips existed. Pilots and owners, however, remembered the poor pre-war performance on floats. They knew, too, that as a skiplane, slush trapped the Beechcraft quicker than any other type.

In 1962, Bristol Aerospace Ltd. in Winnipeg developed a strengthening attachment which fitted to the center section truss. The modification also eased the installation of larger Bristol-built floats. Designated Edo 56-7850s, the new floats supported 680 lb. more than the Edo 7170s of Canada's first Model 18 in 1937.

Flight trials on Winnipeg's Red River took place under the supervision of aircraft maintenance engineer Haakon Kristiansen. Soon, commercial versions went into the field. A Bristol history claimed at least fifty-eight Twin Beechcraft were certified under an STC or Supplementary Type Certificate with the Edo 56-7850s. Almost overnight, the Twin Beechcraft became the favored airplane with commercial air services.

Flush riveting on the wing leading edges reduced aerodynamic drag and engine nacelles had been streamlined for speed. Greater cabin area and increased window size made the ride enjoyable for crew and passengers. With the more powerful engine, amazing loads could be carried.

As ideal as the "new" Beechcraft seemed to be in the eyes of Bristol engineers, it would have seen limited use in bush flying with a standard passenger door. The company offered a "Polar" door which measured 45 in. (114 cm) x 54 in. (137 cm) with reinforced floor sills for heavy loads. Double hinged, the Polar easily admitted 4 ft. (1.2 m) x 8 ft. (2.4 m) plywood sheets or 45 gal. (205 l) fuel drums. Another company in Tucson, Arizona, developed an even larger upward opening door. In any case, almost every Canadian Twin Beech on floats used some kind of modified entrance rather than the small factory issue unit. Exceptionally large and awkward cargo could be carried much easier.

One air service hauled a jeep to South Trout Lake, 122 mi. (196 km) north of Red Lake. Disassembled with the frame cut down the middle, it barely fit inside. On the shoreline, welders "sewed" the vehicle back together with acetylene torches and then drove 3 mi. (5 km) to Favourable Lake Gold Mine. Other loads to the same site included 2,000 lb. (900 kg) generators and 1,800 lb. (810 kg) electric cable reels.

Bristol's sales brochures indicated that the failure of either engine at maximum load was not critical. They pointed out that safe single engine flight could be maintained at altitudes above 5,000 ft. (1,500 m). One paragraph boasted a 7,500 ft. (2,250 m) single engine ceiling and a climb of 225 ft. (68 m) per min. Nearly every pilot with Beechcraft seaplane experience disputed the claim.

"The general feeling they had was that if one engine quit, the other would take you right to the scene of the accident," said an experienced pilot. "I've never had a total failure but I've had blown pistons. As long as you left things alone, you could go a long way. For damn sure, you'd fly farther in a Beech that lost one than any Beaver or Otter that quit."

Many pilots learned the hard way that Beechcraft 18s in any configuration could be a handful when an engine stopped. One man with 1,700 hours experience on wheeled Beeches took off from Rainbow Lake in northwestern Alberta with three passengers and enough fuel to fly to Calgary. After getting airborne at seventy-five knots, the right engine stopped. Almost immediately, the unbalanced thrust created a roll in spite of full opposite controls. No one was hurt in the belly landing.

With heavy floats, struts and fittings combined with the drag of the entrance ladder, no one expected the seaplane Twin Beech to stay up for long when an engine stopped; except Canada's aviation inspectors.

"When they're loaded, single-engine performance is just about zero but the Department of Transport got it in their heads that every twin should fly on one," said a seaplane pilot. "That's a real crock. Not many airplanes hang on when they're hot and heavy. The Beech 18's much safer because there's a million lakes in this country."

A typical seaplane Twin Beech weighed 6,800 lb. including pilot, oil and survival equipment. Approved to take off at a maximum weight of 8,725 lb. (3,926 kg), some models such as C-FCUK of Walsten Air Services in Kenora, Ontario, carried 235 imp. gal. (1,069 l) of gasoline inside four wing tanks and a nose tank. Using nearly 40 imp. gal. (182 l) per hour, this gave a six-hour range at 135 mph (217 km/h).

With full gasoline, only 233 lb. (105 kg) remained for freight/passenger loads in a 450-h.p. Twin Beech. However, some air services out of sight of federal inspectors often carried more. A Vancouver Island pilot remembered days when it was not unusual to fill the fuel tanks and carry 2,000 lb. (900 kg) of fish. "Some of the things the Beech 18 has done are amazing; it's an amazing airplane," he added. Another individual counted twenty-seven passengers emerging from a ski-equipped Model 18 in northern Ontario—outstanding for an airplane that sold after World War II with maximum seating for nine including pilot.

It was not only the placing of heavy cargo inside its 10 ft., 3 in. cu. ft. cabin that added to the Twin Beech's reputation as a hard worker. Plenty of oddball loads were tied outside as well. Norman Wright of Sabourin Lake Airways in Cochenour, Ontario, left his water base with a 12 ft. (3.6 m) billiard table tied between the floats of CF-PSC. Another man carried his share of corpses from drownings, shootings or mine accidents. Bodies were usually fastened inside but not always.

"The ones I hauled on the outside were them that stunk so bad from drowning," he explained. "They'd be in a body bag and we'd put them between the float struts and it was just like trying to tie a bag of water. Was almost impossible to snug 'em down and you couldn't put them inside, they smelled so bad."

As many as eight telephone poles have been seen on the bellies of Twin Beech seaplanes. Pilots used a "come-a-long" or small hand-operated mechanical jack to cinch them tightly. Properly balanced, the poles had little aerodynamic effect. Boats, on the other hand, were another matter.

"You didn't fly boats on the side; you brought them stern first between the floats and used a couple of cables to wind them tight," said Bert Archer who flew for Wheeler-Northland Airlines from Goose Bay, Labrador. "Somebody told me never to fly over 80 mph (129 km/h) with a boat on a Beech but that's the only speed I could get anyway."

Most pilots could accurately guess what Twin Beeches carried in spite of a lack of weigh scales in bush country. They survived by wresting every possible measure of performance from their overworked airplanes. Hartley Weston, with a Twin Beech on straight skis, found himself assigned to haul fish for Canadian Fish Producers from lakes east of Lynn Lake, Manitoba.

Weston decided to rest during his long duty day and allowed several Indian helpers to load his airplane. During the takeoff, he noticed the run was unusually long. With throttles all the way forward, he "kinda hopped along for a couple miles" and then flew more than half of South Indian Lake before daring to raise the flaps. Unable to return when snow squalls obliterated the fish camp behind him, Weston had no choice but to keep flogging.

"If that thing even coughed once, it would have rolled over and died. I had a passenger too. Boy, you want to see a white knuckler. I don't think he blinked once. 'Hart,' he says, 'how come we're so low?' And I says, 'That's as high as I can get this goddamn thing.' 'Jesus Christ, Hart, we're going to die,' he says. 'Yup,' I says, 'I'm sure of it.' And that didn't help at all."

Each time Weston tried to turn, the twin tails shuddered. To miss an island, he "kind of ruddered her around, square-like."

Soon, a mine headframe at Lynn Lake passed under the belly and he began his landing approach. Without retarding the throttles, he pointed the nose down and slammed into the hard-packed snow. He swerved violently left with full power on the right engine just in time to avoid a skiplane base owned by Chiupka Airways.

"Speed? Who had time to look at airspeed? We didn't even think of instruments. Everything was strictly thinking through the hind end," Weston said.

Later, he discovered his Beech had carried at least 3,586 lb. (1,614 kg) of fish, an overload by more than 1,800 lb. (810 kg).

At one point, air carrier inspectors issued an undated letter which stressed that they intended to keep a watchful eye for illegal practices. In particular, and of grave concern, read the bulletin, "...is the operation of these airplanes in excess of maximum certificated takeoff weights."

Although the Twin Beech performed adequately, owners wanted improved performance. Bristol Aircraft Ltd. printed a catalogue of gadgets and modifications, many of which became standard for northern air services. In fact, bare bones original Beechcraft have become rare, especially on floats or skis. One simple modification changed the horizontal stabilizer's angle of incidence, i.e., the angle at which it met the airflow. A sealing strip also closed the gap between the stabilizer and elevator control to lessen drag.

Engine power could be increased with carburetor ram air scoops. The previous factory system drew warm air between the cylinder heads into the carburetor. Bristol's scoops moved colder air through a fiberglass unit below the engine cowling for a 1.5 in. (4 cm) gain in manifold pressure or power. With all improvements in the "Safety Performance Kit" installed, the Beechcraft flew 20 mph faster and increased payload by 350 lb. (158 kg), claimed Bristol.

"The mods are the key," acknowledged Larry Langford of Vancouver Island Air in Campbell River, British Columbia. "The Beech is the most highly modified civil or military aircraft I know of and the airframe's been approved up to 10,200 lb. (4,590 kg). It's got a tremendous history and it's a great performer."

Perhaps the most radical suggestion came from a Bristol study in 1960. A nineteen-page report pointed out that JATO might have an application for fixed wing operators of many civilian airplanes. The JATO rocket bottles were available in two sizes. The pair to blast the Beech off the ground produced 250 lb. (113 kg) of thrust each for fifteen seconds. Although the concept may have seemed reasonable to an engineering team in a Winnipeg factory building, it did not appeal to air service owners. No commercial Twin Beechcraft used the rocket assist, especially at $410 a "pop."

Transition to Beeches in the bush was generally not considered difficult if pilots had seaplane experience. When promoted from smaller Cessnas and de Havilland Beavers, they needed time to adjust to the tremendous power and higher airspeeds. Landing approaches took place as fast as 100 mph (161 km/h). Some smaller seaplanes settled into the water at 50 mph (81 km/h). Hartley Weston remembered his first Twin Beechcraft takeoff as a "revelation." His previous experience included several seasons carrying fish in Cessna T-50 Cranes and plywood-covered Avro Ansons on wheels and skis from Riverton, north of Winnipeg.

"Got her lined up and hit the throttles and all hell broke loose," he said. "That thing was off the water, it would have put a Super Cub to shame. And I'm thundering off, I'm going up, I'm hanging on and I'm already 1,500 ft. (450 m) screaming like a real cowboy and I had no idea what was happening, this thing left me so far behind. I says, 'Wow! This I like!'"

Takeoffs sometimes surprised unwary pilots. With loads placed too far toward the tail, the Twin Beech porpoised easily, especially when slamming into boat wakes. Although most North American airplanes swung gently left because of aerodynamic forces, the Model 18 could be surprisingly abrupt. The only cure, cautioned a northern Ontario pilot, was extreme left throttle to counteract the yaw or swing.

In the air, the Twin Beech was unusually stable. At altitude, said Weston, who estimated his hours on type as nearly 7,000, the pilot simply adjusted the trim controls, slid his seat back and, if time permitted, read a book. Most pilots felt at ease after logging a hundred hours.

"Years back, we had 25–30 mi. (40–48 km) flights with the Norseman," said Herman Anderson, who flew 8,000 Beech hours in Ontario. "Speed wasn't a factor but as the logging industry blossomed and roads spread deeper into the bush, hauls became longer and further away. Now, a 250 mi. (403 km) trip with a Beech is routine."

Gary Fenton, an ex-Beech pilot who now flies de Havilland Beavers for Tyee Airways at Sechelt, British Columbia, remembered the Twin Beech as much cooler than Norsemen or Otters. Heat, he explained, did not flow backwards into the cabin from the engines. Another pilot, who enjoyed the smooth-running Beech, said his feet nearly vibrated out of his shoes in a Norseman.

"The Beech is nothing like a Norseman. You don't have to work hard and you go up to 7,000 ft. (2,100 m), 8,000 ft. (2,400 m) with a load and cruise along quite comfortably," he said.

The Twin Beech had a few quirks. Some pilots insisted it was impossible to force the wings to stall in a throttled back, straight ahead attitude. When practicing such procedures, pilots find that most airplanes lose lift on the wings, then the nose drops gently and speed increases. In the Beech, however, pilots brought the control wheel back and the tail stalled first. At this point, they no longer had elevator control. One man discovered that these situations could create problems.

"I'm coming down hill, engines off, just z-z-z-zting along and then I yanked her real firm like for the round out (change from a glide to a landing attitude) and the tail stalled. Almost put her straight in; just got enough power to bring the nose up when she hit the water. 'Course, you react with full power and it snaps the tail back up again. I must have got too low a speed with full flap down and no airflow over the tail."

Pilots who understood the aircraft's faults and strong points could land in amazingly short distances. A flight manual for C-GENX listed 2,150 ft. (645 m) over a 50 ft. (15 m) obstacle for

The Hudson's Bay Company's Beechcraft 18D was powered by Jacobs L6 engines. Unlike many corporate airplanes, its pilots rarely landed at regular airports. The crew had little choice but to service CF-BMI themselves in locations like Fort Providence in May, 1941. Underpowered by today's standards, the Bay's Beechcraft flew extensively year round until its loss at Richmond Gulf, Quebec, on August 12, 1941.

Photo: Hudson's Bay Company

When Beechcraft 18A CF-BGY entered service in 1938, federal aviation inspectors insisted on a two-man crew. After reams of correspondence between Wichita, Washington, Montreal, Winnipeg and Hudson, Starratt Airways & Transportation was finally authorized to fly with one pilot and eight passengers.

Photo: Thunder Bay Flying Club

a loaded airplane in calm conditions. One veteran used a spectacular technique which cut his regular distance by half.

"You'd flop in on the water and shove the wheel forward as hard as she'd go. No tendency to flip over at all and she doesn't even go sideways but water comes up and over that goddamn windshield every goddamn time. Its got so much flotation in those Edo 7850s, they just tear the airspeed to pieces right now."

Rochelle Bodnar logged several thousand seaplane hours before her first Beech landing with Rusty Myers Flying Service in Fort Frances, Ontario. A Beaver and Cessna pilot, she had studied the huge twins whenever she could, knowing the opportunity to fly one would eventually come her way. When her first flight finally arrived in C-FZRI on May 26, 1996, Bodnar found the change startling.

"The Beech has such a weird landing attitude," she said. "It's very flat so you feel like you're flying right straight into the water and it sinks like a rock, the Beech. You need lots of power on and keep up the speed. Trouble is, you get the impression it's coming down too fast to land."

Some air service owners consider Twin Beeches as "maintenance turkeys." Maintenance engineer Syl Turcotte of Rusty Myers Flying Service called the rust-prone exhaust system a "corker to keep going." Vibration, he added, caused frequent clamp changing. Engine cowlings were difficult and time-consuming to remove. One man said the aging Beech's problems began when companies skimped on replacing parts. As the airplane deteriorated into collections of metal held together with shoe laces and stove bolts, accidents happened and costs went up.

Harbour Air's Peter Evans in Richmond, British Columbia, stressed that although the Twin Beech was reasonably priced, owners wound up with higher costs because they had two engines and "two of everything else." Keeping ahead, countered Syl Turcotte, meant addressing every snag or problem immediately, no matter how small.

"Give them daily inspections and there's nothing wrong with them," he said. "You watch those float fittings to see if they're smoking (showing black streaks of worn metal dust) and do a serious check in the engine cylinder hold down studs every day and the Beech'll go forever."

Early Beechcraft seemed plagued with starting and battery problems related to solenoid relays. Stranded in wilderness, some pilots simply stood by until someone arrived in a company Cessna 180 with a box of tools and an mechanic. Hartley Weston, however, could not abide the wait, especially on cold October days on lakes near the southern shore of Hudson Bay. Handstarting was the solution.

"You took a rope, tied one end to the ladder and crawled under the wing with the other end tied around your middle," he said. "You hand bombed the propeller with one hand and as soon as the engine caught, you fired yourself backwards and sideways into the lake. By the time you come up, you were getting towed and you pulled yourself in with the rope. It was the only way; otherwise, the propeller ate you alive."

One man near Attawapiskat on James Bay snapped a throttle cable in his right engine. He wired the mechanism directly to the carburetor to produce almost full throttle at start up and took off. At cruise, he had little to worry about and on landing, used the fuel mixture control to "burp" the engine for taxiing. This pilot's ingenuity surfaced again when he found his Beech's exhaust pipes dotted with corrosion holes. He patched them with tin cans and flew home.

Bristol Aerospace thought they saw a niche in the Canadian bush flying scene for a retractable wheel/ski. In 1963, project engineer Haakon Kristiansen, known for his work on the Edo 56-7850 floats, embarked on a program to increase the Twin Beech's winter utility.

Kristiansen and his staff created a unique change-over mechanism which allowed a selection of either wheels or skis with the airplane on the ground or in flight. At normal cruise power settings, no noticeable airspeed loss occurred.

Ilford, Manitoba-based Riverton Airways loaned Beechcraft CF-OWU for development flying. On December 28, 1963, test pilot E. H. Birnie began air testing at Winnipeg. During his first flight, the skis stopped 10 in. (25 cm) from the fully raised position. To avoid an emergency landing, electrical circuit breakers had to be pulled and the landing gear hand-pumped down.

On the third test, the crew landed in deep snow and discovered that both engines ingested snow through the carburetor air scoops. They also confirmed that tires and undercarriage oleo struts helped absorb takeoff and landing shocks. Much of the testing took place at gross weights of 9,275 lb. (4,174 kg). At one point, Birnie dove to 257 mph (414 km/h). He also reported single engine climb rates from 80–120 ft. (24–36 m) per min.

On the thirteenth flight, a failed chain sprocket resulted in a belly landing with minor propeller, fuselage and flap damage. Engineers changed the rubber "bungee" cord retracting system to a helical metal spring cable/drum device similar to a garage door raising unit. When Bristol obtained federal certification, the main skis, tail ski and raising mechanism weighed 401 lb. (180 kg)—quite a detraction from payload.

Unfortunately for Bristol, markets for the Model 5100 Retractable Wheel-Skis did not develop. Flying into paved runways from snow-covered airstrips and remote lakes should have appealed to bush air services but records show that only nine kits were sold.

The first production set went to H. C. Paul of Winnipeg. Companies like Northwest Territorial Airways (later renamed NWT Air) in Yellowknife and Northward Aviation of Edmonton also tried them. St. Felicien Air Service of Roberval, Quebec, installed wheel/skis on CF-RRE and flew from Fort Chimo on Ungava Bay to settlements such as Sugluk, Wakeham Bay and Koartak. Northland Airlines in Riverton, Manitoba, ordered three kits and used them throughout northern Manitoba and northwestern Ontario.

A sales brochure stressed simplicity. Bristol claimed the pilot did not need to leave his cozy, leather-covered seat to free frozen skis. By pressing a button, the hydraulics simply snapped them loose. However, the system turned out to be complicated and overly sensitive for bush country operations. Hand pumps, activators, trims and other components fared poorly in cold weather. Cables on the retracting drum frequently slipped.

"They were nothing but grief. It was the stupidest set up in history," recalled Hartley Weston. "If you're taking off in loose snow, here's all this snow blowing around getting into everything. Then there's the heat from engine melting this snow onto the cable tracks. Instant freeze! So you go to retract, you hear the clutch go boom. It had an overload clutch and it just wouldn't pull them up.

"They were hard to move, oh, they were hard to move on the snow. I hated them. Every night you had to take the Herman (heater) and throw the heat in and melt everything out. I never had to belly flop but it seems everybody else did."

Wheel/skis or not, Twin Beechcraft were too heavy for pilots to rock the wings and free themselves from deep slush. Some veterans carried a hydraulic jack and slipped it under each ski. After freeing the bottoms, they shoved wooden poles underneath. Next, came the pilot's miserable job of lying on his back to scrape wet slush which stopped the Beech from reaching liftoff speed. "Cold, miserable, but what the hell, that was the life," shrugged one man.

Another pilot was impressed with Beech durability on straight skis. Slush, ice or deep snow, it seemed to matter little, he said, you could always come home somehow.

"Them Beechcraft were tough. You'd drive them right through slush you couldn't swim through as long as you didn't stop. I had that stuff up in the bottom cylinders and the propeller beat the living Jesus out of itself. Frozen ice all over the wing and the bottom just covered with bloody ice and, hey, both props could be curled up, so the hell with it."

The bumps, grinds and jolts that Beeches endured took a toll and some were lost as a result of wing spar failures. In Canada, all owners received an expensive surprise from federal aviation authorities. An airworthiness directive or mandatory modification demanded the installation of a strengthening kit of laminated steel strips bolted beneath the wing spar. They spread from the fuselage to outboard of each engine nacelle. Streamlined fairings over these strips reduced aerodynamic drag.

At least one type of kit was necessary for any Twin Beech with 1,500 hours flying time which happened to be nearly every one in Canada. Owners grounded hundreds because they were uneconomical to modify. A few organizations had enough foresight to retain what they knew were money makers. Rusty Myers Flying Service, for example, installed "Aerocon 73 Spar Modification Kits" on their four Beechcraft at an in-house cost of $15,000 each. Later, the "feds" imposed more restrictions including mandatory X-rays.

Transport Canada's strict monitoring policy reduced overloading. Surprise inspections eventually changed the attitudes of pilots and mechanics. All organizations had to train aircrew thoroughly and give annual flight tests. In spite of these innovations, however, the "Twin Tailed Wonder" still had a poor reputation. "Just get above the trees and the thing hardly climbs," was a common remark.

Larry Langford in Campbell River, also heard the terrible tales. He knew the Dubin Inquiry into safety during the early eighties helped change the bush flying industry. With no choice but to comply with regulations, some air services suddenly found their Beeches obsolete. Prices dropped as low as $55,000 in flyaway condition.

"The real payload with the heavy unstripped Beech wasn't much more than 1,500 lb. (675 kg). and the actual payload of a de Havilland Otter was around 2,000 lb. (900 kg) so all the Otters disappeared back east," Langford said. "Nobody worried about Beeches before because the airplane performed and nobody cared about being overweight."

Langford studied performance charts carefully and spoke with successful Twin Beech operators. Rusty Myers Flying Service kept a pristine fleet for tourist customers who expected clean airplanes. They also hired only experienced pilots.

Syl Turcotte described a routine Myers trip to Savant Lake, 138 mi. (222 km) north of Fort Frances, which averaged one hour and fifteen minutes flying time and a fuel consumption of 360 lb. (162 kg). An Otter, he said, stumbled along at ninety-five knots for nearly two hours. Worse, the Stoneboat, as some pilots call the

Otter, needed 432 lb. (194 kg) of fuel over the same distance. This economical advantage of a twin over a single-engine airplane had not gone unnoticed by Langford.

"We can do a trip to Vancouver and back on less fuel with the Beech than a single Otter because it takes less time and they both use nearly the same amount of fuel on the 230 mi. (370 km) round trip," said Langford.

Langford added a Beech to his fleet of Beavers and Cessna 180s. An ex-Slate Falls Airways freighter in Sioux Lookout was inspected by Dave Nilson of Nilson Aircraft Ltd. and flown to Campbell River. Mechanics lifted the blue-and-white airplane into Nilson's overhaul shop where his "Beech Boys" disassembled the wings and fuselage. At the end of seven months, they had eliminated numerous nonessential and expired items.

Cracked belly skins were replaced and the two-blade propellers exchanged for more efficient three-blade units. Mechanics tossed over 150 lb. (68 kg) of blood and oil-stained plywood into a garbage can. A lighter 32 lb. (14 kg) duraluminum replacement floor went inside the Beech. Nilson saved another 27 lb. (12 kg) by exchanging an eleven-piece plexiglass windshield for a streamlined two-panel one. Compact digitalized and miniaturized instruments filled the panel where obsolete heavier ones had been before. When Nilson and crew launched C-FCSN from the "Beech House," it weighed nearly 450 lb. (203 kg) less.

"We like the Beech; it's one helluva airplane and it's got the best radial engines ever built," said Langford. "Customers love it, pilots love it and dispatch loves it. Point the nose up and it's not like trying to squeeze the last 20 ft. (6 m) out of a Beaver. In the Beech, you get a 500 ft. per min. climb at 120 knots so we're climbing faster than a Beaver goes down."

Not everyone adored the Twin Beech. It could be difficult to dock since few had a door on the right. Tall pilots found the cockpit confining and Langford admitted that in the air, the Beech needed more room to turn in British Columbia's valleys and straits.

One of the most important advantages to owning a Twin Beechcraft is the availability of low-priced parts. Only 1,631 de

Havilland Beavers were built compared to over 9,000 Beechcraft. Beaver exhaust segments, for example, cost $800 each but similar Beech parts can be acquired for less than $100. Original military spares like fuel gauges are still available in original wrappings.

"By the time you do all the mods, a paint job, zero time the engine and overhaul the floats, a good Beaver is worth about a quarter million dollars," said Langford. "A top of the line Beech converted to our standards would be worth $200,000 depending on engine time."

In June, 1990, Vancouver Island Air acquired an ex-drug runner Beechcraft 18 from California and turned the stripped hulk over to Nilson Aircraft for conversion to what Langford believes will be the ultimate Beech. Called *The Sea Wind* and registered C-GVIB, modifications include an extended nose to hold 800 lb. (360 kg) of fuel and baggage. Waterproof float compartments are expected to carry another 250 lb. (113 kg). Oversize water rudders provide improved taxiing and streamlined ladders will allow slip-proof cabin entry.

"We're expecting 170 mph (274 km/h) cruise and the same fuel burn as the standard Beech but this one'll go further," Langford explained. "*The Sea Wind* seats twelve plus pilot and incorporates over a dozen changes to lengthen and streamline the basic airframe."

Vancouver Island Air is not the only Canadian company to utilize modified Beechcraft. At least two with Pratt & Whitney PT6 turbines flew regularly from Rankin Inlet on Hudson Bay's west coast for Keewatin Air. Survey organizations adapted some to electronic survey work on floats and skis. For several years, a wheeled Beech flew without incident from short ice runways in oil patch country of northeastern British Columbia.

The Twin Beech as a northern airplane will probably survive longer than many of its contemporaries. Proven to provide high profit margins in a milieu never considered by the Wichita "tin snippers," no one has been able to stop the twin-tailed wonder.

5 Fairchild Husky

Canadian Canoe Carrier

A white, single-engine airplane left Vancouver's international airport and climbed above the murky Fraser River. Pilot Gordon Emberley leveled the world's only flyable Fairchild Husky and adjusted his throttle to cruise through valleys to flatlands east of the Rocky Mountains. After fifteen hours and several refueling stops, Emberley landed at Winnipeg's international airport to deliver Husky C-GCYV to the Western Canada Aviation Museum.

The concept of this radial engine freighter dated back to a period near the end of World War II. With new goals directed toward postwar markets, North America's airplane manufacturers began considering the need for new all-purpose bushplanes. Except for the Noorduyn Norseman, nothing had been built.

Fairchild Aircraft Ltd. at Longueuil, Quebec, thought about reintroducing their successful Fairchild 71-82 line. In fact, one potential customer suggested they rework the 71 with a more powerful engine and slimmer fuselage but Fairchild president Hubert Pasmore quickly pointed out that fabric-covered airplanes were obsolete. All-metal types provided the answers to longevity, low maintenance and profits.

In the summer of 1945, Fairchild engineers drew up several designs to test the market. Chief engineer John A. Butler and flight test engineer A. M. MacKenzie traveled to Sault Ste. Marie to discuss the proposal with director George Ponsford.

"In my opinion, it is another of the funny-looking airplanes that Fairchild have spent so much money in developing across the last ten years," Ponsford said. "The new development is so radical in design as compared to the conventional type to which we have become accustomed."

Ponsford registered seventeen objections and predicted many maintenance and service problems. He told the Fairchild team he would prefer waiting until performance under field conditions had been studied at least a year. With the possibility of big sales looming, Fairchild decided to orient the Model F-11 to OPAS requirements. These included a 450-h.p. Pratt & Whitney Jr. R-985 engine and a cabin large enough to hold an 18 ft. (5.4 m) canoe. Ponsford said that he did not believe "...twenty or perhaps twenty-five aeroplanes would be beyond the bounds of possibility."

After viewing a full scale mock-up in Montreal, Ponsford congratulated Pasmore on his willingness to accept constructive criticism from commercial air service owners. On December 22, 1945, Ponsford indicated he would have no hesitations in recommending purchase. Of course, he added, it had to match whatever competition appeared in respect to price and performance.

On June 14, 1946, Fairchild F-11-1, registered CF-BQC-X, made its maiden flight. MacKenzie's test runs averaged eighteen seconds from full throttle to liftoff at Longueuil. *Canadian Aviation* magazine reported a climb of 675 ft. (20 m) per min. on floats at a gross takeoff weight of 6,400 lb. (2,880 kg) and a 2,400 ft. (720 m) run on glassy water. Ponsford became skeptical and suggested that the gross weight seemed high for only 450 h.p.

Ponsford knew OPAS-built Buhl Air Sedans used a 400-h.p. engine with a maximum weight of 4,500 lb. These "Iron Pots," as some pilots called them, were exceptionally poor performers. Other observers remembered that the 420-h.p. Noorduyn Norseman had to be re-equipped with a 550-h.p. powerplant.

Fairchild compensated for the low horsepower with special slotted flaps and a long narrow wing with good lifting characteristics. A constant speed variable pitch propeller and a clean fuselage also helped increase load-carrying capabilities. Department of Transport test pilot D. D. Murphy felt Fairchild had taken the concept of slimness a little too far, at least concerning control surfaces.

"It was noted that it was not possible to take off in a cross wind from port," Murphy said. "Considerable left rudder is required to counteract the effects of propeller slipstream and there is insufficient extra rudder to counteract weather cocking into wind. It is thought that a large rudder may give better control."

The Husky bore little resemblance to any prewar airplane. Its most outstanding feature turned out to be the rear fuselage's thirty degree upslope. Through a combined trapezoidal-shaped hatch/door opened by a hand crank, handlers could load canoes. A 1946 magazine advertisement claimed one 18 ft. (5.4 m) canoe or two 16 ft. (5 m) canoes fit inside the 240 cu. ft. (7 m^3) volume with a full load of general cargo.

The rear hatch opened in flight for long items such as lumber, lookout tower sections or telephone poles. Fairchild also promoted the Husky's suitability for aerial photography, parachuting, aerial crop dusting and even "for fishing in wet weather." Salesmen underscored a unique express pick-up system for snatching mail from the ground.

Controls like horizontal stabilizers, ailerons and trim tabs, fitted either side and even the doors were interchangeable. To hasten turnarounds, fuel caps were not in the wing but on the fuselage. Seats held nine passengers who entered through large side doors. An operations manager of a West Coast airline remembered counting fourteen passengers in a Husky.

To lessen downtime, the power plant was designed for removal in less than one hour. For routine maintenance, all panels quickly detached and several had chains linked to the engine to prevent loss. Siamese exhaust stacks for each pair of cylinders instead of one per cylinder hastened replacement. For winter operations, nose cowling shutters retained heat. A 50,000 Btu Janitrol Combustion Heater kept the cockpit and cabin warm.

The Husky, in spite of so many practical features, did not take the bush flying market by storm. One customer said looks alone created sales resistance and added that Fairchild might better have designed something "...more in keeping with the conventional type." Bad looks or good looks, the largest potential customer—the Ontario Department of Lands & Forests (former OPAS)—cancelled its order even though Ponsford requested the first two Huskies off the line. The Husky, he said, could not live up to the performance claims.

Fairchild Aircraft Ltd. produced twelve Huskies. The price for a "Standard" F-11 on Edo 62-6560 floats varied from $29,745 to $36,505 depending on engine hours and propeller. At the time, manufacturers could not compete with a market glut of war-surplus airplanes. Most air service owners put up with the inconvenience of fabric and wood Noorduyn Norsemen or Stinsons.

After certification, CF-BQC went to Nickel Belt Airways in Sudbury, Ontario, which soon purchased three others—CF-EIC, CF-EIM and CF-EIN. The same company also became the exclusive agent for western Quebec. Three other Huskies went to the governments of Manitoba and Saskatchewan and several to concerns such as Toronto's Lome Airways which lost CF-EIS at Chapleau, Ontario, in July, 1948, when the pilot stalled in a turn. Canada's Huskies went from owner to owner until Gordon Emberley landed the last flyable one at Winnipeg.

The sharpest criticism was directed toward the 450-h.p. Husky's lack of short field performance. One pilot sardonically remarked that it never did take off—it simply ran along the water until the earth dropped away. Nevertheless, Fairchild staff were not unaware of the problems and expected customer demand for more thrust. Former chief of aerodynamics and flight testing R. D. Richmond said in a *Canadian Aviation Historical Society* journal that 800-h.p. Wrights, 600-h.p. Pratt & Whitney R-1340s and even 520-h.p. Fairchild Rangers had been considered.

In 1947, the factory made an effort to improve performance. On June 11, D. D. Murphy and A. M. MacKenzie taxied wheel-equipped CF-SAQ for takeoff at Longueuil. After two normal traffic circuits, they returned and stood by while mechanics attached a 208 lb. (94 kg) Aerojet Jet Assisted Takeoff Motor or solid propellent rocket under the cockpit.

MacKenzie waited until the tail lifted at 25 mph (40 km/h) before activating the rocket switch. With 911 lb. (410 kg) of cabin ballast and 90 imp. gal. (410 l) of gasoline, the Husky left the runway at 55 mph (89 km/h) in 625 ft. (188 m). In normal operations, a seaplane version at 6,300 lb. (2,835 kg) was expected to take off from glassy water in 2,000 ft. (600 m). The system was an improvement but Husky owners balked at the cost. The Saskatchewan Government Air Service became the first and only customer. Former AME John Finch watched a public demonstration at Regina's airport in 1952.

"There was a horrible roar, a big puff of smoke and not much action," he said. "Pilots watching it thought there must have been a goof of some sort. It certainly didn't give the airplane the kind of jolt it needed."

The empty seaplane weighed in at approximately 3,900 lb. (1755 kg). With 96 imp. gal. (437 l) of gasoline, still air endurance averaged nearly five hours at a fuel consumption of 22.67 imp. gal. (104 l) per hr. Payload was estimated at 1,435 lb. (646 kg) Pilots soon found out that the Husky's average takeoff took much longer than the sales figures.

"On the scene came the Husky and we expected an efficient freight carrier," said ex-Boreal Airways pilot William Peppler. "I was inclined to say, 'Hey, this must be a good airplane,' because it was supposed to incorporate all the features bush pilots wanted. So, I was set to think it would be the greatest airplane ever built."

When CF-BQC made an appearance in Red Lake, high-time pilots derided the unorthodox shape but as the strange machine went to work, they soon changed their minds. The wide doors allowed oversize nuisance items like camp stoves, boilers and full-size plywood sheets to fit easily inside. Better yet, "turkeys," tourists in wilderness lodges, could enjoy linoleum or carpeted floors since the long rolls fit easily through the Husky's back hatch. Mine managers loved the ability to carry squared timbers badly needed for shoring underground shafts.

Pilots slowly accepted the underpowered airplane. After logging a few hours, they discovered that the "Pregnant Guppy" required specialized techniques. Operated properly in spite of the meager 450 h.p., the Husky fared well. Accident statistics show that not one was destroyed because of lack of takeoff room.

"You knew there was none of this fooling around with getting into a small lake. That's why we didn't get into too much trouble if you respected the limited performance capabilities and you chose long lakes," said Peppler.

For takeoffs on calm warm days, it was best to wait for an appropriate breeze. The windier and rougher, the better the Husky performed, Peppler added. He noticed, too, that placing loads as far forward as possible enabled the Husky to reach the step position quicker.

The 19 sq. ft. (5.7 m^2) slotted wing flaps could be lowered fully in fifteen seconds to a maximum of 45 degrees with a ceiling crank. Some versions used electric flap motors but pilots who flew Huskies with the manual system "...developed a mighty biceps on their right arm," said Hartley Weston. Another pilot remembered "crawling" into the air at slightly above 40 mph, (64 km/h) thanks to the massive flaps.

"One selected half flap, then trimmed full nose up initially and power was then applied," Weston said. "No one ever looked at the manifold pressure. It was balls to the wall every takeoff once the spray line advanced to a spot even with the front spreader bar. Then you slowly advanced trim full nose down and never touched the wheel until it flew itself off the water."

Most pilots enjoyed the Husky in the air. They found the front seats comfortable and equipped with retractable arm rests. Adjustable fore and aft, the pilot seat tilted so far backwards, one mechanic said it seemed like a cot. A depressed floor allowed plenty of cockpit headroom and the single-piece, easily read instrument panel contained all instruments and switches.

Engine, propeller controls, trim tabs, carburetor heat and interior heating were located on a central pedestal. Few pilots bothered with a factory-issued partition between the front seats and passenger compartment but at least one could have used some sort of separation on a particularly unpleasant winter flight.

En route in CF-BQC from the Cree-Ojibway settlement of Poplar Hill north of Red Lake, Hartley Weston carried what he

Delivered to the Manitoba Government Air Service at Lac du Bonnet on August 10, 1947, CF-MAN was destroyed beyond repair in 1979. Sales brochures stressed component interchangeability as an important feature. Elevators and rudders, wing flaps, trim tabs, left struts, fuel cells, etc., could be exchanged with ease. Billed as all-metal, the Husky's control surfaces were fabric-covered and detachable wing tips were plywood and veneer. *Photo: Western Canada Aviation Museum/Winnipeg*

When delivered to the Manitoba Government Air Service on August 8, 1947, CF-MAO had 40 in. x 48 in. (102 cm x 122 cm) doors on each side. It carried eight passengers on bush seats and had a large storage compartment under the pilot's floor, accessible through a tiny outside door.

Photo: Western Canada Aviation Museum/Winnipeg

described as ten vicious, ill-tempered, stinking dogs. Also settled in the rear end were the Native owners with wives and numerous children. His flight manifest called for landing somewhere in an unmarked bush-country lake.

At the time, Indian trappers customarily preflighted dog teams by stunning them on the nose with an ax and stuffing the dazed animals into a burlap bag.

Shortly after takeoff into turbulent air, every dog vomited and defecated. The overpowering stench nearly blinded Weston and soon, the children and adults contributed their share to the repulsive accumulation upon the Husky's floor. If events had ended there, Weston said, he would have marked the situation down as nothing more than another routine day in the life of a Canadian bush pilot.

"The dogs started howling and to put it mildly, things were rapidly going to hell when a couple broke loose and tore into the ones still in the bags," he added.

The adult trapper closest to the animals attempted restoring order with an ax but his swings went wide in the rough air. Weston knew the melee would soon reach the cockpit. Looking ahead, he saw the weather changing from high ceilings to low with reduced visibility in snow squalls. Behind him, flashing teeth edged closer.

"My reflex action upon viewing the hordes converging upon my space was immediate," he continued. "A quick shove on the wheel to head straight down pasted the whole parcel to the ceiling, then a quick reversal slammed them again. This had what was to me a remarkable soothing effect but the airplane looked like a slaughter house with all that half-digested macaroni, dog shit, blood, urine and Christ knows what else."

Weston landed, unloaded quickly and returned to Red Lake. Faced with a monumental cleaning task, he decided on a well tested method discovered by his predecessors. After collecting a half-dozen of the hungriest pups available, he left them overnight in the Husky. In the morning—a clean airplane.

Bill Peppler learned to "fine tune" the 450-h.p. Husky for peak performance. For many weeks, he took part in a mammoth line-cutting project in central Quebec where the Husky was the only airplane capable of moving three canoes simultaneously—all inside. This unique feature ensured that Boreal Airways would get the contract. Operations manager Phil Lariviere further impressed the clients when he carried five canoes—two on the floats and three in the cabin.

"The surveyors used canoes all summer and at freeze-up in mid-October, they'd leave them on the spot and come out," Peppler said. "After January, we flew everybody back in and they'd travel with dog teams. We were on skis then so we'd take the canoes ahead and they'd be waiting for them after break-up."

Peppler participated in other work which proved the Husky's practicality. A drilling company contracted Boreal Airways to move mountains of camp gear. Exploration parties needed tents and two-by-four wood frames. Previous Norseman hauls meant the frames had to be cut before the trip and spliced together at the camp.

"There was only one airplane that could take those extra length two-by-fours and 16 ft. (5 m) drill rods," Peppler said. "If you carried a 1,500 lb. (675 kg) payload, hey, you could sure put a lot of two-by-fours in there."

Every bush camp and remote air base needed fuel which usually came in 45 imp. gal. (205 l) drums weighing almost 400 lb. (180 kg). With Beavers and Norsemen, loading could be slow and dangerous. A Beaver pilot, for example, usually cut two poles, removed the side doors and tied his poles together to prevent slippage as the drums slid to the shoreline. Choppy water made the task more hazardous. Often, the pilot worked alone and dreaded the possibility of losing his grip on a drum and smashing the fragile floats. A Husky, however, needed only a few moments sailing backwards to a beach.

"You'd get the heels of the floats as far onto the beach as they'd go, then lay each drum down and roll it out the hatch," said Peppler. "Plop, plop, plop and you'd be ready to go again in ten minutes. We'd be gone for our second load before the Beaver or Norseman pilots got their first drum out."

At the time of the Husky's debut, fish freighting had been responsible for the success of many fledgling airlines. Money-hungry owners sent low-time pilots north with tired Avro

Ansons, Cessna T-50 Cranes or anything which could carry a fish tub. The factory-fresh Husky blended quickly into the flow of hard-working fish freighters. One pilot claimed he carried twenty tubs each flight.

Heavy but compact, these loads were valuable. Pilots jettisoned their cargo only if their lives depended on it. Allan Compton of Riverton, Manitoba's Northland Airlines, found himself aboard a Husky when he and his chief pilot heard a loud noise after takeoff.

"It made a helluva bang and we didn't really know what happened," he said. "Since I was getting checked out, it was my job to get back there and throw out the fish. Lazarenko (airline owner) would have killed us if we didn't keep the tubs, so when I emptied everything through the tail, the scales came flying back and covered the floor with slime. It's a wonder I didn't slide out the ass end but we dumped 750 lb. (338 kg)."

The noise came from a snapped float bracing wire. During the landing, they had no way of knowing if the floats would separate with the weight of the fuselage on them. The Husky skimmed the surface gently and settled into the water without further trouble.

Aircrew sometimes contended with an annoying problem when flying from rough water. One pilot pointed out that the fuselage flexed on takeoff or in turbulent air, sometimes enough to pop open a rear door. Passengers were asked to leave their seats and give the handle a sharp pull to re-secure the latch.

A Husky with Island Airlines in Campbell River, British Columbia, came equipped with a microswitch to warn the pilot of an unlocked door. It was also wired to prevent lowering flaps with the door open.

"When the airplane flexed, I had no flaps to land with so sometimes I'd find myself running back to shut the door and then run back up to the front," admitted a pilot. "She'd go a little nose high and then she'd level out. I don't do that any more, but back then..."

In winter, ski operations brought more headaches. The short-coupled design produced a rough ride on snow or ice because of a tendency for the tail to lift. Getting stuck in slush happened frequently.

"If you had a load, about half was on the main legs and the rest on that tiny, little tail ski," Dave Nilson said. "At Wardair (Yellowknife), who leased CF-EIM, it was my job to get outside and wiggle the tail around with a rope while the pilot blasted the engine in thirty below zero."

The Huskies turned nicely in snow, pilots said, but in slush, the 450-h.p. engine lacked the power to break free, unlike the Beaver or other lighter airplanes. Fairchild planned a tricycle-geared version which probably would have worsened the situation. Bogged down Huskies caused many cold overnight stops.

"If you got into certain conditions, you stayed there until the next morning to let things cool overnight until that slush turned to ice," said Peppler. "When mid-March sunlight softened the snow, there was no way you'd get off because the Husky just couldn't overcome the drag of sticky skis."

Boreal Airways devised a practical solution to ski pedestal breakage. Mechanics riveted a steel plate inside the fuselage at the junction of the ski attachment point and tail. Instead of weak aluminum, the iron became a solid, nonbendable skin.

Willard Meister, a corporate Beechcraft King Air pilot in Toronto, remembered long winter Husky hauls from Moosonee with Austin Airways. On good weather days, he left "Moose" on a thrice weekly scheduled run to the coasts of James and Hudson Bay. Mail, snowmachine and outboard motor parts tucked in with grocery orders and an occasional passenger made up the loads in -35°F (-37°C) temperatures.

"There was a saying around Austin Airways, that the Husky was ideal for the mail runs because it could only carry a Beaver load—that's about 1,200 lb. (540 kg)," he said.

In spite of the need for engine tents and a pair of plumber's blow pots wherever he stayed, Meister found the Husky a "pilot's airplane," i.e., roomy, comfortable in cruise and light on the controls. Austin Airways used CF-EIQ from 1952 to 1954, and CF-SAQ from 1952 until 1965. In fact, Meister and other Austin pilots, after becoming familiar with Husky quirks and marginal performance, preferred them over the Norseman for long hauls.

Fairchild Aircraft had experimented with assembling prefabricated houses after losing several aircraft production contracts but lack of profits forced suspension of the project. The factory then switched to millwork through a subsidiary company but this sideline also did poorly. In serious financial straits, Fairchild suffered another blow when the postwar RCAF decided against a proposed twin-engine trainer.

In 1950, the directors liquidated Fairchild Aircraft with losses of nearly one million dollars.

Boreal Aircraft acquired tools and inventory to produce spare parts for operational Huskies. In 1957, a diehard group with chief investor Bernard O. Brynelsen as president, understood the potential of a more powerful Fairchild F-11 and commissioned a survey for a new Vancouver-based organization called Husky Aircraft Ltd.

Studies by W. M. Armstrong & Partners Ltd. indicated that a new Husky at a production cost of $66,400 would retail at $85,000. Husky Aircraft Ltd. could penetrate the bush market with a likely twenty-five sales per year by 1960 since little domestic and foreign competition existed. Helicopters were slow and carried 75 percent less payload and had 30 percent higher operating costs than Fairchild Aircraft.

"Consequently, bush aircraft compete with more basic forms of transportation. Although they cost more than pack horses or canoe backpackers, aircraft can transport much more in the way of passenger and cargo further and much faster," read the report.

Husky Aircraft selected the air-cooled, 540-h.p. Alvis Leonides 503/8 radial engine to replace the 450-h.p. Pratt & Whitney. Dry, it weighed 680 lb. and could be taken to 3,000 rpm. Designated an F-11-2, the redesigned airplane had a gross weight of 7,300 lb. (3,285 kg)—900 lb. (405 kg) more than early models. There were few changes in the main structure. All modifications were applied forward of the fire wall.

First flight took place on July 8, 1956, and performance figures justified the estimates. An extensive test program in

CF-EIM followed. Department of Transport's chief test pilot Walter Gadson later flew the certification trials and criticized the Husky's tendency to swing right instead of left as with most North American bushplanes. Instead of long takeoff runs—one pilot recalled a partially loaded 450-h.p. Husky using 3 mi. (5 km)—the Alvis version leaped onto the step within seconds of full throttle and rarely needed more than fourteen seconds to become airborne. Dave Nilson, who flew both, remembered his first flights.

"When you finally get an airplane that has enough power, you open the throttle and everything tightens up and starts to move, you know it's good."

On September 9, 1959, A. M. MacKenzie, former test pilot and then vice-president sales, began canvassing for customers. The "Super Husky" or F-11-2B, as he called it, carried a payload of 1,558 lb. (701 kg) and took off in 650 ft. (195 m) on floats. With seating for thirteen including pilot, it could stay aloft for over eight hours at an economical 110 mph (177 km/h).

According to historian Kenneth M. Molson, Husky Aircraft, with the help of Vancouver Aircraft Sales Ltd., converted only one F-11-1 to the F-11-2. In spite of the Armstrong & Partners forecast, the Beaver and Otter became unbeatable competition. Also, few air services stocked 100/130 fuel and aircraft maintenance engineers were not accustomed to Alvis Leonides engines.

In 1958, the Alvis Leonides Husky had a rare opportunity for a practical demonstration when an outbreak of fires occurred in the Nelson district, 232 mi. (374 km) east of Vancouver. In desperation, the B.C. Forest Service chartered every airplane they could find for suppression and transport. In less than a week, Husky Aircraft developed, installed, tested and modified an aerial water drop system consisting of an internal 150 gal. (683 l) flat bottom tank with its forward end raised 6 in. (15 cm). A cable from the cabin to the cockpit ceiling released the load and a leakproof chute channeled water through the rear clamshell doors of CF-EIM.

To load, engineers installed 2 in. (5 cm) vertical pipes leading through the forward side windows to the tank. While taxiing at 45 mph (72 km/h), water entered the pipes and filled the tank in twenty-two seconds. The pilot judged quantity through an instrument panel rearview mirror. Dumping the 1,500 lb. (675 kg). load took six seconds. Husky Aircraft claimed the water discharged in a "single blob" and created a 35 ft. (11 m) by 200 ft. (60 m) wetting pattern.

At Nelson, temperatures reached 95°F (35°C) from August 13 to August 28. Two pilots made 340 drops in seventy-four hours flying with average three minute turnarounds from lake to fire. When the load dropped, said pilot K. W. Quest, no violent changes in trim occurred. Rate of climb at full gross weight was 1,000 ft. (300 m) per min. at 87 mph (140 km/h). The Husky handled well on the water and left the surface cleanly at 60 mph (97 km/h).

"The Husky fought fires alongside a de Havilland Beaver. Each aircraft picked up water from the same source and worked together on the same fires," read a Husky Aircraft report. "The Husky carried twice the quantity of water per trip and could make three round trips for every two trips in the Beaver."

Enthusiasm for the system prompted further development. Brynelsen and his associates planned improvements with collapsible watertight materials to increase tank capacity to 180 imp. gal. (819 l). Oddly, no water bomber sales occurred and aerial fire fighting remained the bailiwick of Beavers and Otters. Few operators wanted to take a chance on the "new" Husky and its unfamiliar British engine. Low-cost, surplus Noorduyn Norseman were still available and land-based fire fighters such as Grumman TBM Avengers were well established in B.C.

Although Husky Aircraft converted only CF-EIM, several operators recognized the virtues of the upgraded concept. Campbell River-based Island Airlines, a company founded in 1959, became one of the first coastal Husky operators. Under the supervision of chief engineer David Nilson, they converted CF-EIR and CF-SAQ to F-11-2s.

"The concept had already been proven but we needed an engine mount. I designed all the cowlings and controls for CF-EIR and fiddled around for six months with the idea of easy maintenance and repair," Nilson said. "From the test flight on, there was little trouble and it'd carry an Otter load but keep up to a Cessna."

Including Island Air's conversions, at least six Huskies were re-engined with Alvis Leonides. Most flew in British Columbia and became quite popular. Mechanics, however, had a difficult time "keeping ahead of the engine," as one put it. Setting the valves every fifty hours caused costly down time especially if they needed regrinding. Worse, when major overhaul came due, the Alvis had to be sent to Great Britain.

When functional, the Leonides engine allowed the Husky to do incredible work especially in high terrain because of an automatic mixture control with "altitude compensators." Pilots had a choice of either high or low settings. On high, the Husky cruised at 145 mph (233 km/h). Vancouver Island Air chief pilot Roland Bartlett spent time on Island Air's CF-EIR.

"It'd go through a lot of fuel but on low setting, you'd be down to 125–130 mph (201–209 km/h) on floats and burn less fuel per hour," he said. "We passed just about everything on the coast."

Dell D'Arcangelo of Black Creek, south of Campbell River, remembered engine fires occurred more frequently than in any type he knew. Occasionally, vibration caused leaking fuel lines and ear-shattering backfires which he stopped by opening the throttle and sucking flames back into the exhaust. One pilot said an idling Leonides sounded like a rattling toolbox.

Gerry Norberg, a summer contract pilot before moving on to Air Canada Douglas DC-9s, never logged a minute on Fairchild Huskies but talked a chief pilot into allowing him along for a ride. Stationed at Prince Rupert in mid-1971, he was fascinated by North Coast Air Service's CF-EIM. As he sat on a box of freight during a grocery run to the Queen Charlotte Islands, Norberg heard a strange sound as they cruised above Hecate Strait.

"A bit of grinding noise, just ching, ching, ching and then, the engine just went KA-BLAM! and smoke everywhere inside. (Chief pilot) did an unbelievable job and then KA-BLAM! we hit the ocean and all I could see was this blue smoke everywhere. I yelled for a fire extinguisher but he hasn't got one."

The Husky did not burn.

After several hours drifting in rough water, Norberg and his chief pilot were towed to shelter by a tugboat. They learned that a broken master cylinder rod sheared several bottom cylinders. One penetrated the engine crankcase.

"The whole bottom half of the engine was just gone; just wasn't there. Fantastic engines, those Leonides, if they're running good. I was suitably impressed," Norberg said.

A mixture of Alvis and Pratt & Whitney Huskies flew in northern and western Canada. During Manitoba's heavy floods in 1950, the provincial air service used the rear hatch for dropping hay to marooned livestock. The 2 ft. (0.6 m) bales fit easily through and, on impact, burst open and scattered. Only two casualties occurred—falling hay bales broke the necks of a horse and cow.

In a sales letter, Husky manager L .J. Anderson pointed out the virtues of the F-11-2 as an aerial fish seeder. The Husky could slow fly 25 ft. (7.5 m) above the water while a crew released fish from a cabin tank. At that height, less than 1 percent fish mortality occurred. To study aquatic life, pilots landed on lakes to let surveyors drop nets through the rear as they taxied in a wide circle.

Pilots who saw their first Huskies noticed that the fin and rudder seemed small relative to the airplane's size. With lesser windvaning surface, taxiing Huskies downwind was much easier than the large tailed de Havilland Otter which demanded skill even in moderate winds. However, the lack of tail surface on a Husky became a concern in strong crosswinds or while cruising in turbulent air. "Some guys didn't like flying it because the tail was kind of wishy-washy," a pilot said. "In turbulence and what-not, they'd swish-swash backwards and forwards and people'd get airsick quick."

Although controllability may have been lacking, the design of the Husky tail and hatch suited shuttle service work. Pilots loaded baggage far rearward for easier sorting and unloading. Passengers on Beavers and Otters had to disembark at every stop while pilots repacked the load. One man, accustomed to these multistop flights, remarked: "Just hard work, oh God, it was hard work."

Another individual described a Friday evening pickup flight from a timber cutting camp on British Columbia's coast. Besides three passengers, he loaded a heavy electric generator for Campbell River. It was his habit to help his 450-h.p. Husky into the air by yelling, "So lift, you son-of-a-bitch! Lift!" on takeoff. On this occasion, two black leather-jacketed passengers thought the message was directed at them. Shortly before easing back on the control wheel, the pilot glanced behind and nearly fell out of his seat with laughter. The "goddamn biker types" were trying to lift the generator off the floor to lighten the load.

Island Air flew from Campbell River to Tahsis twice daily to move logging crews for companies such as Crown Zellerbach. Every airplane in the fleet kept busy hauling fifty men across 54 mi. of rugged mountains and through poor coastal weather. The Alvis Leonides F-11-2 proved ideal for such runs.

"I preferred the Husky because we climbed to at least 5,500 ft. (1,650 m) direct to Tahsis and only had about 20 mi. (32 km) to do it in," said Bartlett. "In the Otter, you'd be temping out and getting around a couple hundred feet a minute so it was all you

Although sparse, the roomy Husky flight compartment had plenty of headroom. If desired, a 50,000 Btu Janitrol Combustion Heater Unit could be fitted. Cockpit walls were heavily insulated but cabin insulation was optional. Before production began, Fairchild Aircraft Ltd. predicted $16.34 as a direct hourly flying cost.

Photo: Robert S. Grant

could do to make it. With the Husky, it'd just climb right up there, no problem."

Most coastal work took place at sea level. Occasionally, construction bosses called upon the Husky for high-country charters. Jack Ross drew the unenviable task of delivering lumber for a camp at the 7,000 ft. (2,100 m) level of a mainland mountain range. He and a crewman tied the wood into bundles with rope secured one foot from the end of each one. This enabled the bundles to splay outward and spin down like maple seeds.

"We were dropping out the back hatch in a steep turn in thirty mile per hour winds to stay over the camp," Ross said. "The guy in the back, we tied him with a rope so he couldn't slide out. You had to watch that airplane for the tail dropping out in a turn so every turn had to be coordinated. We never broke a stick."

Ross appreciated the seats and roomy cockpit. He did not care for the Husky's poor forward vision because the shelter of the rounded engine prevented residue, oil and dirt from blowing off the windshield. This, coupled with the instrument panel's reflections on the glass, hindered the view. Ross's employer painted the panels black but to no avail.

"It had a flat windshield and just the angle of it in the fuselage was a little bit too flat and the rain didn't beat off too well," added Bartlett.

Husky pilots fought constantly with the airplane's heating system. Perhaps an engineering marvel in the designers' eyes, the Janitrol could not be counted on. Jack Ross described it as an "antiquated kind of barrel of gas dripping onto a blow torch." If pilots overlooked shutting the switch off before landing, "The next time you lit the thing, it was going to go bang on you."

Mike McCluskey and his fellow pilots demanded functioning heaters for chilly runs along British Columbia's winter coast. Their employer, however, decided against costly Janitrol overhauls and issued gray cot blankets instead. "So here you are, sir, here's your heater for this trip," laughed McCluskey.

Hard use eventually caught up with the Huskies. On skis or rough water, wings tended to pivot backward and forward on their hinges. In time, cracks appeared on the fuselage where the rear wing spar entered the bulkhead. Island Airlines, recalled Nilson, was responsible for a mandatory repair to restrengthen the area. He also filled in holes which had been designed into the airframe bulkheads to save weight but weakened the structure.

Windstorms destroyed at least two Huskies and a hangar fire demolished CF-EIQ at St. Jean, Quebec, in 1954. One registered CF-SAA survived an exciting air ambulance career with the Saskatchewan Government Air Services. As a reward, officious civil servants relegated it to scrap until the Canadian Museum of Flight and Transportation in Surrey, south of Vancouver, acquired the remains in 1976.

Seven Fairchild Huskies were involved in flying accidents. None were caused by design faults. Some resulted in fatalities but most left survivable messes of buckled metal, broken wing spars and bent floats. One registered CF-EIR dipped a wing in Discovery Passage near Campbell River in 1977. No injuries occurred and the airplane received a thorough wetting but little structural damage. Nevertheless, it never flew again.

"You couldn't get parts because they'd have had to make everything from scratch," Bartlett said. "CF-EIR wasn't damaged enough to write it off; any other airplane would have been rebuilt."

One Husky survived intact. The well-worn model delivered by Gordon Emberley in August, 1984, now sits on display at Winnipeg's Western Canada Aviation Museum. Several others have been salvaged and they, too, will eventually become available for public viewing.

The circumstances surrounding the Husky's demise are complex. The airplane entered the market during a period when war-surplus airplanes dominated the scene. When upgraded versions appeared, few pilots and potential customers deigned to take a chance, remembering only tales of long lakes and loads equivalent to cabinfuls of puffed rice.

Given time, evolution would have cured the Fairchild Husky of its troubles. Nevertheless, this unique airplane had the chance to show that Canadian ingenuity did not end with the Noorduyn Norseman.

6   De Havilland Beaver

Wilderness Workhorse

At Resolute Bay, 1,100 mi. (1,771 km) south of the North Pole, the two-blade propeller of a dust-covered airplane turned over several times. Blue smoke belched from the de Havilland Beaver's exhaust and disappeared behind the tail. With plenty of back-and-forth shots of throttle to move its gigantic oversize tires, the pilot taxied past several heavy-lift helicopters and a sleek Lear jet.

Inside the Beaver, the pilot wondered whether he had tied his load properly. Three 45 imp. gal. (205 l) red drums of aviation gasoline sat lashed in place by yellow nylon ropes. A bag of mail and several cases of soggy, semifrozen steaks and soft drinks occupied every remaining inch of space.

At the same time in another part of Canada, a Beaver idled toward the east side of Eddontenajon Lake, 240 mi. (386 km) southwest of Fort Nelson, British Columbia. Behind the pilot sat four tourists weighing more than 800 lb. (360 kg). Oversize passengers from Europe and the United States were not unusual loads but the day was hot and the wind calm.

Both pilots eased the throttle of their Beavers to takeoff power. They accelerated slowly but soon reached a speed which lurched them into the air. Seconds later, with safe airspeeds showing on their gauges, they began long steady climbs. One turned toward the valleys of Ellesmere Island and the other map read to a narrow channel on the Stikine River, not far from Wrangell, Alaska.

Before the advent of the Beaver, flights into the Arctic and mountainous regions with low-powered fabric and tube airplanes were hazardous undertakings. In other regions, small lakes and high trees took their toll in injured pilots and wrecked airplanes. De Havilland in Downsview, Ontario, decided that the world needed something with short takeoff and landing performance.

With this in mind, sales manager "Sandy" A. F. MacDonald drew up a questionnaire for commercial operators. Soon, he announced de Havilland's decision to create a five-place, all-metal airplane powered by a British 295-h.p. Gipsy Queen engine. Many industry greats such as C. H. "Punch" Dickins combined their expertise with de Havilland's design team. One contributor was Ontario's Lands & Forests deputy minister Frank A. MacDougall who visited the factory frequently.

"When the Beaver aircraft was being designed, I spoke to D. Hunter, the chief engineer, and asked him to so stress the bolts at top and bottom end of the wing strut that they couldn't fail," he wrote to Thomas C. Cooke, supervisor, Air Service Section, eighteen years later. "In short, at this point, we suggested he disregard his design book."

By September, 1946, de Havilland staff completed a wooden mock-up of what they thought a state-of-the-art bushplane should be. Instead of the Gipsy Queen, the company decided upon the 450-h.p. Pratt & Whitney Junior R-985 Jr. engine. On August 16, 1947, test pilot Russ Bannock flew the prototype and after 150 hours of development flying, George Neal took over seaplane certification trials.

An initial order for four came from the Ontario Department of Lands & Forests which accepted CF-OBS on April 26, 1948. When production ceased in 1967, 1,631 of these short and stubby wonders were built.

A walk around a typical DHC-2 Beaver showed that the manufacturer had listened to bush pilots. Removable, wide side doors which hooked on each wing strut made loading easier. A 45-imp. gal. (205 l) drum—surely the most common item carried beyond roads and railways—fit nicely through. The pilot had his own private entrance and all the upholstered seats detached quickly from bakelite-covered metal floors. The rear bush seat was a slip of canvas with a metal rod through it which could be hung up out of the way when not in use.

One pilot, anxious to please his customers, transported an exceptionally unwieldy load. Although highly dangerous, the flight provided a demonstration of what a Beaver could really do. A contractor wanted a hydro pole moved to a remote lake. Unable to tie one on the outside because it would hinder the propeller, the pilot removed his right front and left rear doors and inserted the pole through the cockpit and cabin. Several feet protruded from the front and some from the rear. In spite of the drag, he survived the twenty-minute flight.

Fuel filler necks were no longer on the wings nor did pilots need to stand on cold, dead airframes and drag heavy, grit-covered gasoline hoses across delicate plexiglas windshields. They simply opened a waist-level panel on the left side of the fuselage and inserted a nozzle. Even belly fuel gascolators came oversize, so huge they could be manipulated by hands encased in gloves or mitts. Oil could be poured into the engine during flight since the tank's filler neck had been placed at the bottom of the control wheel pedestal.

An all-metal airframe alleviated nuisance punctures from trees or ice chunks on ski-strips. Rubber shock absorbers built into landing gear struts made touchdowns pleasant regardless of terrain. Well-balanced controls allowed pilots to fly dawn to dusk and return unfatigued at the end of the day. A slotted wing flap system from the wing roots to the inboard end of the ailerons provided excellent slow speed handling.

The standard off-the-shelf de Havilland Beaver had an average basic weight of 3,278 lb. (1,475 kg). Fully loaded, final production models could take off at 5,090 lb. (2,291 kg). Three belly tanks held 79 imp. gal. (359 l) of fuel and the engine burned between 16–20 imp. gal. (73–91 l) per hr. while cruising as high as 115 mph (185 km/h). A route study showed a Beaver on Edo 4580 floats with pilot, oil and gasoline for 50 mi. (81 km), taxiing away from the dock at 3,685 lb. (1,658 kg). This allowed a 1,405 lb. (632 kg) payload or six passengers and 415 lb. (187 kg) of freight.

Journalist Ronald A. Keith wrote one of the first pilot reports and described a ten-second takeoff on wheels with a 10 mph wind. Test pilot Neal reported five-second takeoffs in 25 mph (40 km/h) winds. A full-page advertisement in January, 1948, *Canadian Aviation* showed a float-equipped Beaver off the runway in 775 ft. (233 m) with a 4,750 lb. (2,138 kg) gross weight during a calm day—a far cry from the multi-mile run of the Norseman.

Airline owners of the late 1940s accustomed to slow climb rates from Norsemen, Fairchilds and Bellancas were pleased to meet the de Havilland Beaver. During the first year, the Quebec North Shore Paper Company in Baie Comeau believed their CF-FHE could do more to prevent forest fire losses than any other piece of equipment. In Vancouver, Central B.C. Airways' founder Russ Baker considered the Beaver as "the most marvelous aircraft of its type that has ever been built." Operators across the country placed their orders.

"If you could have seen their eyes after the Buhls and Stinsons; it was really something when the first Beaver came to town," said AME Joseph Holmburg in Sault Ste. Marie, Ontario.

The first Beaver left Downsview with Punch Dickins as pilot on June 1, 1948, for an extensive tour during delivery to Central B.C. Airways Ltd. Dickins demonstrated CF-FHB to every potential customer he could find before crossing the Rocky Mountains. Russ Baker put his Beaver to work immediately hauling freight and passengers throughout the province's rugged interior and coast.

Fresh water or salt, it mattered little to CF-FHB. Like all factory Beavers, it had been cleaned thoroughly with a Binks water-wash system before treatment with zinc chromate corrosive proofing. It had a 100 ft. (30 m) turning radius in zero wind and with the 20 in. (51 cm) draught, pilots had no reason to worry about shallow bays and tidal flats. Type-approved to carry canoes up to 16 ft., 6 in. (5 m) in length with a 12 ft., 8 in. (3.8 m) beam, the Beaver could handle almost any assignment.

When the Granduc Copper Mine opened in 1954, Baker's Beavers hauled in 300 tons of freight from Stewart. Some landed with floats on glaciers and flew off empty. Later, CF-FHB worked on the sprawling Kitimat Alcan project; at that time, the largest development ever undertaken by private enterprise.

Beaver CF-FHB moved on to Northward Aviation in Edmonton where it flew regularly from Yellowknife until sold to Saskatchewan's Norcanair in April, 1969. The last flight occurred eleven years later from La Ronge to Ottawa when it became an important addition to the National Aviation Museum's collection.

As corporate airplanes, Beavers were ideal. One registered CF-CAT carried the colors of a Caterpillar earth-moving machinery distributor and covered a 500,000 sq. mi. (1,295,000 km^2) territory in British Columbia, Yukon and the Northwest Territories. Another registered C-FXGG and painted black, found a niche in British Columbia's fish farming industry.

Fish farming generally required an amphibious airplane. Young fish raised inland must be taken quickly from hatcheries to saltwater pens stationed near communities like Tofino or Powell River. Vanessa Jago, an ex-White Rock, British Columbia, resident and experienced Beaver pilot, described transferring bucketfuls of smolts into C-FXGG.

"There were a lot of short trips. The fish were too valuable to waste time with so we'd take about 800 lb. (360 kg) which had a value of nearly $40,000. We also flew managers who weren't really interested in looking at fish from the air but more in going down to watch the grading processes."

Anyone who logged flying time in Beavers remarked on the light control pressures. Journalist Keith reported: "...the flying comfort is more than one has any right to anticipate in a bushplane." Operations manager Pat Doyle of First Air in Ottawa remembered it as a "dream." However, the easy manner in which Beavers flew sometimes led pilots into complacency.

"Yes, the Beaver's easy to fly but it has more ways to kill you than most airplanes I know," admitted Ignace Airways operations manager Brad Greaves in Ignace, Ontario. "You have to be on top of it and ahead of the aircraft; particularly in winds—that's where the Beaver shows its ugly side."

One pilot pointed out that Beavers handle so well, novices and veterans forget they have a mechanical machine with the potential to do great harm. In most airplanes, only part of the wing loses lift before stalling. With a Beaver, the entire wing comes sharply down, sometimes sliding toward the inside of a turn if a pilot happens to be banking. Harbour Air's operations manager Peter Evans in Richmond, British Columbia, remarked that "...everything feels good, looks good but when it stalls, it really goes."

Gusty days can be hazardous when taking off near the stalling speed. A blast of wind or "cat's-paw" can quickly jump a Beaver into the air. When the wind passes, the airplane often drops abruptly back to the water. Many pilots have dipped wing tips into a lake and in some cases, lost control. Six men died north of Fort Frances, Ontario, in May, 1983, when their chartered Beaver cleared the water only to lose its lift and roll over.

A striking example of what can happen in a low airspeed steep turn took place at Fenton Lake, British Columbia, in October, 1964. The pilot was no novice—his log book showed nearly 12,000 flying hours including 350 hours in Beaver CF-OBX. After takeoff, he reduced engine power, entered a forty degree bank and leveled at 500 ft. A passenger heard him say, "I wonder what's wrong?" The Beaver descended and smashed into the water in spite of the pilot bringing the control wheel as far backward as it would go. The accident report simply stated: "Loss of control for undetermined reasons."

Steep, low-airspeed turns are often necessary in a peculiar task carried out nearly exclusively in British Columbia. Log buyers request Beavers because they need six-passenger seating and the ability to slow to 80 mph (129 km/h) at 400 ft. (120 m) above the water. The small turning radius allows easier inspection of log booms. Once customers locate valuable yellow cedar or fir, the pilot lands on the boom's calm side. Treated with respect and caution, the Beaver does this kind of work well.

"You have to control the ball in the turn and bank indicator at all times in those tight turns low to the water so the radius is smaller," said Harbour Air's Trevor Bird.

Few seaplanes fly regularly into the High Arctic regions north of the North American mainland. Huge drifting ice pans hinder shoreline access and summer days rarely become warm enough to clear sea lanes and lakes. Standard wheel airplanes are useless for anything other than prepared airports. Boulders, frost heaves and gullies become hazards as does the tundra's "goo and guck," as one harried despatcher called the desolate damp surface of the High Arctic plains.

Worse, weather shuts down islands for days. Summertime storms spawned by air masses crashing into mountains stop the most sophisticated airplanes. Strong winds grind sand particles from cornices and plateaus into fine powder which seeps into every part of an airplane. Only rugged types with solid airframes and sturdy engines to absorb "Islands" flying survive. The Beaver seems to have been designed for this kind of work. Accident rates dropped quickly once it became available with a unique landing gear.

Pilot/mechanic Weldon W. Phipps spent several seasons searching for a low-cost alternative to helicopters. After several seasons in the High Arctic, he wondered why he rarely sank to his ankles while walking the damp summer grounds. Phipps calculated the area on his boot soles and concluded that Arctic airplanes needed wider low pressure tires for better weight distribution. He installed a 36 in. pair on a Piper PA-18 Super Cub.

The concept worked. Phipps tested Douglas DC-3 45 in. tires on his Beavers. To reduce weight, he shaved their ten ply to six and pumped in only enough air to keep the wrinkles out. "Doughnuts" or "Big Wheels" provided a cushioning effect on landing and sufficient flotation to taxi over soggy permafrost. Commercial operators were quick to capitalize on Phipps' design.

Tundra flying required specialized techniques. In southern climate, grassroots pilots appreciated lush grass carpets on which to land. In the Islands, the same condition usually spelled soft ground and trouble. High Arctic pilots learned that when poppies, bell heather, saxifrage and other colorful plants grew in clumps with bared areas between, the surface might support a tundra-tire airplane.

In 1961, the Ontario Department of Lands & Forests which operated more than forty Beavers, developed a laminated pair of wood skis with 3/16th phenolic-covered bottoms. The fleet already flew at a 4,820 lb. (2,169 kg) wintertime gross weight but the new units allowed a 280 lb. (126 kg) increase over factory skis. These small increases were important to Ontario government pilots flying along the fringes of Hudson and James Bays. Caribou surveys and wolf control flights made up much of their winter work. The long distances dictated a need to conserve every ounce of fuel and carry all the survival equipment possible.

In Quebec, air service operators found the Beaver perfect for fur buying expeditions. Indian people established winter camps with little understanding of the differences between short lakes and long ones. Large Fairchild Huskies or Noorduyn Norsemen could not handle the task.

"Around September, the Indians piled into their canoes and made their own way to a hunting ground somewhere in the bush," said Bill Peppler. "They'd let the trading post manager know the approximate area they'd be trapping after freeze-up so we'd start out about December 27 for the camps."

Peppler carried flour, tea, sugar, lard or whatever the Natives wanted to barter. These expeditions, with pilot and fur buyer, often lasted days. Before returning to base, Peppler's Beaver would be packed tightly to the ceiling and behind the front seats with animal hides. In winter, the fur emanated almost no odor. Warm weather float flying, however, brought a distinctive aroma as fat, blood and hair created what one loader called a "fetid shit-stinking atmosphere."

Peppler's Boreal Airways trips included many with wall-to-wall dogs. Unlike Hartley Weston's customers in the Fairchild Husky, Peppler's canine passengers were not always semisavage. Jammed inside the 144 cu. ft. (4.32 m3) cabin close to Peppler's head, the animals licked his neck from takeoff to landing.

"You could hear this sniff, sniff and then you'd feel a cold nose under your ear and hope he wasn't going to take a chunk out of you," he said.

Ron Gangloff, proprietor of Red Lake, Ontario's Lakeview Restaurant and ex-Green Airways pilot, carried an item special to wild rice harvesting. Rice boats are not heavy but the large collecting screen or speedhead create considerable drag. Gangloff secured the speedhead and tied the boat section so the motor extended under the wing strut.

"It took off good and flew no problem. We just went out one way, turned around and landed because we didn't have enough rudder to keep straight. We were doing eighty-five and actually, it wasn't shaking much at all. You leave a little bit of flap on. Shit, maybe one or two pumps, not even close to climb; one pump maybe."

Not all challenging loads went to backwoods destinations strapped to a pair of Edo floats. A pilot with Gulf Island Air, according to 1993 December/January issue of *BC Aviator*, arrived at his company dock in Campbell River, British Columbia, to find CF-FHT plastic-lined and loaded with five pigs. Each one was tied into a potato sack with only its head and slimy snout protruding. In the pristine airplane, the aroma of porcine feces and urine nearly suffocated the pilot.

"Now it's fair to say that the pigs didn't like it any better than I did, but they had the advantage of not minding the smell," the pilot said. "It was a hot day and as I taxied out of the river, the smell really became bad and the pigs were squealing, well, like pigs. The smell became more intense with the roar of the engine as I guess the pigs were scared. I had to stick my head out of the pilot's window for the whole trip."

When the pilot returned, nearly asphyxiated by the essences emanating from his rank clothing and slippery boot soles, he staggered into the company office. Despatcher Evelyn Crum pointedly ignored him. She did, however, manage to suppress her breath long enough to hand him a peppermint.

Three reliable aviation-wise witnesses described one of the most bizarre flights in de Havilland history. A pilot neglected a pretakeoff inspection and overlooked a tie-down/anchor log he had secured to the tail. Airborne, he wondered why his controls felt strange. After landing, he discovered he had flown with the log swirling behind the airplane.

Overlooking safety items on a checklist can happen to any pilot. Stanley King, a veteran of Georgian Bay Airways in Parry Sound, Ontario, cautioned novices that the aviation world consisted of two types of pilots—those who forget their flaps on takeoff and those who will. In Quebec, one man ran a Beaver into a stand of spruce. Another in Ontario remembered his flaps milliseconds from a shoal of moss-covered rocks. He barely managed to "rap the flap" and jump into the air.

Most pilots claim Beavers cannot normally become airborne without the extra lift supplied by flaps. One who now captains Air Canada Douglas DC-9s, and prefers to remain unidentified, testified that on certain occasions, the Beaver will leave the water without flap. He described a long multistop day during which he landed on a high mountain pond 150 mi. south of Watson Lake, Yukon. He had already flown seven hours with Dogrib Indian families, several exploration groups and tourists for lodges.

"I didn't have a load on this time which was a good thing and it was a lake about three, four miles long and I don't remember how it happened. I just forgot to put them (flaps) down. Anyway, got up on the step and just going and going and going and I was so tired, I just kept going until it flew itself off."

Amphibious Beavers require extra-long water takeoffs. Most weigh at least 354 lb. (159 kg) more than standard seaplanes. Wheeled floats do not provide as much buoyancy as regular Edo 4580s. Nevertheless, sales brochures of the 1950s insisted that no appreciable performance loss occurred. With full belly tanks, amphibious versions carried 444 lb. (200 kg) less payload from the water and 670 lb. (302 kg) less than a Beaver on wheels.

Mike McCluskey said, water "packing" into the space around the four amphibious wheels slows the Beaver considerably. Another pilot added the airplane becomes nose heavy on landing. For safety reasons, most pilots use fuel from the front tank first, then center and finally, the rear to keep weight as far toward the tail as possible.

Journalist Bonnie Dickie described the Beaver as "Queen of the Bush" but not everyone believed it to be the best STOL (Short Takeoff and Landing) machine in spite of its phenomenal success. AME Gordon Hughes of Northland Aircraft Services in Ignace, studied the type in detail and believes de Havilland built the Beaver with excessively light materials. He contended that de Havilland sacrificed strength for performance.

"You take something off and put the same damn thing on again, like wing bolt inspections," he said, referring to a compulsory airworthiness directive. "If they'd built the things properly in the first place, you could forget about them for life but you hammer those bolts off every year and damage them every time."

Dave Nilson in Campbell River also knows de Havilland products well. He agreed with Hughes and claimed the Beaver was "designed in a bit of a hurry as a stop gap thing" to keep de Havilland in business after World War II. Belly tanks crack frequently and leak, he pointed out, but many owners are forced to solve this problem by applying a thick coat of fiberglass to reduce vibration.

"Worse, the fuel system drains everything to the back where it goes through a selector and then comes all the way to the front of the airplane," Nilson explained. "The Beaver didn't have anything except a hand wobble pump to get fuel to the carburetor and that's asking too much. It's really something that could have been improved a whole bunch."

Another mechanic insisted that few other types could match the performance but maintenance costs have skyrocketed and outweigh the advantages. Engine problems on hard working bushplanes, said Ignace Airways' Paul Hawkins, kept his staff busy.

"You spend a day on the airframe and a week on the engine at inspection time," he said. "Works out to oil leaks, magneto changes, spark plug changes and repairing engine cowlings—the Beaver's enough to drive anybody crazy."

Mechanics weren't alone in finding faults. Pilots whose daily work consisted of numerous brief hops in areas where fuel was readily available were satisfied with the range. In other localities, however, it fell short. With standard belly tanks, endurance is less than four hours. De Havilland provided optional 36 imp. gal. wing tip tanks. Awkward to fill, these were not as popular as belly tanks preferred by companies like Les Ailes du Nord in Sept Iles, Quebec. This organization used Beavers to service communities as far east as Blanc Sablon on the Quebec/Labrador border in the early 1970s.

"What really baffles me are those friggin' little inside rear door handles," said another pilot. "Almost everybody has to fight to open them at the dock. It's too horrible to think of what would happen if we went upside down in a lake."

The same pilot went on to describe the Beaver's poor "crashability." Hold down fittings from seat to floor barely have the strength to hold the seat in place. "You crash with those things, believe me, your ass is going right through that windshield."

Occasionally, pilots have been caught with dead batteries. One operations manager blamed this not on the airplane but on their inability or unwillingness to interpret ammeters properly. With barely enough electrical charge to "tickle" (turn over the propeller), handspiking or swinging by hand often becomes the only alternative to an evening in a mosquito-infested cockpit.

The swinger works from behind the propeller after placing the magneto switches to "on." If the blade is not at the correct angle, it must be moved. This can be dangerous.

"If you've got somebody that can flick the switches on or off, you don't have to climb back in every time it doesn't catch," said Mike McCluskey. "You've got to move that prop around with your foot because you can't reach over the top. It's hard but once everything's in the right place, the Beaver's easy to hand start."

After the Pratt & Whitney R-985 fires on all nine cylinders, they are generally reliable. Dave Robertson of Green Airways called them "round pounders" and Langford considers the R-985 as the "best radial every built." Nevertheless, in spite of their good reputations, they have been known to quit, as one West Coast pilot testified.

He felt an abnormal roughness after takeoff. By releasing his seat belt and looking ahead and over the nose, he discovered a large bulge in the cowling. A cylinder had blown loose from its hold down studs and caused the dent. In spite of serious internal damage, the engine continued running until he landed.

Another pilot shuddered when he described his flight across 130 mi. (209 km) of 12 ft. (3.6 m) ocean rollers. His Beaver began shaking before he sighted land but the engine kept working until he reached a sheltered bay. Had it quit completely above the open sea, he probably would not have survived.

Engine failures in Beavers became so commonplace that some air services considered them "nonevents," even when pilots new on type were undergoing check rides. Rochelle Bodnar was deep in B.C. wilderness near Quesnel with C-GIPL. Her employer, a Beaver owner and tourist lodge operator for decades, sat in the passenger seat idly flipping the pages of a trade magazine.

"It's my last checkride, right? And I'm flying along thinking, 'Holy cow, this is it, I'm finally moving up,'" she recalled. "Gradually, I noticed there's a little mist on the windshield here and it's getting worse, but John's (the owner) not saying anything and we can barely maintain altitude."

Bodnar, accustomed to an incident-free career at this point, became quite concerned since the Beaver had blown a critical cylinder with oil spray obscuring forward visibility. She still had 10 mi. (16 km) to fly to her employer's lodge. Worse, when the destination finally came into view, the lake was glassy and she would have to land directly into a setting sun.

"Everybody knows a Beaver blows jugs, so it was okay," Bodnar said. "I'm trying to do what's right but it doesn't look like we'll make the lake. The airplane's just covered with grease and oil and smoke's trailing behind us but the boss didn't look worried since he had tools at the lodge. But me, I'm worried about getting down."

Bodnar, eyes fixed on high trees visible through a side window, managed a perfect glassy-water landing. Her employer put down his magazine and waited for a boat to tow them to shore. Two days later, Bodnar flew back to her base and went on to log over 1,500 hours on de Havilland Beavers, always aware that the airplane possessed remarkable engine-out stability.

Beavers have endured recklessness from foolish pilots and the desperation of frightened ones. For example, reliable witnesses watched a Beaver loop several times near Moosonee on James Bay; other bored pilots have spun their airplanes; one found himself stranded above an impenetrable cloud layer. At the time, he lacked instrument flying experience.

"Somebody told me about putting a Beaver into a sideslip through cloud and kicking it straight as you came out the bottom," he said. "So, down we went. It didn't stall and we broke out at 200 ft. (60 m). I know we weren't supposed to do such things but there were no holes around and I was stuck."

This pilot eventually captained a huge multi-engine passenger jet. Without question, the skills developed behind the dimpled, greasy cowling of an overworked Beaver influence his decisions as he manipulates an airliner into international airports.

When production ended nearly thirty years ago, de Havilland executives believed bushplane markets had been saturated. Some may have thought that pilots no longer needed to learn the rudiments of professional flying in anything but electronic simulators—they were wrong.

Today, the demand for a six-to-seven-place utility airplane has increased. Since nothing comparable is in production, Canadian and American firms have gone to great lengths to improve the basic Beaver. The standard bush-oriented airplane has become what journalist Robert G. Halford called "more refined."

With the exception of sixty DHC-2 Mk III Turbo-beavers produced at de Havilland between 1963 and 1968, turbinization did not begin in a strong way until the mid-1980s. Extremely expensive to purchase when available, turbine-powered Beavers usually belong in the realm of the very rich or government air arms.

Enlarged windows, lighter components, teflon-lined fittings, three-blade propellers and modified wing kits are only a few refinements available to backwoods bush airlines or tourist outfitters. Taken together or one at a time, some kits have made tired airframes into safer performers.

Fortunately, Canadians will be able to see examples of Beavers forever. The prototype rests quietly at Ottawa's National Aviation Museum, the second may be viewed at the Canadian Bushplane Heritage Centre in Sault Ste. Marie, Ontario. Another occupies a place of honor in Winnipeg's Western Canada Aviation Museum. Bashed and beaten, pampered or pushed, these workhorses represent one of Canada's finest technical achievements.

7   De Havilland Otter

Short Takeoff/Heavy Hauler

A few yards below the de Havilland Otter's wheel/skis, the pilot spotted several gigantic black boulders thrusting upward through the sea ice. He peered into the murk but saw only the nothingness of a full-blown Labrador whiteout. A small party of geologists waited in the Inuit village of Nain.

Suddenly, the dark hills surrounding the community loomed ahead. He rolled the Otter steeply left keeping a series of small wooden houses in sight. The instant the wings became level, he brought the throttle back, pushed propeller pitch forward and slammed the airplane hard upon the 2,000 ft. (600 m) gravel airstrip.

Few bushplanes could have survived the abrupt turn this Labrador Airways' pilot needed to avoid the whiteout and save his life. The Otter's thick, high-lift wings permitted a steep angle of bank that would have sent others crashing to the earth.

The concept of the de Havilland DHC-3 Otter began taking shape not long after the Beaver's startling success. By 1950, a design team had tabled specifications for an airplane with comparable takeoff performance. Besides STOL capability, the "King Beaver," would have more than twice the cabin volume with an increase of only 33.3 percent engine power.

Engineers decided the nine-cylinder, 600-h.p. Pratt & Whitney R-1340 would appeal to bush airlines who used the similarly powered Noorduyn Norseman and Bellanca Skyrocket.

The R-1340 was still in production and thousands of these engines were built by Pratt & Whitney Aircraft of Canada.

The huge airplane—renamed the Otter—made its first flight on December 12, 1951, at the hands of test pilot George Neal. Spectators who stood in the wet snow that day in Downsview could hardly believe their eyes when CF-DYK-X left the runway in less than 600 ft. (180 m) After a few minor dorsal fin modifications to compensate for propeller torque, de Havilland built another 465 which went to customers around the world until production ended in 1967.

Otters sold well to military air arms in Chile, Costa Rica, New Zealand, Norway, the United States and many others. The Royal Canadian Air Force acquired 69 and stationed them across the country for Search & Rescue, training and paradropping. When foreign air forces and armies withdrew their Otters from service, many returned to Canada as civil bush freighters.

Only 107 new models went directly to civilian buyers. Noorduyn Norsemen were still plentiful and cheaper compared to "Stoneboats," as some pilots called the Otters in later years. New prices started at $80,000. Equipped with Edo 7170 floats and radio, one sold to the Ontario Department of Lands & Forests fully equipped for $110,664. In 1996, the average used price exceeded $300,000.

With major airlines like Canadian Pacific, Eastern Provincial, Pacific Western or Wardair, Otters carried a pilot and eleven passengers although a type approval dated eight years after the maiden flight indicated seating for seventeen. In federal service, they wore the blue-yellow scheme of the Royal Canadian Mounted Police and for provincial fleets, Manitoba chose orange, and British Columbia and Ontario selected yellow.

Most first time Otter passengers were awed by its size. The wing span reached 58 ft. from tip to tip—4 ft. (1.2 m) more than the Fairchild Husky and 7 ft. (2 m) wider than the Noorduyn Norseman. Not fast at a 120 mph (192 km/h) cruise on skis or 110 mph (177 km/h) on floats, a well maintained Otter burned an average of 30 imp. gal. (137 l) of 80/87 gasoline per hr. Inside, the cabin had 345 cu. ft. (10.4 m^3) of freight space. Not a trace of fabric existed on the all-metal tapered fuselage or single strut wings.

A gigantic set of full-span, double-slotted flaps, whose outboard trailing edge portions acted independently as ailerons, provided incredible slow speed control. With hydraulically selected flap settings, pilots approached as slow as 55–60 mph (89–97 km/h). They could be landed in little more than a few lengths of the 41 ft., 10 in. (13 m) fuselage.

The Otter could be easily recognized long before it could be seen. Because of an exhaust system composed of four stovepipelike stacks or augmenter tubes below the cockpit doors, they hit the skies with a peculiar pocketa-pocketa sound. In the stacks, exhaust gases created enough suction to draw cooling air around the engine and from behind the accessories compartment. Factory salesmen believed these pipes developed a small amount of thrust.

"The Otter was big. Everywhere you went, people stopped and listened," said Tom Henry, a former Nakina, Ontario-based pilot. "We were all used to screaming Norsemen and Stinsons."

De Havilland's first Otter went to the RCAF on November 1, 1952. After several seasons it returned to the factory on indefinite loan as a demonstrator and test bed. In 1969, it became CF-SKX for Lamb Airways, The Pas, Manitoba, and soon left that organization to fly as a geophysical survey platform for Geoterrex in Ottawa. The prototype's career ended tragically when a wing separated during dive testing near Dunrobin, Ontario, on May 1, 1970.

As time went on, Otters showed their age with long streaks of oil and soot down their bellies, crazed plexiglass and badly worn seats and ceilings. Author Karl E. Hayes labeled it an overworked road grader. Ontario government pilots called them "Stationary Objects in the Sky" and an American magazine published a report on the "Head Shaker."

As word spread of the Otter's slowness, suggestions came in concerning the replacement of airspeed indicators with calendars. Pilots hardly helped the Otter's reputation when they lowered the flaps and practiced flying backwards on windy days.

As a UC-64, CF-FQX had a flap-aileron interconnect mechanism which drooped ailerons to fifteen degrees. Constant maintenance forced most commercial operators to remove this system. Flaps were lowered from neutral to 40 degrees through a cockpit ceiling crank. *Photo: Robert S. Grant*

Several ski types have been used on Noorduyn Norsemen like CF-GSR at Red Lake, Ontario, in 1978. During March, 1938, test pilot Leigh Capreol dived a Norseman to 205 mph and recorded no upward or downward ski deflection. One operator claimed that deep crusty snow cut the vertical side walls. As a result, Capreol insisted metal sheeting be installed for protection. *Photo: Robert S. Grant*

In Northway Aviation Ltd. colors, C-FGUE flew regularly from Arnes, Manitoba, after a colorful career with Queen Charlotte Airlines, BC Airlines and Tyee Airways Ltd. on British Columbia's rugged coast. One of the world's most well know Norsemen, C-FGUE, was replicated on a British plastic model kit and appeared in several movie productions. *Photo: Robert S. Grant*

When first flown, the regal SR-10F did well as a limousine for private owners. Licensed for five passengers, the huge airplane had surprisingly short lake performance. This one, CF-HVP, at Trout Lake near North Bay, spent much of its career working for northeastern Ontario's tourist industry. Only eighteen SR-10Fs were built. *Photo: Larry Milberry*

With full fuel, claimed Winnipeg's Bristol Aero-Industries, a seaplane Beechcraft D18S/C45H like C-FZNG could takeoff in nineteen seconds at a 8,250 pound gross weight and climb at 1,150 ft. (345 m) per minute with both engines or 225 ft. (68 m) per minute with one.   *Photo: Robert S. Grant*

An ex-pilot claimed he carried thirty-four fish tubs and two passengers in a Beechcraft 18 on skis. At Pickle Lake, under contract with Kelner Airways in 1987, C-FXUO came under heavy supervision from the airline owners and carried only legal payloads to mining camps.   *Photo: Robert S. Grant*

Beechcraft C-FTBX has flown with Kenora Air Service on Lake of the Woods since 1978. Almost all current seaplane Beechcraft use Winnipeg-built Edo 56-7850A floats. Most bush versions were also equipped with 20G floors and many had one generator removed to save weight. *Photo: Robert S. Grant*

Beechcraft 18 CF-ZRI's flight manual suggested that the throttle be immediately closed if fuel starvation occurred because of improperly selected gas tanks. If not, power surges and propeller overspeeding could occur. When using highly leaded fuels, engines had to be operated at slightly higher cruise settings.
Photo: Robert S. Grant

Beaver CG-EXK in Lynn Lake, Manitoba, was Calm Air's only single-engine airplane in 1982. Before production, de Havilland's questionnaire to potential customers determined that 83 percent wanted short takeoff performance but the majority protested against wing tip navigation lights and 86 percent insisted on ash trays. *Photo: Robert S. Grant*

Equipped with a Baron/STOL modification package, Beaver C-FLUA flies 350-400 hours annually from Ear Falls, Ontario, south of Red Lake. The kit consists of fibreglass droop tips and airflow fences on the wing mid-upper surface. In 1993, owner Ted Trippier estimated twenty-four dollars per hour more revenue since C-FLUA flew 8 mph (13 km/h) faster and needed less maintenance due to lower vibration and quicker climbs to cruise altitude. *Photo: Robert S. Grant*

With three on board, journalist Ronald A. Keith reported a ten-second takeoff run for a Beaver on wheels. Pilots at Walsten Air Service in Kenora, Ontario, can testify that CF-MAQ may take slightly longer. Nevertheless, few ski planes exist that have a 1,676 lb. (754 kg) disposable load. *Photo: Robert S. Grant*

One pilot, assigned to carry an oversize refrigerator in a Beaver, removed both rear doors and slid the cumbersome object in horizontally. Two feet of refrigerator protruded from each side but he took off anyway. "Awfully loud, but the Beaver performed great," he said. Kakabeka Air Service's C-GUNE rarely flies anything more unaerodynamic than corpulent tourists north of Thunder Bay, Ontario. *Photo: Robert S. Grant*

George Ponsford, chief, division of air service, Ontario Department of Lands & Forests, considered cloud seeding with de Havilland Beavers at 25,000 ft. (7,500 m). The project did not materialize but C-FOCJ, the thirty-ninth Beaver built, would likely have been assigned to the task. It now flies regularly at much lower levels with Harbour Air, Richmond, British Columbia.   *Photo: Roach/Killin*

Before de Havilland Otters arrived on the transportation scene, such as C-FMEL shown here at Werner Lake east of the Ontario/Manitoba border in 1983, designers introduced ejector cooling cowls for additional thrust. The stovepipelike exhausts helped account for the peculiar Otter sound.

Photo: Peter Schaffer/Kenora, Ontario

The Ontario government operated seventeen de Havilland Otters during the late 1970s and early 1980s. Pilots flew them in roles never intended for the stalwart "Stoneboats." Game enforcement patrols, outpost cabin inspections and water bombing were some tasks assigned to Otters such as C-GOFA near Red Lake, Ontario in 1981.

Photo: Robert S. Grant

De Havilland Otters on "straight skis" (no wheels) must be parked carefully or they become stuck and cannot be shaken loose by hand. Usually, pilots of aircraft like C-FDDX pack a runway by taxiing several times over a selected area.

Photo: Robert S. Grant

Green Airways, Red Lake, Ontario, acquired C-FMEL from Ontario Central Airways in the late 1980s. Flown year-round, it became a favorite with mining exploration crews for hauling dismantled diamond drills and core boxes.

Photo: Robert S. Grant

Like the Fairchild Husky, the FBA-2C had many interchangeable components. Stabilizers and elevators on aircraft like CF-RXJ at Nestor Falls, Ontario, could be switched without extensive rerigging. The simple steel tube, aluminum-covered airframe meant high strength and quick field repair.

Photo: Robert S. Grant

Still flying in Hudson, Ontario, CF-SDC carries Starratt Airways & Transportation colors for Tudhope Airways. On skis, the FBA-2C has never been considered a good performer. Current owner Glen Tudhope leaves his Found on floats over winter and depends on a de Havilland Beaver to service nearby Indian settlements. *Photo: Robert S. Grant*

Powered with a 290-h.p. Lycoming and three-blade propeller, Air Alma's C-FSOQ showed slightly increased takeoff performance. However, additional fuel consumption and shorter endurance forced a return to the 0-540-A 250-h.p. engine.   *Photo: Larry Milberry*

In 1953, Cessna Aircraft Company in Wichita, Kansas, boasted that the Model 180's "Para-Lift" flaps allowed it to "...descend more slowly than a man in a parachute." Vancouver Island Air Ltd. in Campbell River, British Columbia, rarely needs short lake requirements since most trips takes C-GVIZ above coastal bays, inlets and channels.   *Photo: Robert S. Grant*

In 1970, Found FBA-2C CF-SOT hauled tourists from Temiscaming, Quebec, northeast of North Bay, into tourist camps. Some Founds flew with a small ventral fin under the tail but in the field, operators removed them.   *Photo: Robert S. Grant*

In the late 1960s and into the 1980s, Lamb Airways, The Pas, Manitoba, used a fleet of Cessna 180s on Arctic surveys. When not counting caribou or searching for minerals, they flew regularly to northern Manitoba and Saskatchewan Native villages. One pilot recorded a trip with a Cree elder, an eleven-year-old girl, three plump women with three babies, full fuel and a cabin crammed with groceries.

Photo: Robert S. Grant

Later model Cessna 185s were powered by 300-h.p. IO-520-D engines. In Yellowknife, Aero Arctic used C-GTAA to freight parts and relieve crews assigned to the company's helicopters. At cruise with oversize tires, airspeed indicated over 150 mph (242 km/h).

Photo: Robert S. Grant

Only the strong survive years of flying over the world's toughest terrain. Waweig Lake Outfitters owner Don Plumridge's Cessna 185 C-GDTM has endured high winds, small lakes and deep snows north of Lake Superior. With a forty-nine knot flap down stalling speed, Plumridge has accessed lakes too short for lower powered Cessna 180s.   *Photo: Robert S.Grant*

In springtime, it was not unusual to see aircraft such as Cessna 180 CF-KPF break through the ice at Red Lake, Ontario. Usually the last airplane to change over to floats, they were kept working because of their light weight relative to Beavers, Otters and Norsemen.　　　　　　　　　　　　　　*Photo: Dale Flieler*

Cessna 180s, such as this one of Vancouver Island Air, are ideal for quick transportation into British Columbia's interior. Their lightness allows access to stone-covered beaches which could quickly puncture the floats of heavier airplanes.　　　　　　　　　　　　　　*Photo: Larry Langford*

"If that thing ever collided with a brick wall, it flies so slow, you'd have time to get out of the seat and run out the back door before it stopped," remarked former Ontario government pilot George Beaushene in Sault Ste. Marie.

Otter Serial Number Two still flies regularly every summer from Kenora, Ontario, on island-dotted Lake of the Woods. Registered CF-GCV, it served briefly as a test airplane for development flying at Downsview. With three belly tanks filled to their 178 imp. gal. capacity, C-FGCV's payload totalled 1,793 lb. (807 kg) at a gross seaplane takeoff weight of 7,967 lb. (3,585 kg). Few air services carried full fuel and were able to cram more revenue freight aboard. A glossy twenty-four-page de Havilland sales brochure claimed Otters like CF-GCV carried 2,525 lb. (1,136 kg) within 200 mi. (322 km) on floats or 2,810 lb. (1,265 kg) on skis.

Otter CF-GCV flew with Eastern Provincial Airways in February, 1954, into wind-ravaged Atlantic coastal communities like Cartwright, Makkovik or Nain. After surviving Labrador, CF-GCV crossed Canada for Pacific Western Airlines, then briefly flew from a small lake west of Fort Nelson, British Columbia, in 1966. Loaded with fire fighters, it easily handled fast-running rivers like the Liard during forest fire fighting activities. On October 14, 1974, CF-GCV met with an accident at Williston Lake near the colossal Peace River dam site. At the time, the logbooks showed 12,410 hours flying time.

Salvaged, Otter CF-GCV returned to central Canada with Silver Pine Air Services, Pine Falls, Manitoba, and a year later, Walsten Air Service became the current owner. Silver and yellow, the world's oldest Otter's duties were no longer as strenuous as they were during its youth. Pilots still complained.

"God, it's hot in that cockpit and GCV's floor temperature's unbelievable," recalled pilot Mike Stuart. "It's so bad, I wear out shoes pretty quick because every time I land, I have to dip my feet in the lake to cool them off."

Pilots of water-bombing Otters considered warm weather flying a specialty. De Havilland offered a 193-lb. pair of tanks mounted separately on each float with eighty gal. of water in each.

6 ft. (2 m) long and with a 22 in. (56 cm) diameter, they were filled by a tube extending downward to the keel of each float. As the pilot maintained 35 mph (56 km/h) across a lake, dynamic force pushed water up the tubes into the tanks.

"A control lever located on the floor at the right hand side of the pilot's seat is connected by means of cables and pulleys to the front end of each tank," said the DHC-3 Flight Manual. "Pulling the control lever upward disengages a lock and rotates each tank in an outboard direction 130 degrees to empty the contents."

Pilots found the outside tanks awkward to climb over. De Havilland described an alternate 176 lb. (79 kg) "water dropping gear" consisting of a single 9 ft., 8 in. (3 m) tank mounted between the floats. It held 190 gal. (865 l) and could be filled by touching down at 60 mph (97 km/h) and maintaining a steady run until the tank filled. Total time on the water depended on wind and surface conditions but averaged fifteen to twenty seconds.

In 1966, aeronautical engineer J. K. Hawkshaw of Field Aviation in Toronto developed a new system for the Province of Ontario's Yellow Bird fleet of Otters. Enclosed within the Edo 7170 floats, the "Ontario Integral Float Fire Bomber" arrangement eliminated the drag associated with roll-over tanks. After landing, the pilot electrically lowered a square probe. In 600 ft. (180 m) or twelve seconds, he scooped up 220 imp. gal. (1001 l) of water.

Initial trials took place in St. Petersburg, Florida, with pilot supervisor Thomas C. Cooke and check pilot Reg Parsons who picked up more than 600 water loads in two weeks. Every load slamming into test Otter CF-ODY's floats meant a full gross weight takeoff. Airborne, the pilot selected an arming switch above his instrument panel and kept flap at a climb setting. The load exited at maximum drop speed of ninety-one knots in less than a second through a 4 ft. sq. (0.4 m^2) door on the float bottoms. Each door shut with hydraulic jacks and visual flag indicators and cockpit warning lights confirmed door closure.

"The end result was highly successful and I must say, we now have the ultimate in water bombers for float aircraft," said Parsons.

Fire fighting in a cumbersome single-engine airplane demanded exceptional skill. Pilots could not realistically expect to survive an engine failure above the flames, turbulence and low terrain. Curiously, the Ontario government paid Otter pilots $60 and land-based Grumman Tracker pilots $100 per day in 1977. Several thought the scale should have been switched.

"If a Tracker engine calved, the guy flew home, but we didn't," said one pilot. "In a day, we'd do nearly a hundred loads and they rarely did more than a dozen after flying all the way back to their airports and back out to the fire."

One pilot took time to record his thoughts. He had already retrieved a survey crew on a remote lake: after helping load their boat, outboard motor, tent and fish samples, he returned CF-ODX to Kenora, and found himself assigned to aerial photography in Otter C-GOFA. At the end of several hours at 9,200 ft. (2,760 m), his employer dispatched him with a crew of orange-suited fire fighters and equipment to a fire. He dropped his passengers close to the flames, took off again and went into "water bombing mode."

"Power back but not to the stop so the engine doesn't 'pop,' flaps to takeoff, down we go," he wrote. "Wind's picked up, whitecaps paralleling the cream-colored wind streaks as we touch. Back on the control column, speed below forty, up on power. Keep slow until the probes go up. Tanks full and with a bit of work, we'll be airborne. One float out, then the other. She's off.

"Now I have a loaded single-engine water bomber. Peachy. The Otter hates climbing so aim for a narrows between an island and a shoreline but OFA just might struggle above the trees. Near the fire, she flies heavy. Speed's stable at seventy knots. Watching for cheekos (standing dead trees). Power on, nose up. A colony of tree-nesting herons slides underneath, their necks twist to follow me as they watch.

"Close now, don't bomb into smoke, watch for trees. Jesus, it's rough. Hot spot under the nose, smell of burning wood. Wait a second. Press. Now! A glance at the shadow tells me the water's out. Lights flashing and the hydraulic click says the bomb doors are closing. I get the hell out."

No one has lost their life while water dropping in an Otter, despite the hazards. One pilot struck several poplar trees after a long day but flew home. Another hit a spruce with his wing and he, too, landed safely. In one case, Otter C-GOFG ran out of takeoff space while on a pick-up run. Burning gasoline destroyed the airplane but the pilot escaped unhurt. Many Otter pilots, however, have had frights when bomb doors did not close.

"Any situation where a door or doors are suspected of not being closed prior to touchdown must be considered serious in the utmost," noted a flight manual.

No Otter water bomber has flipped inverted although those who experienced an opened door on landing said the airplane went through several horrific gyrations. Such episodes served to underscore the ruggedness and versatility of the type. Water bomber one day, passenger carrier the next and freighter after that—superb in all roles.

Otters also excelled as aerial photography platforms. The 5 ft. x 5 ft. (1.5 m x 1.5 m) cabin with a length of more than sixteen feet allowed room for cameras and photographers. In fact, CF-ODJ spent an entire season in 1955 on wheels flying northern Ontario photo missions. Technicians had installed a Lear L-2 autopilot and an extra circular window in the rear.

"The slow climb was no problem during May to July when the sun was at its highest," explained photographer Cor Dikland. "The fact that the Otter took so much time to reach our photo altitude (9,200 ft. [2,760 m]) wasn't a disadvantage because most of our areas were far enough that the aircraft had time to get that high."

Seaplane Otters generally climbed at an agonizingly slow 150–200 ft. (45–60 m) per minute. One contract awarded to Sabourin Lake Airways in Red Lake, Ontario, depended not on climb ability but rather a rapid rate of descent. In 1979, between fuel hauls to Indian villages in CF-VQD, the airline chased rockets for a NASA/NRC project for solar eclipse research.

"Our Otter, orbiting at 10,000 ft. (3,000 m), watched for parachutes which lowered a payload back to earth. The Otter'd follow them down, load the equipment and return it to the scientists," said ex-owner Norman Hegland.

The Otter's huge tail often posed problems on windy days. With a vertical surface of over 60 sq. ft. (5.4 m^2), steerage in the seaplane configuration was poor. Coval Air's Dell d'Arcangelo in Campbell River, British Columbia, remembered the frustrations of battling high winds, fast currents and 15 ft. tides when approaching docks in narrow bays. Some commercial air services installed oversize water rudders which hung slightly below the floats when raised for takeoff.

An amphibious Otter pilot from Powell River, British Columbia, nearly destroyed his airplane on takeoff. He had landed in a small slough behind a rock dam to pick up tree planters "plus all their bloody stoves and garbage." After he "he-hawed and bullshitted around" waiting for a band of fog to dissipate, he loaded eight men.

"And that goddamn dam's coming up and I was on the step and of course, an amphib Otter's not the best performing thing," he said. "I had full aileron deflected over to the left and I'm going. Jesus, God, she's got to go. And just as the dam went out of sight, we went into the air and those water rudders hung down a fair bit because they hit the dam. Boom! Bang! This bastard, I staggered out and into the sea fog so I just pulled the power back and sort of landed, kept it on the step and we come out of it in 300 yards (273 m), eh?"

Normal unhurried takeoffs into wind usually mean easy times for Otter pilots. Herb Neufeld who flies CF-ODV for Vermilion Bay Air Services, 22 mi. (35 km) west of Dryden, Ontario, marveled at how well the airplane handled maximum loads from small "puddles." With plenty of "wallowing and roaring," the Otter gets on the step smartly and airborne quickly, he said. Taxiing, however, takes patience.

"That thing's terrible in the wind. It's so big that docking can be really tricky," he explained. "You've got to be right on because you got 8,000 lb. (3,600 kg) there and it doesn't have to be moving fast to punch a really big hole in something if you hit a rock."

Campbell River-based Ken Leigh pointed out that oversize water rudders made turning easier. With engine idling, average pilots could turn downwind in twenty-knot winds but few Otters had the costly modification. They had no choice but to become proficient at sailing backwards with flaps down and propeller slowly ticking over.

"Anybody can fly one of these turkeys," remarked an Athabaska Airways pilot in La Ronge, Saskatchewan. "But when it's windy, dock hands should be able to sit in their lawn chairs and wait and watch and enjoy the show when there's a pro in the cockpit."

Complaints concerning the "underfloated" Otter surface each season. Often, the Edo 7170s buried their noses underwater while turning downwind on gusty days. Canadian Airlines Airbus 320 captain John Jacobsen remembered his disappointment when faced with an Otter for the first time. His career until then consisted of hundreds of Norseman hours along Hudson Bay and James Bay.

"In a strong wind, you could horse the Norseman around because it was overfloated but you didn't dare do that with the Otter without capsizing," he said. "That de Havilland tail was just too big and in tidal waters, forget it."

In the late 1970s, several air services began adapting the Otter to larger Edo 7850 floats. According to Allan McNeil, who logged nearly 12,000 hours on type, the revised arrangement worked well.

"At first, I was prejudiced toward 7170s but after getting used to the 7850s, there's no way I'd want anything else," he said. "You hardly need more than 1,000 rpm to turn in winds we sailed in before. The Otter suddenly became easier to dock and crosswinds go much easier."

Although the Edo 7850s eliminated windy day worries and improved downwind takeoffs—a procedure not unusual with lightly loaded airplanes—they were expensive. Norman Hegland estimated floats, attachment fittings and labor averaged $40,000 in 1981. Obtaining the special float has been difficult since Bristol in Winnipeg manufactured less than sixty pairs. When found, they "sure make life a helluva lot easier," said one pilot.

External loads seemed to be an Otter's forte. A Pickle Lake air service tied 700 lb. (315 kg) road grader tires below the wing struts. Septic tanks and satellite dishes roped to floats rarely raised an eyebrow.

A close call occurred at V. Kelner Airways at Pickle Lake after a pilot left his dock with a tightly tied stack of pressed cardboard tubes. Used for forming cement pillars to support satellite dishes, the flight went well until heavy rain materialized south of the Ojibway community of Webequie. The cardboard absorbed moisture, weakened and began disintegrating. Luckily, the pilot reached a lake before the tubes broke loose and created a dangerous aerodynamic unbalance.

"Yeah, the Otter's slow for sure, but it handles good loads out of short lakes," admitted Jack Hooker, manager for Miminiska Sportsman's Lodge Ltd., 204 mi. (328 km) north of Thunder Bay. "One year we tied picture windows to the side. It flies a little slower, but the Otter got where it was supposed to go."

A strange Otter flight took place near Ear Falls, 42 mi. (68 km) south of Red Lake, after an overanxious amateur pilot "wrinkled" his Cessna 206 seaplane. A helicopter attempted slinging the remains but "pickled" (dropped), the load in turbulence. Another team dragged the badly battered airplane to an island and wondered if it would fit the outside of an Otter. If so, money and time saved would be tremendous.

Chief pilot Lee Martin of Lac Seul Airways carefully measured the wrecked fuselage and decided it would fit. Helpers used heavy cables to fashion a double loop and fastened it to the 206's wing root fittings. They also lashed ropes snugly around the fuselage.

"We cut a short tree, about five inches thick, and propped one end on the side of the float and laid the other against the ladder," said Martin. "If we hadn't, the 206's tail would have been against the Otter and the nose facing out. We taped the broken windshield and cowling shut and padded whatever space we could find with seat cushions."

Martin estimated his load at 800 lb. (360 kg) He emptied the Otter cabin except for some light aluminum parts before taxiing into deep water from the sandy beach work site. The destination was only 35 mi. (56 km) away.

Immediately, Martin saw that the Otter did not list toward the side on which the Cessna 206 rested. If he could raise the float during the first few seconds of takeoff, he would continue. If not, another helicopter would try again. Air service owner Tom Hannaway sat beside Martin to monitor the load.

"When we got close to normal lift off speed, I started feeding in aileron and the float popped right out of the water," Martin said. "As a matter of fact, everything trimmed exactly right except for the aileron which could be kept level with one finger. I'd say it flew about the same as a big boat."

Lac Seul Airways became well practised in the moving arts. Martin carried a Piper PA-18 Super Cub fuselage and two Otter wings in separate flights. Other northern Ontario agencies often found themselves compelled to transport oversize loads as well. A photograph exists of an Ontario government Otter southbound from MacDowell Settlement, a Cree-Ojibway village 96 mi. northeast of Red Lake, with a de Havilland Turbo-beaver wing mounted vertically on each float.

Leuenberger Air Services at Nakina, Ontario, 35 mi. (56 km) east of Lake Nipigon, has been in the bush flying business since 1960. In this organization, Otters are preferred for moving prospecting parties and tourists, and supplying Indian settlements north of a base at Cordingley Lake. Included in their many destinations is the "metropolis" of Martin Falls Reserve #65 or, as locals know it, Ogoki Post. This 19-acre (7.6 ha) plot of wooden homes has a post office, sawmill and school but no running water, sewage system or garbage pit.

On the 105 mi. (169 km) map reading run, Leuenberger air crews do not benefit from short-skirted flight attendants nor are their cockpits cluttered with complex electronic navigation devices. In winter, coordinating freight hauls with washdays helps since laundry on the lines and chimney smoke indicate wind direction.

In open-water seasons, pilots like John McElwain judge approaches by wind patterns on nearby lakes and swamps. Landings take place on the fast-running, shallow Ogoki River.

McElwain admitted he hated Ogoki trips since the rapid water made docking tricky.

"With an Otter in an east wind above fifteen knots, you can't turn. One year, somebody went sailing down the river and over the rapids, but got away with nothing more than a good scare," he said. "The only way's to face the wind regardless of current and at low water, channels get narrower and sharp rocks pop up where there weren't any before."

De Havilland designers figured they had thought of everything when they roughed out the first sketches of their King Beaver. On hearing this, McElwain shrugged, "Well, almost everything."

"The Stoneboat's got a double cargo door on the left side and a smaller one on the right," he said. "It always seemed to me that Ogoki trips called for large freight like lumber, fuel drums or furniture and everything that fit through the side door. Trouble is, the narrow one always wound up on the dock side."

Occasionally, this factory oversight caused embarrassing incidents especially when the entire population of settlements like Ogoki Post lined the riversides to watch the crazy *wump-teh-go-shey* or white man. Once, a thoughtful group of construction workers insisted on helping McElwain park Otter CF-SOX. Soon, a water rudder jammed under a makeshift dock. A self-appointed assistant decided to release the only rope.

"And there went my airplane, sailing down the river to Hudson Bay and me standing there with nothing to do except wonder how I'd find my next job," McElwain laughed. "Suddenly, this Indian woman in a boat came out of nowhere. She told me to jump in and drove through the rapids to the Otter. Never got a chance to thank her and never holed a float."

Many customers are surprised at the unorthodox nose down attitude an Otter assumes after takeoff. With 98 sq. ft. of flap area, the huge craft ignores its size and gets into the air as low as 50 mph (81 km/h). After "just kind of levitating with the stick right back in my gut," as Gerry Norberg described a STOL departure in northern Manitoba, the Otter is no rocket. Nevertheless, the thick wing has allowed many pilots to perform terrifyingly steep turns at low airspeeds—the same maneuver which saved the Labrador Airways pilot.

Few pilots enjoy winter flying and cold cockpits. Factory equipment included a 50,000-Btu Series 50 Janitrol heater on the upper forward side of the engine fire wall. Assembled from switches, valves, ignition units and other small parts, the unit depended on fuel from the airplane's belly tanks. Liquid spraying into a tubular combustion chamber produced a coil-like whirling flame. A complex unit, the Janitrol often malfunctioned and forced pilots and passengers into fur-lined boots and smoke-tanned leather mitts.

Frost-bitten limbs were not the only hazards. A Quebec-based pilot's oil cap vanished after takeoff. Oil spread down the fuselage side and congealed into long, hard stringers. Landing quickly, he pried the frozen mess from the metal, warmed it with his hands and crammed it back into the tank like a handful of spaghetti. The same pilot later became badly stuck in snow on a remote lake in -38°F (-39°C).

Trudging through knee-deep slush, he dragged several jackpine poles back to the mired Otter and dug beneath the skis with a short-handled shovel. Jamming poles under each ski, he started the engine, moved the Otter toward a drier area and eased on takeoff power. After pounding around the lake several times unable to struggle airborne, he stopped. Stepping outside, he found a 10 ft. (3 m) pole frozen to the tail ski.

Most Otters used special order de Havilland wheel/skis weighing 301.7 lb. (136 kg). Activated by a selector unit and hand pump between the front seats, hydraulic pressure moved an actuator to swivel a linkage around the axle. Hand pumping them up required at least one hundred strokes. Many pilots preferred partial wheel down in rough snow to absorb landing and taxiing shocks.

Superior Airways staff in Thunder Bay, were encouraged by owner Orville Wieben to develop a pair of "straight" skis, i.e., without wheels. The angle iron and steel bar design was not light or streamlined but extremely strong. Lee Martin remembered them well: "What they lacked in workmanship, they made up in

The Otter's 345 cu. ft. (10 m^3) cabin and reinforced cargo floors allow heavy loads to be "bulled" aboard. This crew at Kenora, Ontario, in 1980, worked dawn to dusk loading government and civilian Otters with fire pumps, gasoline generators and groceries for forest fire camps.   *Photo: Robert S. Grant*

weight and what they lacked in engineering, they made up in weight. There were no compound curves and the pedestals looked like they came from truck springs with a small tip turned up at the front."

Stopping an Otter in snow almost always meant "instant stuck." With engine power at full throttle, the airplane would do little except tip nose down. On lucky days, pilots might gain enough momentum to continue the takeoff. Often, Martin said, he repeated the process several times.

Some air services assigned helpers to flights away from home base. If shoveling did not suffice, they exited and yanked a rope tied to the tail as the pilot slammed the elevators and rudder to break the ice's grip. The factory flight manual recommended leaving flaps up for more effective "tail wag." Unlike Beavers or Cessnas, Otters could barely be rocked by hand because of their weight and high wing struts.

De Havilland Otters achieved notoriety for poor crosswind handling, particularly on wheels from airports. One pilot reported encountering many "some kind of hairy situations" in crosswinds. Lee Martin never forgot a "mean" wind he battled during a ferry flight to the mid-United States for new paint. Before his arrival at a refueling stop in Mena, Arkansas, 98 mi. (158 km) west of Little Rock, snowstorms had inundated the area. When plows cleared the only suitable runway, high banks left barely enough room to turn Otter CF-DDX. Book figures recommended against crosswinds of more than 17 mph (27 km/h).

"The wind was on the right and I had all the rudder I could get on and riding the brake to keep it on the runway until we got enough speed to keep straight," Martin said.

Switching from seaplane Otters to wheeled ones required caution. The first few land takeoffs often surprised anyone accustomed to a milieu without crosswinds or long lakes. Slow to accelerate, an Otter seemed to crawl down a runway and then suddenly, the tail would snap up.

One pilot touched his propeller while leaving Oshawa, Ontario, for Watson Lake, Yukon. Resourceful, he shortened the remaining two blades with a hacksaw and flew on. His employer did not appreciate the get-home-it-is after mechanics replaced the propeller with a new one.

Watson Lake Flying Service developed changeovers into an art form. On the brink of freeze-up, they flew morning seaplane trips and returned to base. Waiting mechanics quickly removed the bulky Edos and attached wheels. Pilots climbed in for fast landplane trips and in the evening, mechanics reconverted the Otter back to floats for the next morning. A changeover rarely took more than three hours.

As Otters aged, old-guard bush pilots retired into management or found better paying positions outside of aviation. When younger ones took their place, the airplane began losing its popularity. Gary Cutts, formerly of Red Lake's Green Airways, said he felt like an actor in a slow-motion movie when he plunked himself behind an Otter's control wheel.

"With the Beech and the Norseman, you reduced power, you came down, but in the Otter, throttle back and it floated up and ballooned and wallowed all over the sky," added David Robertson. "You never quite know what an Otter'll do. You'd be up 200 ft. (60 m) and drop 300 ft. (90 m) and if you were lucky, it'd touch down at the midpoint of a wallow."

Many incidents demonstrated the Otter's strength. One Otter, verified a group of Vancouver Island pilots, survived a collision with a glacier during cargo dropping on British Columbia's 13,104 ft. (3,931 m) Mount Waddington. While supplying a mountaineering team, the pilot could not escape from a shaft of descending air. He struck ice at the 9,000 ft. (2,700 m) level severely damaging 5 ft. (1.5 m) of one wing. The impact canted the engine to the right and shifted the control wheel. Both front struts penetrated 2 in. (5 cm) into the fuselage. The pilot flew home. Later, the damaged airplane went to Calgary via truck for rebuild.

Another individual landed an amphibious Otter with wheels down in a salt water bay. "When he went in, it was nothing but a wall of water. It pirouetted and came around upright," said a witness. The shaken pilot did not report the incident. Next day, another pilot noticed several tell-tale wrinkles during his preflight inspection.

De Havilland Otters often caught fire after forced approaches. Mechanics attribute this to the landing gear struts penetrating the flexible, bagtype gasoline tanks beneath the forward portion of the cabin floor.

"There are three tanks and the center's made up of two sections," said Gordon Hughes. "Being rubber, they'll rupture on impact with any kind of load. A metal tank might have prevented a lot of fires, and why de Havilland went for the rubber ones, I'll never understand."

In recent years, engine failures have occurred with alarming regularity. Even though Pratt & Whitney produced 34,966 direct drive and geared R-1340s (the last in 1960), parts shortages have developed. All have been overhauled again and again with a trend toward decreased reliability.

"It's an engine failure waiting to happen; there's no doubt in my mind," lamented Al McNeil. "It's going to blow a jug (cylinder) or just simply cease to function for no particular reason other than they're old."

David Nilson attributed many stoppages to improper distribution of air. Most breakdowns occur in the top three cylinders. The Otter's exhaust system is enclosed at the rear and exhaust discharges through the augmentor tubes. Sounds good, remarked another mechanic, but the engine never cools properly.

"You can fly that damn thing pretty slow and still be comfortable with a load. It's easy to handle in gusty conditions and takes quite a sea chop and can land on pretty heavy water. It's a real tough airplane but that engine...," said a pilot.

An operations manager admitted that the Otter, as it was originally envisioned, made it a "super airplane" but passengers have lost confidence. If customers saw "...one of those things farting, popping and blowing smoke and landing in the middle of the chuck out there, you can't blame the suckers for taking their business elsewhere," he pointed out. No fatalities occurred within this man's organization, a fact he attributed only to his policy of avoiding flights over mainland whenever possible.

A pilot in northern Ontario lost count of failures he experienced during his multidecade career. Some engines simply blew up, a few seized. Some were new and others old. For certain, he stressed, no one could ignore an Otter which decided to stop flying.

"You'd be sitting there, just flying along, fat, dumb and happy, moose meat and bunch of turkeys in the back and Boom! There she goes and down you go."

The Otter flight manual offered advice for pilots caught with a dead engine. They must decide whether "...to ride aircraft safely to the ground for a crash landing," and then go through a list of shut-down procedures. In case of fire, they are expected to sideslip into soft ground, sand or shallow water and absorb the impact with the wing and tail. One paragraph admitted an engine fire excluded "...a bail out at low altitude."

Allan McNeil carried out a textbook forced landing near Red Lake after noticing an oil temperature rise. Minutes later, it returned to normal and then swept past red line limits before the engine stopped. The glide to a nearby frozen lake did not take long and ended successfully.

"I'm sitting there having a cigarette and a cup of coffee, when it dawned on me the prop was still turning," he said. "I say, 'What the hell?' Before long, Dave Harvey (Wings Ltd. AME) shows up with his tool box. 'Hold it, Dave, watch this,' I said, and flipped the prop over about ten times with my little finger. Like the whole gear case was toast. Nothing."

Rarely does the Pratt & Whitney R-1340 stop completely in spite of horrifying smoke and severe vibration. Veteran pilots recommended holding takeoff power on until clear of obstacles before retarding the throttle. Sometimes a cylinder shatters when power settings alter pressure inside the engine. McNeil compared the situation to someone pushing against a locked door. When the door opens, pressure disappears and the pusher falls.

"So you always, always make sure there's a lake around when you bring the power back, even if you go 5 mi. (8 km) out of your way, eh?" cautioned McNeil. "Never, never, never pull the throttle all the way back when you're coming down, never. If you hear a pow-pow-pow, you're really screwing your engine. Keep a little power on and go very slow with that throttle."

Not all complaints centered around the Otter's engine. Although not certified for icing conditions, a few pilots discovered that thick wings could be detrimental rather than life saving. One man, desperate to escape low ceilings, climbed into the murk to avoid hilltops. He soon reached a point where high power settings and extra flap would not prevent an altitude loss.

"Okay, the next lake I see, I'm landing, that's it," he said. "So I just cranked into a steep turn and the thing stalled right now. It was going down about 4,000 ft. (1,200 m) a minute. I just got the power on when I hit the lake and I swear them skis, if they didn't touch the wings, they should have. That thing don't like no ice at all."

There will probably always be a place for heavy haulers like Otters. Logging, tourism and exploration demand airplanes with floats or skis. The problem, current users know, is that Stoneboats are wearing out and no North American company manufactures spare parts, particularly for radial engines.

All is not lost, however. Allan McNeil learned this during a lumber run to Pauingaussi, a Cree Indian village 114 mi. (184 km) south of Norway House, Manitoba. By coincidence, Otter C-GSUV, flown by chief pilot David Martin of Silver Pine Air Services, Pine Falls, taxied from the shoreline at the same time as McNeil in C-FVQD.

Like many pilots, neither could resist some friendly competition. A few leather-jacketed residents stood watching with hands in pockets and wet, hand-rolled cigarettes clamped between their lips. They had seen Otters before but rarely two leaving Paunigaussi at the same time.

"So, I get on the step and he hasn't punched her yet," McNeil said. "I'm going to blow by this guy when all of a sudden he was pulling away from me so fast and I'm sitting there. We're talking at least 40–50 mph (64–81 km/h) difference and that's saying something for an Otter."

McNeil had been surprised by a 1,000-h.p. Polski Zaklady Lotnicze (PZL) radial engine. Currently in production, Polish PZLs can be bought factory fresh from North American distributors. Consequently, mechanical breakdowns have been nearly eliminated. With full loads, the converted Otter climbed nearly five times faster. Airspeed jumped to 144 mph (232 km/h) and a four-blade propeller with replaceable hubs produced extra thrust.

The PZL's fuel consumption averaged 40 imp. gal. (182 l) per hr. instead of thirty. Users admitted, however, that it required more careful handling in cold weather than the R-1340s. A large shutter described as looking "like something borrowed from a Kenworth (truck)" regulates oil temperature.

"The pilot can't daydream. If he lets down without monitoring the manual air shutters, the oil congeals," said Frank Kelner of V. Kelner Airways. His air service in Pickle Lake leased PZL-powered Otters in 1987.

Polish engine sales have slowly penetrated the bush flying industry but turbine powerplants seem to be the answer to extended Otter life. The first changeover took place at Seattle, Washington, in 1972 with a Garrett AiResearch TPE-331 fixed shaft engine. The fragile Garrett proved unsuccessful. Six years later, C-FMES-X flew a trial hop from Edmonton with a 662-h.p. Pratt & Whitney PT6A-27 and four-blade reversible Hartzell propeller.

Ray Cox of Cox Air Resources had developed the conversion to reduce maintenance costs and increase productivity through higher cruising speed and more payload. Also, added Karl Hayes, a turbine Otter would overcome the shortage of aviation gasoline which threatened to ground all piston airplanes.

Since the "Cox Turbo-Otter" project, some conversions have gone to Alaska and South America. One called the "Vazar Dash Three" and re-engined by Vazar in Bellingham, Washington, flew over the North Pole from Vancouver to Stockholm, Sweden, for a parachuting club.

Whatever the future holds for the de Havilland Otter, no one can deny that this slow, noisy machine has sustained many operators. Whatever pilots, mechanics, owners or passengers choose to call it, this grand but undramatic lady will continue making contributions to northern transportation.

8   Found FBA-2C

The Flying Half-Ton Truck

Several sea gulls swept past the dock and touched lightly on the glassy surface of Eldon Lake at Lynn Lake, Manitoba. A few yards away, two pilots strolled toward an airplane loaded with cardboard boxes and red plastic fuel kegs. Their training flight had to be done quickly. Soon, the season's moose hunt would begin and every airplane within hundreds of miles would be in demand.

One pilot had never seen the Found FBA-2C. Powered with a 250-h.p. Lycoming 0-540 engine, the "no-frills utility aircraft," as *Aviation Week* called it, could outperform the popular Cessna 180. "Maybe," the new pilot thought, "but I sure as hell don't have a choice and I need this job." New to Calm Air, a company formed at Lynn Lake in 1962, he intended to prove himself with whatever they gave him, whether it turned out to be an eggbeater on a board or a shiny de Havilland Twin Otter.

As the check pilot explained the FBA-2C, his eager acolyte became distracted by an attractive Cree girl perched nearby on an upturned fuel drum. She would be his first passenger to Brochet, a small community 78 mi. (126 km) northwest of Lynn Lake.

A sharp, "Are you listening?" from the check pilot drew him back to business.

Preflight inspection completed, the new pilot stepped onto the Edo 2870 float and sneaked another peek at the girl who smiled coquettishly back. With eyes intent only on her long, blueberry blonde hair and pretty face, he opened the Found's door and reached behind him for support before gripping the seat.

Suddenly, he lost his balance. Flailing frantically for the strut—he had been flying Cessna 180s—and milliseconds before his already chilled body felt the shock of cold October water, he remembered.

The Found FBA-2C had a cantilever wing.

No struts.

The check pilot shook his head. He had watched many first-timers fall into Eldon Lake. A keen aviation nut, he knew that only a few airplanes like the pre-War Fokker Super Universal depended on strong multispar wings without external struts or wires.

The check pilot watched the trainee drag himself onto the dock. Without waiting for him to drain his rubber boots, he ordered him into the Found.

The Indian maiden tittered silently.

The concept of one of the few all-Canadian bushplanes originated during the 1930s when four brothers worked for pioneer airline MacKenzie Air Services of Edmonton, Alberta. They saw many types which, with the exception of the Noorduyn Norseman, had been impressed into northern transportation from some other facet of aviation. They also noticed that not every airplane struggling out of the hinterlands carried full loads. Customers complained about Bellanca, Fokker, Junkers or Norseman rates whenever they wanted to move a few pounds of freight. The brothers—Bud, Dwight, Grey and Mickey—decided a market existed for a lighter flying half-ton truck.

In 1946, they formed Found Brothers Aviation Ltd. in Agincourt near Toronto. A year later, they moved to Malton. The first airplane, a two-seat, fabric-covered tricycle gear design of welded steel tube called the FBA-1A made an unofficial maiden flight on June 3, 1949, when it became airborne during a fast taxi test. It landed hard, bounced 8 ft. (2.4 m), struck the runway again and slammed back into the air. On the third "landing," a nose wheel snapped and the airplane skidded to a stop. A 140-h.p. high wing monoplane, the "Green Hornet" went on to log twenty hours without problems. Registered CF-GMO-X, the FBA-1A served as a test bed and proving ground for developing their ideal bushplane.

With experience from the FBA-1A program, the Found brothers returned to the drawing boards. Financing delayed the arrival of the FBA-2A until August 11, 1960, when test pilot Stanley M. Haswell flew the maiden flight. John David Eaton of the T. Eaton Co. became interested and signed for delivery of the first two production machines for Georgian Bay Airways in Parry Sound, Ontario.

Found Brothers Aviation had planned to market the FBA-2A with a tricycle landing gear but switched production to the tail wheel FBA-2C. Pilot J. C. Temple carried out its first flight on May 9, 1962. Several weeks later, this model went down at Brampton because of fuel starvation. Although the loss hindered deliveries, production continued. By the time test pilot George Ayerhart flew the last FBA-2C in 1967, twenty-six had been built.

Promotion took place through pilot reports, product information guides, editorial comments and cover photographs in Canadian as well as other North American, British and European publications. At one point, N. K. Found even responded to a query from the Central Library in Peking but no sales took place.

On wheels, the impressive Found FBA-2C lifted off in 400 ft. (120 m) at 55 mph (89 km/h) and climbed at 1,200 ft. (360 m) per min. As a seaplane, cruise averaged 125 mph (201 km/h) using 13.5 imp. gal (61 l) per hr. for a 720 mi. (1,159 km) range. The competitive 235-h.p. Cessna 180 could not match the Found.

N. K. Found claimed the company sold another FBA-2C in Quebec when one flew formation with the more streamlined Cessna 185. One pilot remarked that the overly sensitive Cessna needed to be flown hands-on at all times but the stable Found had "...solid control feeling somewhat like an Anson."

A typical Found weighed 1,891.5 lb. (851 kg) with Edo 2870 floats and received approval for a maximum 2,950 lb. (1,328 kg) takeoff weight. A sales brochure claimed that with a reduced fuel load from 56 gal. (255 l) to 23 gal. (105 l), it legally carried over 750 lb. (338 kg) for 200 mi. (322 km) With full tanks, payload dropped to 526 lb. (237 kg) with a 600 mi. (966 km) range.

On skis, loads could be increased by 133 lb. (60 kg). A seaplane's average takeoff run lasted 1,000 ft. (300 m) and aviation writer John Gallagher in Toronto used 850 ft. (255 m) in a wheeled Found. One pilot watched a Found fly away with 1,500 lb. (675 kg) and another claimed the seaplane version would leave the water in fifteen to seventeen seconds with or without a full load.

Inside the Found's 120 cu. ft. (3.6 m^3) cabin, carpetless aluminum floors distributed cargo weight evenly and a canvas flap served as a rear hammock seat. Behind the hammock, a huge baggage area enticed dock boys into loading freight toward the tail—dangerous since the unbalanced airplane became unstable. Between the seats and below the instrument panel, a pedestal served as a support for engine and propeller controls. Pilot Bert Archer called the arrangement a "tee-pee," and found it a nuisance when entering the airplane.

Pilots lamented the lack of outside visibility through the slightly distorted windshield and several reported poor defrosting. "So you wind up looking through a little round hole no bigger than four inches," said one. Another described the Found's outside view as "awful terrible." *Aviation Week's* David A. Brown pointed out that an absence of a window behind the wing restricted visibility in right turns.

Luxuries were hard to find. The royalite interior, manufactured by the Naugatuk Chemical Company, absorbed noise poorly. Even at reduced throttle settings, noise levels were disturbingly high but the Found brothers made it clear they believed customers wanted a workhorse, not a flying yacht.

"As a freighter, every available pound should be used for payload," explained Bud Found. "Spilled cargo or residue from carrying fresh fish can penetrate and accumulate in soundproofingwhich can create a hazard through corrosion and extra weight."

The FBA-2C may have shaken eardrums of passengers but no one complained about its unbelievable strength. The flying truck's steel tube airframe covered with aluminum sheeting was a quantum leap beyond its fabric-covered contemporaries. This simple structure could be easily maintained and repairs completed quickly without costly jigs in faraway maintenance shops. Crumpled stressed skins of Beechcraft 18s or Cessna products could rarely be repaired in the field.

"Cessna had already got their foot in the door but they didn't have better airplanes," said AME Ross McEwen in Parry Sound. "They nickeled and dimed people to death worse than the Found."

The Found brothers struggled to ease workloads of the men and women who maintained FBA-2Cs. Hinged engine cowlings dropped down for easier access and hands could reach the battery without gouging knuckles. The hinged cowlings also made cylinder changing simpler. With good intentions, factory workers ran control cables through small openings throughout the fuselage.

"The control system was the worst I ever seen to work on because everything was awkward to get at because of little holes in the floor and you had to work with strings down through there to pull the cables through," explained McEwen.

Rudders and elevators were interchangeable. Four bolts held each wing in place, and if removed, the push-pull controls did not need rerigging after reinstallation. The pitot tube was in the center; ideal for parking on treed shorelines. Many so-called bushplanes had their pitot tubes near the wing tip where they became entangled in trees.

The 1964 price for a bare bones Found FBA-2C listed at $17,029 FAF Toronto. Floats added another $6,700. Customers had a choice of paint but only to the "standard FBA scheme." If extras such as turn and bank indicator or an altimeter were required, they cost another $1,160. The pilot seat was the only one delivered with the airplane. If the right seat passenger needed to ride on something besides an orange crate or baggage, the buyer paid another $160. Ordering three airplanes or more resulted in a $1,000 discount.

Most FBA-2Cs went to Canadian commercial customers—no foreign sales occurred. In early 1961, sales staff attempted to sell their utility freighter to the Manitoba Government Air Service, a branch of the Department of Mines & Resources. Every warm weather season, this provincial organization found itself plagued with forest fires. The FBA-2C, said Found vice-president W. H. Bayley, could be a valuable asset.

"It would appear that FBA-2C utility freighter, float-equipped, could provide a wider range of detection and more detailed fire inspection at the start of a forest fire, particularly due to aircraft mobility and its capability in many cases to put two or three men near the site at the earliest stages of fire," Bayley wrote on July 11, 1963.

At the time, other Canadian manufacturers concentrated on government air services through a Federal Equipment Purchase Program. With this plan, the federal government paid fifty percent of capital equipment cost. N. K. Found stressed to the Manitoba officials that the Found sold for approximately $20,000, therefore the purchaser needed only $10,000.

Director of the Manitoba Government Air Service H. P. Smith responded favorably by showing interest in an evaluation of the FBA-2C for game patrols, wildlife census and other forestry-oriented tasks which "...could be done with a small aircraft to some advantage over a larger craft."

Keeping close tabs on the Found's progress, Smith requested a demonstration a year later. This encouraged S. R. Found to bring CF-RJV to Lac du Bonnet, 60 mi. (97 km) northeast of Winnipeg, during a sales tour to Vancouver. On wheels, the airplane put on a good show with a 1,000 lb. (450 kg) payload and a 1,400 ft. (420 m) per min. climb. Manitoba Government Air Service personnel were impressed that the FBA-2C could carry 10 ft. (3 m) drill rods and poles.

Found Brothers Aviation kept up a stream of correspondence and telephone calls with high level officials in Winnipeg. The Manitoba Government Air Service already operated several de Havilland Beavers and Otters as far north as Churchill. On March 22, 1965, N. K. Found received disheartening news: "I now regret to advise that the final decision taken has been in the negative," said H. P. Smith. "Our policy for this year, anyway, will be to rent light aircraft, if necessary until such time as we can more fully justify the need for this type of aircraft."

Despite this setback, the future still looked promising for Found Brothers Aviation. The factory received orders for sixteen FBA-2Cs. Two went to Georgian Bay Airways in Parry Sound, as promised, and others crossed the country to Prince Rupert, British Columbia, for North Coast Airlines and Pacific Western in Vancouver. British Columbia Air Lines, in Vancouver, acquired several, and timber company Mahood Logging Ltd. bought CF-RJV for servicing remote camps near Powell River. In central Canada, Calm Air of Stoney Rapids, Saskatchewan, used several before moving on to become the multiengine turbine airline it is today.

In the field, wrote historian Kenneth M. Molson, the FBA-2C neither distinguished nor disgraced itself but opinions varied. Not many pilots enjoyed it and only a few air services took a chance on this new Canadian product. Georgian Bay Airways staff often became unofficial demonstration pilots.

"We'd heard it was a 'Made in Canada' product and that they were trying to find a good bush type replacement for the Cessna 180," recalled pilot John Jacobsen. "The feeling at the time was that the Cessna 180 was just too light and not standing up to the wear and tear of bush flying."

The staff at Georgian Bay Airways noticed some of the FBA-2C's shortcomings almost as soon as the first one (CF-OZV) taxied to their L-shaped docks. A lack of cowl-flaps added to the streamlining of what someone called a "tin box with wings" and office manager Duane Clarke labelled it the "Flounder." Wayne Parton, a 12-year-old dock boy at the time, remembered his surprise at the absence of wing struts. With nothing to grip, parking the seaplane version could be tricky on windy days.

"They tried to overcome that by putting a couple of handles on the wings and it looked to us like it was underfloated which in actual fact, turned out to be true," Parton said. "Every time anybody put a decent size load in, the back of the floats went under. We'd had Stinsons which were dromedaries when it came to performance, so we hoped we'd see something that was going to take off and climb almost vertically."

The Found brothers believed that the bush flying business would welcome four-door access without wing struts. All openings swung a full 180 degrees to an unobstructed floor from fire wall to rear cabin bulkhead. Richard Petersen, an AME who maintained CF-RXJ for Northwestern Flying Services in Nestor Falls, Ontario, thought the idea was a good one.

"You didn't have to climb over all the seats and get on the float and watch out for the strut," he said. "In the Found, you just opened your own door and a couple of steps, you're on shore—we never missed that strut at all."

Another pilot pointed out that when he walked along the float toward the tail to unload, he no longer worried about gouging his back on a sharp door frame corner. Inside, he stacked loads ceiling high and didn't need to disturb passengers or rearrange freight. More than one Cessna 180 pilot had exited head first from a tightly packed airplane.

"That 180 was nice but you couldn't get nothing through them doors without fighting the strut," an exasperated individual added.

Other pilots resented the missing struts and claimed they needed something on which to tie external loads. On skis, the FBA-2C could not be pushed when stuck in snow or slush, unlike Cessnas and Stinsons.

The 36 ft. (11 m) wing proved exceptionally strong. Canada's National Research Council in Ottawa tested it intensely and found the structure capable of bearing heavy flight loads. Occasionally, it supported the pilot's weight.

"It was real handy for bush operations. If you were coming into a dock on the right side and you were packed to the ceiling, all you had to do was climb up on the wing, run out to the tip and jump off. No can do in a 180," said Petersen.

Wayne Parton remembered the wing flexing and rivets popping in the spar area. Ross McEwen pointed out that aviation inspectors issued an airworthiness directive or AD after small cracks had been discovered. Wing bolts had to be replaced every 1,000 flying hours. One bush air service remanufactured the fittings to a smaller size. Ironically, the process involved shaving metal instead of changing to stronger materials. The four bolts on each side worked well—the Found FBA-2C has never lost a wing.

One of the greatest testimonies to survivability took place in the mid-1960s at Parry Sound, when a bizarre pilot mix-up occurred. Veteran Nick Robertson had been assigned to check out a recently hired man on CF-OZW. While waiting for the new pilot, he met a stranger on the dock. Thinking he was the trainee, Robertson ordered him into the left seat while he sat in the right. With the single throw-over control wheel in the hands of the stranger, they took off.

"This guy had never been on floats before and he just thought, 'Jesus, how lucky can I get?'" said McEwen who watched the Found's unusual arrival. "I'm telling you, that thing never slowed up. When she hit the water, it didn't even float, just went right on down and the two of them got out. When we dragged that thing out, the fuselage was still intact—said a lot for the strength of the Found."

Neither pilot received more than a few bruises. The "correct" pilot had been waiting in the office during the accident and the so-called trainee was never seen again. The same company had another pilot fly through electrical lines near a boys' camp south of Parry Sound. He parked the wrinkled airplane at Georgian Bay Airways' dock. Without reporting his brush with disaster, he purchased a bus ticket and disappeared into the depths of southern Ontario.

Many pilots who flew Founds admitted the airplane had a "...good solid feel, not like a de Havilland product but a lot similar to the Twin Beech." With spring-loaded controls, the FBA-2C was hands-off stable and needed only light touches to change direction. At first, mechanics found the springs overly stiff so they simply altered the size without informing inspectors or factory representatives.

No one seemed to like the direct linkage flap handle above and between the front seats. After reaching up with the right hand and squeezing a trigger button on the pipelike handle, the pilot chose either zero, twenty-three or forty degrees. With wet hands, flaps were sometimes accidentally dumped from takeoff position of one "notch" to zero with a sudden loss of lift. One pilot remembered the tremendous strength needed to make any selection when speed went beyond 90 mph (154 km/h).

"You pulled down on that bar until you came out of the seat," said Lee Frankham. "As the airplane slowed, so'd the pressure and it'd come easier the rest of the way."

Bert Archer disliked the poor rate of climb with one notch. He learned that holding the flap handle midway between zero and takeoff produced a better climb. N. K. Found admitted that Found Brothers Aviation planned an extra stop to improve climb. Tourist lodge owner/pilot Tinker Helseth recommended "cleaning it up right away after takeoff (i.e., flaps to zero as quickly as possible). No use fighting it."

As an option, the company offered Federal metal bottom skis for $1,120 which included six urethane pads as shock absorbers. On skis, however, the Found turned out to be an exceptionally poor performer.

"The suspension system on the skis was, they tried to copy the de Havilland puck system except they didn't seem to have their geometry right and we ended up breaking and cracking these things all the time," said Parton.

Air Alma, 28 mi. (45 km) east of Roberval, Quebec, became one of the first winter Found operators. This air service carried snowmachines and 45 imp. gal. (205 l) fuel drums routinely in CF-SOQ. Georgian Bay Airways also sent Founds on skis to Timmins or Moosonee. In ice hummocks and snow drifts at native settlements on both sides of Hudson Bay and James Bay, pilots hated the airplane.

The main gear legs were positioned too low and the tail ski excessively high to reach a proper takeoff attitude. Some pilots tried jumping into the air by slamming flaps full down. This did nothing more than reduce speed, destroy lift and extend the takeoff run.

"You couldn't get the nose up enough unless you got the thing going a million miles an hour," said Parton. "In deep snow, this wasn't particularly catastrophic because it just never got off anyway. I found if you went up on one ski, you'd get a little more of an attitude and that put the tail lower which seemed to pry it out.

"You ended up rebounding off the mains and the tail and you were thrashing and crashing as those hard hummocks pounded the airplane to death. I remember rivets coming out."

Archer said the FBA-2C was "just hell on skis." It required wider turns and bogged down in slush quicker than Cessnas and no pilot dared stop before packing himself a smooth area. Vibration destroyed "straight" skis so quickly the Found could only be flown with wheel/skis since the rubber tires absorbed some of the shock. Petersen said winter work "...busted up the undercarriage bad."

During the 1950s, the Canadian government embarked on a program to build a radar station chain from coast to coast. Construction contractors established the Mid-Canada Line but by the mid-1960s, technological advances had rendered these stations obsolete. Two Bay Construction, a salvage barge company in Moosonee, won a contract to remove as many of the electronic components as possible and contacted local airlines.

At the time, Georgian Bay Airways had barely penetrated the James Bay-Hudson Bay area during cold weather seasons. The company's pilots had little choice except to fly into the north with no elaborate flight watch systems and few fuel caches. Worse, electronic navigation aids were almost nonexistent and airplanes left Moosonee with minimum survival and maintenance equipment. Like their predecessors of the 1930s and 1940s, the men who crewed the Beavers, Norsemen and Founds were completely on their own.

Parton, then a low-time pilot, left Moosonee in CF-OZU with two Cree Indian helpers for a radar site at Cape Henrietta-Maria on western James Bay. Other pilots warned him of the area's hummocks and rock-hard snow drifts. Apprehensive but eager, he circled a potential treeless landing strip barely discernible in the snow.

"I ended up slowing down as much as I dared and we touched and didn't break anything," he said. "A huge storm rolled in so we slept in some buildings—all unheated—at 40 below. All we had was a .22-caliber (rifle) and we could hear polar bears trying to break in all night."

The storm lasted four days. When it stopped, Parton and workers returned to the parked Found. They found the Lycoming engine packed solid with wind-hardened snow and the interior inundated. Removing the snow and warming the engine with a blow pot took a full day. By the time they finished, darkness returned and they had to endure another cold night. Next morning, the Found's performance on skis almost kept them there again.

"We knew right away we couldn't haul anything out of there in that Found or we'd break it," he said. "With two people and enough gas to get back to Moose, we had a problem. Later, Two Bay went back with a Cessna 180 and broke a few landing gear legs."

Parton returned to Moosonee and never again flew a Found on skis. He did, however, receive a severe fright while flying floats soon after breakup. The Found depended on two 28 imp. gal. (127 l) rubber cells, one in each wing, for fuel. A sales brochure described the mechanical fuel gauges as reading with "...minimum fluctuation due to fuel slosh." A simple float and red needle behind plexiglass covers, they were usually reliable. Parton learned that operators and pilots could not always believe the factory sales pitches.

At Fort George, Quebec, both tanks had been filled to the brim for the first leg of a charter to Timmins via Moose Factory with two Bell Canada employees and tool boxes. After takeoff, Parton turned south, expecting a pleasant flight. As they were "chugging along," it occurred to the trio that cutting directly across James Bay from Eastmain, a Cree settlement 48 mi. (77 km) south of Fort George, would save time. Parton "double checked" his instruments.

"Everything's in the green and we have bags of fuel so away we go," he said. "About ten minutes out from shore, I do another quick check and holy shit! Zero! My first reaction was to turn back so as I did a 180-degree turn, she snuffed and we won't make it to shore. This thing glides like a crowbar."

Descending 2,000 ft. (600 m) per min., Parton had no choice but to glide toward the gigantic wind-blown rollers of James Bay. Knowing small floatplanes were not designed for ocean-size swells, he feared the Found would overturn on landing. Unexpectedly, the engine caught.

"But again she snuffs, so there's nothing left to do," he said. "Down she comes and slams into the water. Ka-boom! Ka-boom! And we're down but the tide's going out and the tail's slapping the waves. We threw out their gear and tried to anchor but had nothing to hang on to, this stupid airplane—no struts."

Parton and his passengers straddled the float spreader bars to prevent the tail from filling with sea water. Two hours later, a de Havilland Beaver diverted from another coastal flight, circled the distressed Found and dropped two 10 imp. gal. (46 l) drums of gasoline. Both kegs landed out of Parton's reach. Luckily, the third drop was successful and a keg floated underneath the Found. With great difficulty, Parton replenished the gas tanks and managed a "hairy" take off.

Parton was certain his tanks were full when he left Fort George. After the terrifying open-sea splashdown, he had climbed onto the wing and found them empty with caps secure. Word spread quickly along the coasts that a Georgian Bay Airways pilot had run out of fuel.

Several months later, a mechanic noticed that some Founds tended to siphon gasoline through the fuel caps, especially when flying in a nose-up attitude. An airworthiness directive based on operator concerns confirmed his suspicions. A slight adjustment to the cap and the problem never reoccurred.

"Underfloated" became one of the most common complaints heard from pilots. At least one Found—CF-OZU—flew with 15 in. extensions to the standard Edo 2870s. Designed for increased stability on the water, the heels dragged just before liftoff and lengthened take off runs.

"If you pulled that thing out of the water, the floats acted like a sort of spoiler and porpoised you back in," said one pilot. "The extensions made it worse, not better."

Georgian Bay Airways' use of two Founds from Parry Sound provided an opportunity to compare CF-OZU's extended floats and CF-SDB's standard models. A mechanic remarked that anyone who flew CF-OZU needed a yachting cap since it was the "fastest boat on the lake." On the other hand, CF-SDB outflew Cessna 180s and 185s with ease. Sales brochures called the FBA-2C a "Baby Beaver."

"I didn't mind flying the Found, provided nobody threw a Beaver load at you because it wouldn't handle it," said Bert Archer. "You'd take a walk-on load, no sweat, unless they had baggage."

Another pilot worried about a Found's taxiing capabilities on windy days. Legal full loads, he said, were barely safe. He never considered overloading the Found unless he had a light breeze and a chance to taxi directly toward a dock.

Other pilots despised the FBA-2C's rapid sink rate with the engine idling. The nose down attitude was much steeper than most types and pilots had to be alert to break the glide for touchdown. Archer recalled that descents always meant "...power on. Cessna, you could throttle them right back, but you kept power up on that Found." One man frightened himself in CF-SDB after a glassy water approach.

"I had over 200 hours on the Found by then and considered the airplane to be my friend," he said. "I relaxed just a fraction too much and too soon and the floats dug in. Before I knew what the hell happened, she went ninety degrees to the water and almost on her back. Water came up over the windshield and through the doors before the damn thing flopped back right side up."

Founds, like most bushplanes, suffered mishaps and mechanical breakdowns. A severe thunderstorm destroyed one in northern Manitoba and another struck a huge rock near Inuvik, Northwest Territories, and survived. One of the strangest incidents took place near Campbell River, British Columbia, when Lee Frankham shut the switches off and the engine stopped.

"But the propeller didn't and it just sat there and went around and around," he laughed. "Everybody stepped out and I phoned the base to say it didn't have any compression and it sure as hell didn't—the crankshaft broke."

Found Brothers Aviation underwent management changes when sales were slow. Business might have improved if several proposed modifications, such as an extra flap setting, had been made. However, the new managers decided to shunt the FBA-2C program aside to concentrate on the Found Centennial 100. Powered by a 290-h.p. Lycoming, this creation had six seats and a cabin volume 10 cu. ft. (0.3 m^3) more than the FBA-2C. Test pilot George Ayerhart flew the prototype on April 7, 1967.

Designed for a 3,500 lb. (1,575 kg) gross weight and a 1,350 lb. (608 kg) disposable load with full fuel, the builders expected 150 mph (242 km/h) on wheels. However, the 290-h.p. engine did not deliver the expected performance and only four were constructed. During the summer of 1967, a salesman disgustedly snapped that the, "Damn thing won't get off the water with full fuel."

In November, 1968, financial backers withdrew. In March, 1969, a public auction terminated what remained of Found Brothers Aviation. Although not everyone missed what one pilot called the "Floundering Found," some did.

"I thought when I first saw the Found FBA-2C, we had a real bush airplane and I still think so. It's too bad they couldn't have stuck with it and got the bugs out," said Dick Petersen.

Found enthusiasts point out that financial reasons compelled the brothers to place their dream aside from 1952 until 1957. During this gap, Cessna moved in with a general utility airplane. When Found Brothers Aviation finally offered a practical flying half-ton, few northern air services willingly gambled on a Canadian product. One veteran said the FBA-2C was "shot down by Cessna" before it had a chance.

9 Cessnas

Adaptable, Agile and Seldom Stuck

Not again, God, not again, he thought, as wagon-wheel-size snowflakes slammed into the plexiglas windshield and slid swiftly up and over the roof. In moments, forward visibility dropped to almost zero. Only by opening the left window could the pilot see the sharp-tipped spruce tops rushing by below. White breakers came into view and he banked left to follow the shoreline to Kegashka, a small French-Canadian fishing community on the North Shore of the Gulf of St. Lawrence.

Using the black-roofed homes, snow-flecked fish nets and a row of green boats for reference, the pilot circled carefully and soon landed his Cessna 180 across the rock-hard drifts. An ice ridge slammed the tiny airplane back into the air, but down it came again. Everything held together and he slowed to taxi toward a frozen-in fishing boat.

The Cessna 180 had left a base in Lac Rapide, east of Sept Iles. Equipped with long-range tanks, the all-metal minifreighter had flogged on without a hint of trouble until 20 mi. (32 km) west of Kegashka when the wall of snow appeared. Warm inside and cruising comfortably at 135 mph (217 km/h), the trip had almost been boring for the young pilot.

Writers often overlook the Cessna utility line while researching radial engine wonders like Norsemen and Beavers. They ignore the fact that countless, inexperienced pilots with fresh commercial licenses began their careers in these diminutive airplanes. Battered by windstorms, smashed into cementlike ice ridges and overturned on glassy water lakes, Cessnas worked unnoticed and efficient.

Cessna Aircraft Company of Wichita, Kansas, probably took little notice of markets in faraway Canada when they delivered their first Model 180 in February, 1953. Nothing more than a redesigned, oversize Cessna 170, it became an instant hit throughout the United States. With a six-cylinder, 225-h.p. horizontally opposed Continental piston engine, the "Wichita Wonder," as operators called it, had no competition.

In April, 1953, Cessna claimed their "greatest low cost floatplane" needed an 1,830 ft. (548 m) water run to lift a gross weight of 2,700 lb. (1,215 kg). "Para-lift" flaps, a 500-lb. (225 kg) cargo capacity, yard-wide doors and a $12,950 price tag offered what *Canadian Aviation* magazine called a "...fresh, promising solution to the problems of Canadian bush flying."

Cessna increased the Model 180's horsepower to 230 and public relations specialists touted it as "America's Fastest Airplane in the Medium Price Field." With four aboard in complete comfort, they said, the wheeled version had a 750-mi. (1,208 km) range and a 150-mph (242 km/h) cruise with a 1,200 ft. (360 m) per min. climb.

When production ended in 1981, 6,193 were sold. Originally offered to business travelers, Cessnas carried far more than attache cases. The distinctive aromas of fish slime, sweaty bottoms and gasoline-soaked interiors became standard as users accepted them in every corner of backwoods Canada.

In 1961, Cessna applied new ribs, redesigned stringer patterns and stronger wing spars to the Model 180 airframe to produce the "Cessna 185 Skywagon." They included a 260-h.p. Continental engine and expected the upgraded Cessna to replace hundreds of overworked Model 180s. With floats, the 185 legally flew 1,125 mi. (1,811 km). One magazine quoted an empty weight on wheels of 1,520 lb. (684 kg) and maximum takeoff weight of 3,200 lb. (1,440 kg)—600 lb. (270 kg) more than a Cessna 180. With long-range gasoline tanks filled, payload reached 996 lb. (448 kg).

Tail wheel Cessnas turned out to be tricky to handle with the 3/4-in. chrome vanadium steel landing gear. Men of experience, said writer James Sharp, believed only two kinds of Cessnas existed: those that have ground looped and those that will. With long fuselages and billboard-size tails, crosswinds on paved runways could never be taken casually. Veterans with thousands of hours on type sometimes lost control.

"If you put the Cessna 185 or Cessna 180 down too early with too much speed or sink, the gear acts just like a spring to bounce you back into the air," said one pilot. "Once that bounce came, you don't got no choice but to hold that control wheel all the way back or else slam the power on and go around again."

On floats or skis, the Cessna line was easy to land. Light compared to de Havilland Beavers or Noorduyn Norsemen, they seldom became stuck in slush or snow. On rare occasions when they did, passengers stepped outside to rock the wings in order to break the skis free.

Cessna decided to appease owners weary of ground loop repairs by introducing the steerable nose wheel, six-seat Model 206 in 1964. Uncomplicated to handle, it came with a level floor for easier loading. However, the Wichita designers ignored Canadian carriers who preferred tail wheel airplanes. A wheel/ski tricycle gear airplane did not work well because they needed more space to turn and bogged down quickly in the snow. Worse, the Cessna 206 seaplane version lacked a pilot's door—inconvenient when parking at docks.

Nevertheless, at least the double cargo door on the right rear side was a huge one. It measured 40 in. (102 cm) wide and 37.5 in. (953 cm) high and easily handled cumbersome objects such as coffins. In fact, a flying funeral director made regular Cessna 206 runs to Native settlements north of Sioux Lookout, Ontario, during the late 1970s and never had a customer complain.

Lamb Airways of The Pas, Manitoba, happened to be one of the bush country air services which understood the Cessna 180's workhorse potential. During Canada's 1967 centennial year, they used seven in a hodgepodge of paint schemes and colors. Flown by pilots of all experience levels, Lamb Airways 180s worked as far south as Winnipeg and northward into the Arctic islands with cargos ranging from politicians to magnetometers and caribou meat.

Some British Columbia outfitters found Cessna 185s useful for hauling sheep and goat meat from land-locked hunting camps. Aerial survey companies like Spartan Aero Services in Ottawa installed a camera hatch and flew photo missions above 20,000 ft. (6,000 m).

An overland winter freighting company bought a Cessna 185 in 1962 and patrolled trucking routes north of Winnipeg. When construction machines malfunctioned, owner Svein Sigfusson became obsessed with the quick delivery of tractor parts. He flew in dynamite, pumps and shovels to remove beaver dams or create slush to reinforce river crossings. His Cessnas paid for themselves by reducing downtime and boosting morale for frost-bitten mule skinners slugging temperamental machines through boreal forestland.

Cessna's all-metal monocoque fuselage and wings appealed to air service owners disgusted with constant fabric repair. David Nilson was present when the first wave of Cessna 180s invaded British Columbia.

"The Fairchild 24s and that kind of thing were great, but Cessna became the standard because they were the best around," he said. "That doesn't mean they were really good; it's just that there was nothing else and the Cessna surprised us because it wasn't really designed for floats."

Most "bush-tuned" Cessnas spent their working careers on floats. Although float brands such as Edo, Wipline, Aqua and several others crowded the market, the Edo 2870 produced by the Edo Company of Farmingdale, New York, became the most popular. Later, Canadian Aircraft Products or CAP units manufactured in Richmond, British Columbia, proved satisfactory, if not differing in required take off techniques.

"The 185 I flew out of Watson Lake had CAP 3000s which people thought were a lot harder to fly," said Gerry Norberg. "Instead of hauling back and yanking back and forth to get off the water, you'd just leave the thing neutral with two notches of flap and let it climb out of the lake on its own."

Another pilot found the CAPs "scary" until he logged several hundred hours on them. He claimed they had a "fairly short spot" or fine balance point between less drag and more lift. On landings, the CAPs tended to snub the front ends and demanded more concentration than Edos or Wiplines. In late fall, pilots dreaded flying CAP-equipped Cessnas because of the rounded float tops. Many unwary souls overlooked a frozen skim of ice on the metal float and plunged into an October lake.

By the time most pilots reached their first bushplanes, the glitter of Wichita-fresh metal had long faded. Including 180s, 185s and 206s, 12,532 were built. Writers began calling the Cessna line a "production classic" or an "aviation anachronism" when comparing them to sleek, shark-nosed turbines.

Herb Neufeld learned to fly in an elementary 100-h.p. two-seat trainer called a Cessna 150. When he climbed into his first Cessna 180, he considered it a "powerhouse." Pilots like Neufeld rarely forgot their first glimpse of a Cessna 180. Jane Etzkorn saw a photograph of one she would later fly at Jellicoe, 24 mi. (39 km) east of Geraldton, Ontario. It was being dragged from the bottom of a muskeg lake. Ron Gangloff came upon his hanging vertically in a tree after an inexperienced owner misjudged a landing approach.

"They have their place in the north all right," Gangloff said. "You talk to air services like Green Airways, Sabourin, Big Trout Lake and Bearskin (all in northwestern Ontario) and ask them what they started with."

As overworked "Chevy pickups of the air," Cessnas were usually the last on a flight line slated for state-of-the-art electronics or modernized light weight instrumentation. Brad Greaves remembered his early flying on Cessna 180 CF-IWD north of Sioux Lookout. Black trim on bare metal, it sported a faded bandage wrapped around the tail section. A closer look revealed an aluminum strip fastened with rivets spaced every inch along the edges. No entry for the home grown modification could be found in the log book. Nevertheless, CF-IWD was a "super performer" in spite of a bedraggled appearance.

Cessna's marketing specialists originally used the word "economical" but as the airplane aged, many operators disagreed. A Cessna 180 on floats burned slightly more than 11 imp. gal. (50 l) per hr. and a Cessna 206 with a 300-h.p. engine gulped 15 imp. gal. (68 l) per hr. Seaplane kits with structural beefing and float attachment fittings were optional and increased factory prices. A bare bones Cessna 185 on wheels sold for $18,950 in 1961.

"I'd just as soon do without them but there are times when you don't want a Beaver," said Vancouver Island Air's Larry Langford. "It's cheaper for us to fly the 180 and at least it's got a bulletproof carburetted engine."

By "bulletproof," Langford meant that Cessna 180 engines pose few mechanical problems. He preferred them instead of the more powerful Cessna 185s for his routine two-passenger loads. Much of Vancouver Island Air's work deals with quick trips to Seattle, Washington, or pleasure flights with pairs of whale-watching, hand-holding honeymooners. The Cessna 185 could easily do the same task but expenses accelerate.

"On short hauls, you go out and buy new cylinders for a 185 about every 700 hours and when you're paying $1,000 a jug and it seems like every second inspection one gets replaced, then you look at the economics," Langford said.

Cessna 185s lack carburetors. Instead, gasoline is injected directly into the cylinders through a series of nozzles. At first, the concept sounded practical but the complex pumps, fuel return lines and header tanks often delayed engine starts. On seaplanes, misfires sometimes led to unplanned scenic tours down sharp-rock rapids.

Norman Biegler, a Vancouver Island Air pilot, stressed that fuel-injected engines were susceptible to poor warm-weather starting. They sometimes developed vapor lock in the lines after shutdown. To start, these lines needed purging by what one mechanic called a "fair amount of cranking," often to the point of a dead battery. Rochelle Bodnar worked briefly for a West Coast organization which owned Cessna 185 C-GWNS. Company staff derisively called it *Will-Not-Start* to match the last three letters of the registration. Pilots dealing with holidaying Chicago cops who have just spent days on hot highways only to be told their fishing flight is delayed, rarely appreciate vapor lock.

"Fuel-injected engines seem to be more susceptible to thermal heating and cooling so they start cracking from the spark plug to the exhaust valve," said Langford. "Carburetors can pass rust or dirt right through, but the same stuff plugs a fuel injector nozzle."

Air services using skiplanes and coastal operators flying off perpetual ocean swells in high winds, often find wings cracking where they enter the fuselage. These "stretches" can be strengthened with triangular metal patches but the wings frequently need complete reskinning. One mechanic remarked that 5,000 hours flying time meant that the time to sell a Cessna had arrived.

David Nilson remembered spending hours trying to convince the Wichita wizards that Cessnas corrode in salt-laden milieus. During the mid-1950s, he often returned corroded cables and fuselage fittings to the factory. In early models, several components were formed from magnesium.

"The Cessna 180's rudder bar went through some magnesium pillow blocks," he said. "All it took was the saltwater dripping off your boots to start these things boiling away until there was almost nothing left, so Cessna shortly after came out with some made of nylon."

John Jacobsen flew Cessna 180s along the windy tidal coasts and fast-running rivers of James and Hudson Bay. He enjoyed Cessna handling qualities but considered the airframe too lightly built to endure prolonged operations. Nilson, on the other hand, praised the 180's inherent strength and said no Cessna type he knew had a major in-flight structural failure. On floats, he admitted, pilots sometimes "stoved in" or crumpled the rear fuselage where the float fittings attached.

"They've really been good and have done a tremendous lot of work and some of them put in an awful lot of time," he said. "The 180's pretty handy although they sure do blow over easy in a wind."

Ignace Airways, 125 mi. (201 km) northwest of Thunder Bay, runs a fleet of de Havilland Beavers to supply northwestern

Ontario outpost camps but keeps a Cessna 206 on standby. With plenty of room inside—what some pilots describe as "overcabined"—the 206 serves as a backup or quick-trip machine for excess tourist baggage.

Manager Brad Greaves understands the pros and cons of Cessnas and laments the hours chief mechanic Paul Hawkins spends repairing noncritical items. Although salesmen called their aerial wonder "all-metal," the cockpit contains plenty of plastic and vinyl in seats, knobs and control switches. After a few trips in rough air and choppy water, these items wear or shake loose.

In cold weather, headliners crack and seats slide past their stops—nothing of which impresses customers. One pilot in Parry Sound, Ontario, delayed his flight to comfort a shaken passenger after the seat slid backwards at the instant a door popped open on takeoff.

The tourist trade demands quick turnarounds. Unlike Beavers and Otters which use belly tanks, Cessna fuel caps are in the tops of the wings. To reach them, grit-covered gas hoses must be dragged over engine cowlings or sensitive plexiglas windshields. Brad Greaves pointed out that fuelling his Cessna 206 usually takes two men to avoid damage.

Paul Hawkins detested the Cessna 206's oil filler cap location at the top of the engine. Filling the tank without a funnel is nearly impossible since the cap cannot be seen. Many high-time Cessnas have unsightly dents where someone placed their knees while servicing. This kind of damage lowers retail value and raises maintenance costs.

Beyond the watchful eyes of vigilant aviation inspectors, many Cessnas carried far more than their legal limits. One man admitted wrestling a seaplane 180 into the air with 10 ft. (3 m) radio towers tied to the side. A northern Ontario pilot remembered his adventures on Cessna 180 CF-HRY.

"Legally, I don't think you could haul 600 lb. (270 kg) in a 180 with full fuel but we'd always take three guys and gear with full tanks and go north, no trouble at all," he said. "Three feet of floats under the water, she'd still go."

Until recently, the "Mennonite Air Force" in Red Lake, Ontario, used a mixed fleet of fabric and metal airplanes to service wilderness mission stations. Flown almost entirely by American pilots, their Cessnas and their ability to absorb Canadian cold, has resulted in remarkable accident-free safety records.   *Photo: Robert S. Grant*

The same pilot spent many hours in a Cessna 185 for another company and classed the particular airplane as "a piece of junk." In spite of more horsepower and only a slight change in empty weight, the 185 could not outperform CF-HRY. In fact, he frightened himself badly.

"I just got off the water and that was it, the trees were there already," he said. "Like I pulled the nose up, went over the top and pointed the thing straight down on the other side. The same trip could have been done with a 180, easy."

Vancouver Island Air pilot Peter Killin liked the idea that a properly maintained Cessna 185 handled three 180 lb. (81 kg) loggers, their toolboxes and tree harvesting gear. He described typical coastal days which included up to twelve legs of 25–100 mi. (40–161 km) each. Overanxious pilots, he added, frequently flooded the carburetor. Some never learned to recognize the almost imperceptible "whoosh" of a fire until they destroyed several engine hoses and grounded the airplane.

"When you had a hot day, that thing (Cessna 185) was a real bugger. You'd push off from a dock and crank and crank and crank and nothing happens," said an operations manager at Goose Bay, Labrador. "In the air, those Cessnas had hot-running engines so it took time to familiarize new guys with cowl flaps and how to cool an engine."

Veteran Larry Morden of Landseaair in Red Lake pointed out that Cessnas could be intimidating to newly trained commercial pilots. Awed by 230-h.p. bushplanes instead of 100-h.p. trainers, they neglected to remember that they had to fly the airplane and not the engine. In other words, Morden explained, it mattered little what was under the hood; all airplanes had limitations, especially tired bush workhorses.

Heavy-load takeoffs required the light hand of finesse, Morden said. In 185s, most pilots used one notch or "click" on the thumb release ratchet flap handle between the front seats. After blasting themselves onto the step, some added another notch (i.e., twenty degrees) and accelerated. Next, they slammed down another ten degrees to jump into the air. Not everyone agreed.

"Me, I use full power, drop ten degrees of flap, get on the step and just lay back and wait," said Herb Neufeld. "Add another notch, then off with one float, hold the handle and ease off slow on that last ten degrees after she's flying."

Coastal pilots learned quickly when they encountered ocean swells. Rolling one float out of the water may help them shorten the takeoff but sometimes, said a Harbour Air veteran in Vancouver, they play a waiting game. In light winds, aligning parallel with the swell pattern is safer than crashing into them head on. Shaking the airframe into a motionless blur should be avoided whenever possible.

"We go through a lot of windshield V-braces and take a real beating with our 185s," said Trevor Bird of Harbour Air. "If you stay right in the swells, you'll be okay and sometimes you have to ride up and down the first couple to get some speed."

One pilot north of Geraldton admitted complacency nearly got him into serious trouble. After pushing in full throttle, he placed his Cessna 185 onto the step when a severe wind gust struck the airplane and spun it almost completely around. No damage occurred but this pilot unwillingly earned the distinction of becoming one of the first pilots to "water loop" a floatplane.

An organization servicing central Manitoba and Saskatchewan Indian settlements welcomed the opportunity to use a wheel/ski Cessna 185. In spite of cheaper insurance rates and no float repairs, the company learned that land airplanes needed maintenance nearly as much as their waterbound brethren. Often, the tail section shook badly and rudder pedals vibrated so much, pilots could barely touch them.

"You just kind of blocked your feet up so they wouldn't kick back. They'd take the skis off in the spring, wire the works together on a bolt and throw everything back on in late fall without setting the camber and castor of the tail wheel," said one disgusted pilot who left the air service after one week. "The first few times out, that airplane was so wild, you didn't want to get it near the ground again."

Most pilots preferred landing on the two main wheels first and letting the tail settle as airspeed dropped. On slippery or gravel surface airstrips, touching down without the nose centered mattered little since a slight slide did no harm. Some pilots dreaded paved runways especially after winters of easy ski flying. On landing, the airplane "grabbed" sharply and bounded away in the direction of the nose. Such an incident embarrassed Jane Etzkorn at Brochet, 235 mi. (378 km) north of The Pas, Manitoba.

"When I touched, my 185 just darted off the strip and the three guys riding with me screamed," she laughed. "I managed to get the thing back in one piece and thought, 'Oh, my God, Indian people never say anything and I made them scream.' It had to be the absolute worst landing in the world."

Seaplane landings on towering ocean waves are frightening to "flatlanders," a term referring to pilots who learned to fly east of the Rocky Mountains. To reduce the impact of solid swells, pilots prefer transitioning from graceful flight to taxi speed with a nose high, flap on, slow-as-possible approach. Sometimes, nothing helps.

"You're just going to pound. Once you hit that water, forget the control column, you can't hardly hold it," said one pilot.

Flight instructor Dave Hamel of Fort Langley Aviation, 19 mi. (31 km) southeast of Vancouver, spent hundreds of hours familiarizing students with Cessna 180 ocean flying. He pointed out that swells occur regardless of wind condition and, from above, look deceptively smooth. Avoiding airframe damage is not impossible, Hamel said, but pilots must understand different shoreline types and water surfaces. Anyone—old pro or novice—can be fooled.

"A guy comes over a bay and says, 'Ah, great, that looks like a nice beach.' So they come on down to what they think is calm water and Wham! They wonder why the skin wrinkled," said Hamel.

Not all metal-bending incidents take place on coastal waters. A 185 struck a log near Harrison Lake, 10 mi. (16 km) northeast of Chilliwack, British Columbia. The floats did not separate nor did the fuselage wrinkle but, said the pilot, "Those Edos looked as if they'd been machine gunned." He and a mechanic whittled wooden plugs, drove them into each hole and sealed the gaps with industrial tape. A puttylike compound helped waterproof the holes for the flight home.

Cessna 180s, said Bert Archer, can be notorious "diggers." Assigned to familiarize an employee with his company's routes, he decided to do the trip without a control wheel on his side. The new man would do the flying.

"So this guy's getting ready to land and I says, 'Better slow down, you're like a house on fire.' He says, 'What?' So I told him again, 'Slow the damn thing down.' Just then he hits at about 120 mph (192 km/h). I reached over and pulled the wheel back and hit the throttle. She skipped two or three times on the front of the floats and Jesus, we got the hell out of there."

Not all frights occur on takeoff or landing. Peter Evans of Harbour Air heard two loud explosions in his Cessna 185 while cruising at 1,500 ft. (450 m) to Sechelt from Richmond. The engine kept running, no oil streaks coated the windshield and both fuel tanks held plenty of gasoline. Deciding to play it safe, Evans gently turned and declared an emergency with Vancouver Airport's tower.

"I looked out at the wing-leading edge and couldn't see anything and then glanced back. Holy Christ! It looked like a shark took the back of the flap out, just chewed it right off," he said. "So I wondered what the hell did that and then looked around some more. Now, I really got scared."

Evans discovered that his left horizontal stabilizer had crumpled. If propeller slipstream ripped it away, he knew the airplane would be uncontrollable. In spite of the blast of air, it held and he landed. While taxiing in, Evans looked down at his floats and discovered the reason for his unexpected landing.

Previous owners had installed storage hatches in the floats and secured them with rivets. Rarely used, they had been wire-locked shut but customer traffic on the floats elongated the rivet holes until the cover broke loose. The first noise occurred when the hatch struck the wing and the second, when it ripped the stabilizer. Repairs cost $6,000.

Deceived by the thin metal covering of Cessnas, tourists often ask if they are built from "Reynolds Wrap." John McElwain can testify to what kind of punishment a Cessna 206 can absorb.

At God's Lake Narrows, 135 mi. (217 km) southeast of Thompson, Manitoba, McElwain had been despatched to pick up groups of Native people on several isolated lakes. On the final leg home, he flew into some light drizzle and rain showers. Almost within sight of the company dock, he estimated daylight would last long enough to complete the trip. As he lowered flaps and eased his engine power gently back, the wet windshield and dim light hindered visibility.

Descending, McElwain touched a rudder pedal gently to avoid a powerboat wake. Almost home, another 80 ft. (24 m) to go and it's Miller time, he mused. In that instant, John McElwain thought he was going to die.

"There was a bright blue flash off to the right as I was slammed into my shoulder straps. One of the rear seats sailed past my head and wiped the magnetic compass out and bounced back," he said. "I felt the airplane falling and I shoved the throttle and prop to the wall as my left hand pushed the control column to the stops and then pulled it back to my belt buckle.

"I couldn't see a thing and it was, oh, so dark, and I held the nose up, waited and smash, we were on the water. Afloat. Alive."

McElwain's propeller had severed one of four thick electrical lines and dragged the remaining three to the water. Accident investigators concluded he could not have seen the unmarked wires. McElwain said, "No matter how bad things look, keep flying the airplane. It's not over 'til it's over."

The Cessna 185 normally carried 32.5 U.S. gal. (148 l) in each of two wing tanks but could be ordered with an optional 42 U.S. gal. (191 l) per side. Cessna's marketing agents claimed the seaplane version could fly 1,125 mi. (1,811 km) between fuel stops. Pilots on forest fire detection missions in the Yukon appreciated the extra range.

"I'd go out at midmorning. The route covered the whole end of northern British Columbia from Fort Nelson to the Alaska border," said Jerry Norberg, who flew three seasons from Watson Lake. "We didn't fly high, usually below the mountain tops and along the valleys. Once in a while, we'd take fire fighters into the same fire I'd reported."

Norberg also carried geologists from Dease Lake, British Columbia, to Burwash Landing in the Kluane Lake area west of Whitehorse. His passengers wanted landings at nearly every potential mineral rich shoreline they could find. When necessary, he stretched his time to six hours. High-altitude lake landings posed little problem. One Cessna 180 had alighted at 14,300 ft. (4,290 m) on Alaska's Mountain McKinley in 1977.

"You would always get in but your ground speeds were high and you really hit the water faster even though the airspeed indicator showed about 80 mph (129 km/h)," Norberg said.

British Columbia MacMillan Fisheries, B.C. Packers and other conglomerates often contracted Cessnas on a six-to-eight-week basis during the herring season. The work required an airplane with endurance and comfort. Cessna seaplanes filled the niche with well-padded seating and long-range fuel tanks.

"My job was to find concentrations of milky white spawn and pass their locations to the boats who moved in with their nets. They were caught, cleaned and the caviarlike roe went to overseas markets," said Mike McCluskey.

All pilots dreaded engine failures over open ocean. Once down on warehouse-size rollers, small airplanes could capsize in minutes. McCluskey had at least one close call while carrying a major fishing corporation's vice-president.

"The engine started running rough so I headed for shore and reduced power thinking it was a cylinder. I just nicely got over a sheltered place when the thing stopped dead. No power. No nothing. We got down in one piece but if that had happened fifteen seconds earlier, we'd have been in deep trouble."

Luckily for McCluskey and his shaken passenger, a seiner (fishing vessel) towed them to Vancouver. During the long pull, a cook discovered a bottle of expensive liqueur on the dry boat. By the time they arrived beneath the city skyline, McCluskey and his client had forgotten the close call. Mechanics later discovered a broken piston rod had been forced through the engine crankcase.

Mechanical failures sometimes occur in Cessnas which can quickly develop a glide angle described by Dave Hamel as "...just short of a greased crowbar." During a winter flight, Al McNeil watched his engine stop north of Red Lake in an area of northwestern Ontario well known for its multitudinous water bodies. Unfortunately for McNeil, he happened to be over one of the few areas with nothing except a small frozen pond.

McNeil's solitary Ojibway passenger began screaming as the Cessna 185 settled rapidly toward a site encircled by high jackpine trees. On wheel/skis with wheels down, McNeil did not have enough time or altitude to retract them.

"Like this is a dead engine and it's nothing but a pothole we got. The only thing that saved us was I hit a big snowdrift at about 70 mph (113 km/h) with the wheels. It was like somebody grabbed us. I'd say we stopped about 10 ft. (3 m) from the trees. Big trees."

McNeil experienced a number of serious incidents in his 21,000-hour career. One example underscored a potentially deadly Cessna shortcoming. On a track from Winnipeg to an Native village called Sandy Lake, he carried a load of groceries packed to the ceiling. His outside air temperature gauge showed minus 38°C as ice crystal fog forced McNeil down on a stretch of ice. For a moment, he thought the Cessna 185 had damaged its undercarriage. Instead, the yellow and silver skiplane sank through a snow-covered river.

"I can't go through the front window because they got that cross brace in there and the ice wouldn't let me open the door," he said. "Oh, yeah, here I go, drown like a rat so I got up against the Carnation (canned milk) and put the boots to the door. It popped open and out I go."

McNeil, numbed by freezing water and hindered by winter flying clothing, could barely move. Exhausted, he splashed his way to the 185's tail.

"So, I figured, well, I'll just put my hand there and it'll freeze and I'll take a breather but it didn't stick."

Unable to rest, McNeil dragged himself hand over hand to the wing which had settled to water level. Calling upon his last reserve of strength, he rolled onto the aileron portion, hoisted himself up and stepped off the wing tip. Scarcely able to maintain his balance, he staggered toward the shoreline.

McNeil's numbed hands matched the color of toilet tissue and he had lost all body sensation. Miraculously, two Cree trappers appeared out of nowhere, placed him on a snowmachine and roared away. By the time they reached a tiny log cabin, McNeil had frozen to the seat. He waited while his saviors chopped him loose with a small hatchet.

McNeil continues flying for Sabourin Lake Airways in Cochenour near Red Lake, Ontario. He avoids Cessnas when possible and prefers any airplane without crossbars behind the windshield.

Another pilot strayed too close to a seaplane Beechcraft 18 and accidentally rolled upside down in the wing tip vortices or wake. His recovery testifies to the Cessna 185's ability to hold together regardless of attitude.

"Once we started going over, I couldn't stop it so I thought, I'm dead anyway so might as well continue the roll," the pilot said. "I pushed the nose down and cursed the guy in the Beech as everything dumped on the ceiling but we came out upright."

Since the first Cessna entered the northern scene, this high wing utility line has improved. More powerful engines, modified wings and various landing gears have been tried and nearly all worked well.

"By God, you gotta admit," said a slightly bushed diesel mechanic waiting for a ride to Thompson, Manitoba, from Cullaton Lake, Northwest Territories, 217 mi. (349 km) northwest of Churchill, "them little Cessnas can do just about anything you want them to and you'll get away with it, don't matter what."

He spoke the truth.

Cessnas have served as backbones for many northern entrepreneurs and as starter airplanes for hundreds of junior pilots. Like the Douglas DC-3, Noorduyn Norseman and other greats, the Cessnas are, as aviation writer William Cox wrote in *Plane & Pilot* June 1983, "Utterly timeless."

Epilogue

Many of the airplanes described in *Great Northern Bushplanes* still fly in Canada's remote regions. Their niche, spawned by the nature of the countryside over which they work, survives because of abilities to absorb the constant abuse of rough water, rock-hard snow and Arctic mud.

As government-built airstrips and encroaching roads dominate the transportation scene, their place will gradually disappear. Nevertheless, when futuristic space travelers and computer-guided machines call upon fresh generations of pilots and mechanics, the need for Canadian ingenuity will still exist.

All of them, whether astronauting hundreds of miles above the earth or assembling laser-driven components for ground-bound terminals, owe a debt to every collection of fabric, tubing and wood that galloped down a northern lake. In spite of competitive environments in what experts now call "aerospace industry," the future bodes well as Canadian products and people meet the new challenges.

Specifications

CURTISS HS-2L

First Flight ....Oct 21, 1917 (i.e., HS-1)
Cost New Average Unit $30,000
Wing Span ....74 ft. (22 m)
Length ....39 ft. (12 m)
Gross Weight ....6,432 lb. (2,894 kg)
Empty Weight ....4,300 lb. (1,935 kg)
Fuel Capacity ....152 imp gal. (692 l)
Engine ....360–400-h.p. Liberty
Cruise Speed ....60–65 mph (97–105 km/h)
Seating 5
Payload with Full Fuel ....4,300 lb. (1,935 kg)   empty weight
                                1,094.4 lb. (492 kg)   fuel
                                  180 lb. (81 kg)   pilot
                                  50 lb. (23 kg)   misc.
                                  5,624.4 lb. (2,531 kg)   total
Payload ....6,432.0 lb. (2,894 kg)
                                  -5,624.4 lb. (2,531 kg)
                                  =807.6 lb. (363 kg)

In 1924, Laurentian Air Service Ltd. agreed to sell twelve HS-2Ls to the Ontario Provincial Air Service (OPAS) for $5,500 each.

Some OPAS HS-2Ls had brass camera tubes fitted through the hull. Great care had to be taken to use cotton and lead to retain waterproofing qualities. In service, HS-2Ls were subject to wood rot in main bulkheads and step areas. Sponsons leaked frequently and wood flooring in the cockpit often broke.

Curtiss HS-2L pilots were sometimes watched carefully by envious nonfliers. In 1929, OPAS headquarters in Sault Ste. Marie received surreptitious reports concerning a pilot who took unauthorized female passengers aloft.

JUNKERS W 33/34

First Flight	1926
Cost New	$19,500
	Plus engine/propeller (July 1928)
Wing Span	58 ft. 6 in. (17.5 m)
Length	34 ft.5 in. (10.3 m)
Gross Weight	6,600 lb. (2970 kg)
Empty Weight	4,048 lb. (1,822 kg)
Fuel Capacity	90 imp. gal. (410 l)
Engine	425-h.p. Wasp
Cruise Speed	90 mph (154 km/h)
Seating	10

Payload with Full Fuel	4,048 lb. (1,822 kg)	empty weight
	648 lb. (292 kg)	fuel
	180 lb. (81 kg)	pilot
	50 lb. (23 kg)	misc.
	4,926 lb. (2,217 kg)	total
Payload	6,600 lb. (2970 kg)	
	-4,926 lb. (2,217 kg)	
	=1,674 lb. (753 kg)	

The Junkers Corporation of America on Madison Avenue in New York was the North American distributor. Canadian representative was Canadian Junkers Ltd. in Winnipeg.

At full gross weight, CF-ARI and CF-AMZ took off in thirty-five seconds and climbed 1,000 ft. (300 m) in 1:30 seconds during a flight test at Lac du Bonnet, Manitoba, on May 16, 1933.

Canadian Airways became disgusted with constant landing gear problems on the Junkers. Fourteen occurred on two aircraft; "...a source of annoyance to both operations and maintenance departments," said Tommy W. Siers.

Junkers CF-ASN burned 21 imp. gal. (96 l) per hr. at 1,650 rpm with a two-blade propeller while CF-AMZ used 28 imp. gal. (127 l) per hour with a three-blade propeller.

JUNKERS Ju 52

First Flight ....September, 1930
Cost New $75,000
Wing Span ....95 ft. (29 m)
Length ....62 ft. (19 m)
Gross Weight ....15,500 lb. (6,975 kg)
Empty Weight ....9,250 lb. (4,163 kg) (seaplane)
Fuel Capacity ....275 imp gal. (1,251 l)
Engine ....685-h.p. BMW VII
Cruise Speed ....95 mph (253 km/h)
Seating ....2 crew only
Payload with Full Fuel ....9,250 lb. (4,163 kg)   empty weight
                                        1,980 lb. (891 kg)   fuel
                                        360 lb. (162 kg)   pilot/mechanic
                                        100 lb. (45 kg)   misc.
                                     11,690 lb. (5,261 kg)   total
Payload ....15,500 lb. (6,975 kg)
                                    -11,690 lb. (5,261 kg)
                                    =3,870 lb. (1,742 kg)

Typical cargo for the Ju 52, said Winnipeg's Western Canada Aviation Museum, was four oxen, eight horses, a diesel engine shovel, 20 ft. (6 m) boat or tractor parts.

The trailing edge of the Ju 52's wing had three flaps, the inner two of which could be lowered to allow slow landing speeds.

One pilot seat of the Ju 52 could be tilted back into a couchlike arrangement.

Flight magazine on February 27, 1931, pointed out that the Ju 52 on wheels was expected to carry a 4,680 lb. (2,106 kg) payload for 622 mi. (1,001 km). Landing speed was 48 mph (77 km/h).

FAIRCHILD 71C

First Flight 1932
Cost $21,500 (1942)
Wing Span .... 50 ft. 1.5 in. (15 m)
Length .... 35.7 ft. (10.7 m)
Gross Weight .... 6,000 lb. (2,700 kg)
Empty Weight .... 3,787 lb. (1,704 kg)
Fuel Capacity .... 133 imp. gal. (605 l)
Engine .... 420-h.p. Pratt & Whitney Wasp Jr.
Cruise Speed .... 95 mph (253 km/h)
Seating 7
Payload with Full Fuel .... 3,787 lb. (1,704 kg)   empty weight
        957.6 lb. (431 kg)   fuel
        180 lb. (81 kg)   pilot
        50 lb. (23 kg)   misc.
        4,974.6 lb. (2,239 kg)   total
Payload .... 6,000 lb. (2,700 kg)
        -4,974.6 lb. (2,239 kg)
        =1,025.4 lb. (461 kg)

In August, 1948, the Ontario Provincial Air Service sold CF-OAP for $6,666.66.

Factory representatives claimed that Fairchild 71Cs received nine coats of dope before completion but to save weight, they would reduce the number to five. They also offered celluloid windows instead of heavier, more resistant glass when Canadian Airways complained of poor performance in August, 1933.

Under the eyes of a Civil Aviation Department inspector, tests were carried out with a seaplane Fairchild 71C carrying full loads in calm weather in 1933. Average takeoff runs were twenty-eight to thirty-two seconds.

FAIRCHILD 82

First Flight ....July 6, 1935
Cost New ....$18,791 plus floats
Wing Span ....51 ft. 0 in. (15.3 m)
Length ....36 ft. 10.75 in. (11 m)
Gross Weight ....6,325 lb. (2,846 kg)
Empty Weight ....3,835 lb. (1,726 kg)
Fuel Capacity ....100 imp. gal. (455 l)
Engine ....550-h.p. Pratt & Whitney Wasp S3H1
Cruise Speed ....129 mph (208 km/h)
Seating 11
Payload with Full Fuel ....3,835 lb. (1,726 kg)   empty weight
                                        720 lb. (324 kg)   fuel
                                        180 lb. (81 kg)   pilot
                                        50 lb. (23 kg)   misc.
                                        4,785 lb. (2,153 kg) total
Payload ....6,325 lb. (2,846 kg)
                                        -4,785 lb. (2,153 kg)
                                        =1,540 lb. (693 kg)

The Fairchild 82, claimed the factory, used 23 imp. gal. (105 l) per hour
fuel and had an absolute ceiling of 18,000 ft. (5,400 m).
The British Yukon Navigation Company Ltd. operated a Fairchild 82
throughout January 1936 in -50°F and complimented the manufacturer on
the heating system and absence of peculiar flying habits. Unlike pilots
farther east, Yukon pilots flew routinely at 14,000 ft. (4,200 m) and were
"...the envy of the pilots in Alaska."

FOKKER SUPER UNIVERSAL

First Flight ....June 18, 1929
Cost New ....$19,340 plus floats
Wing Span ....50 ft. 7 in. (15 m)
Length ....36 ft. 7 in. (11 m)
Gross Weight ....5,150 lb. (2,318 kg) (seaplane)
Empty Weight ....3,550 lb. (1,598 kg)
Fuel Capacity ....105 imp. gal. (478 l)
Engine ....Pratt & Whitney Wasp 410 h.p.
Cruise Speed ....98 mph (158 km/h)
Seating 8
Payload with Full Fuel ....3,550 lb. (1,598 kg)   empty weight
    756 lb. (340 kg)   fuel
    180 lb. (81 kg)   pilot
    50 lb. (23 kg)   misc.
    4,536 lb. (2,041 kg)   total
Payload ....5,150 lb. (2,318 kg)
    -4,536 lb. (2,041 kg)
    =614 lb. (276 kg)

Right-hand cabin door installed in Canadian version.

Original cabins were fitted with velour and mahogany veneer and had a volume of 194 cu. ft. (5.8 m^3)

In 1929, Canadian Vickers of Montreal began building Fokker Super Universals under license.

Only one Fokker Super Universal exists and has been rebuilt by Clark Seaborne in Calgary for Winnipeg's Western Canada Aviation Museum.

BELLANCA 31-55 SENIOR SKYROCKET

First Prototype Flight ....February 28, 1946, Edmonton
Test Pilot......................................Stanley R. McMillan
Cost New ....$31,000 (on wheels less engine)
Wing Span ....50 ft. 6 in. (15 m)
Length ....27 ft. 8 in. (8 m)
Gross Weight ....6,450 lb. (2,903 kg)
Empty Weight ....4,616.3 lb. (2,077 kg)
Fuel Capacity ....145 imp. gal. (660 l)
Engine 600-h.p. R-1340
Cruise Speed ....140 mph (225 km/h)
                                            (sales brochure figure)
Seating 10
Payload with Full Fuel ....4,616.3 lb. (2,077 kg)   empty weight
                                            1,080 lb. (486 kg)   fuel
                                            180 lb. (81 kg)   pilot
                                            50 lb. (23 kg)   misc.
                                            5,743.3 lb. (2,584 kg)   total
Payload ....6,450 lb. (2,903 kg)
                                            -5,743.3 lb. (2,584 kg)
                                            =706.7 lb. (318 kg)

Thirteen built in Canada by Northwest Industries, Edmonton.
Used price from Superior Airways, Fort William, Ontario, August, 1965,
$13,500. "...rugged and beautiful in her classical way but unlike the
serene stability of the de Havillands, she could be fickle and terrifying to
the unwary who became too lax in her presence," wrote pilot Don
McLellan in April, 1990.

NOORDUYN NORSEMAN MK I

First Flight ....November 14, 1935
Cost ....$23,500 (including floats and skis)
Wing Span ....51 ft. 6 in. (15 m)
Length ....32 ft. (10 m)
Gross Weight ....6,050 lb. (2,723 kg)
Empty Weight ....3,460 lb. (1,557 kg)
Fuel Capacity ....105 imp. gal. (478 l)
Engine ....420-h.p. Wright R-975-E3 Whirlwind
Cruise Speed ....120 mph (192 km/h)
Seating 10
Payload with Full Fuel ....3,460 lb. (1,557 kg)   empty weight
       756 lb. (340 kg)   fuel
       180 lb. (81 kg)   pilot
       50 lb. (23 kg)   misc.
       4,446 lb. (2,001 kg)   total
Payload ....6,050 lb. (2,723 kg)
       -4,446 lb. (2,001 kg)
       =1,604 lb. (722 kg)

Norseman CF-AYO was featured in *Captains of the Clouds* with James Cagney. After filming, Dominion Skyways billed Warner Brothers, Burbank, California, for $3,400 in damages. RCAF technical officer Owen Cathcart-Jones pointed out that the airline had already been paid $5,300 for fifty hours flying.

On June 20, 1938, a pilot received a severe fright when an elevator torque tube at the base of the control column failed during takeoff. Total loss of elevator control occurred. The defect was remedied and CF-AYO's career extended until August 18, 1953, when it was destroyed in a fatal accident. The wreckage has been recovered for restoration by the Ontario Bushplane Heritage & Forest Fire Educational Centre in Sault Ste. Marie, Ontario.

Some early Norsemen were fitted with hydraulic flaps but pilots disliked the system's slow response. The first Norseman to have a basic screw jack teleflex mechanism installed was CF-BDD.

STINSON SR-9

First Flight 1937
Cost New $24,083
Wing Span ....41 ft. 10.5 in. (11 m)
Length ....30.3 ft. (9.1 m)
Gross Weight ....5,030 lb. (2,264 kg)
Empty Weight ....3,563 lb.(1,603 kg)
Fuel Capacity ....105 U.S. gal. (478 l)
Engine ....420-h.p. Pratt & Whitney
Cruise Speed ....130–135 mph (209–217 km/h)
Seating 5
Payload with Full Fuel ....3,563 lb. (1,603 kg)   empty weight
                                      630 lb. (284 kg)   fuel
                                      180 lb. (81 kg)   pilot
                                      50 lb. (23 kg)   misc.
                                      4,423 lb. (1,990 kg)   total
Payload ....5,030 lb. (2,264 kg)
                                      -4,423 lb. (1,990 kg)
                                      =607 lb. (273 kg)

One organization added a small ventral fin under the rear of the SR-9's fuselage. After two or three landings in rough water, said pilot Tim Taylor in Huntsville, Ontario, the ventral fin disappeared.

The SR-9s began their career with numerous engine choices beginning at 225 hp to 450 hp. The larger engines, said pilot Al R. Williams in Edmonton, made them nose heavy on landing.

One pilot began takeoffs with flaps retracted. As speed increased, he flipped a toggle switch down and the SR-9 "fairly leaped" into the air. The increased air load at 100 mph (161 km/h) raised the flaps to fifteen degrees—what he called the "required flap angle for a robust climb."

BEECHCRAFT 18A (CF-BGY)

First Flight ....January 15, 1937
Cost New ....$77,323.74 (May 21, 1940)
Wing Span ....47 ft. 8 in. (14 m)
Length ....31 ft. 11 in. (13 m)
Gross Weight ....7,170 lb. (3,227 kg)
Empty Weight ....4,742 lb. (2,134 kg)
Fuel Capacity ....133 imp. gal. (605 l)
Engine ....Wright R760-E-2 320–350 h.p.
Cruise Speed ....160 mph (258 km/h) (wheels only)
Seating 9
Payload with Full Fuel ....4,742 lb. (2,134 kg)   empty weight
                                                    959 lb. (432 kg)   fuel
                                                    180 lb. (81 kg)   pilot
                                                    50 lb. (23 kg)   misc.
                                                    5,931 lb. (2,669 kg)   total
Payload ....7,170 lb. (3,227 kg)
                                                    -5,931 lb. (2,669 kg)
                                                    =1,239 lb. (558 kg)

Floats, fittings and ventral fin weighed 840 lb. (378 kg).
Ski undercarriage weighed 724 lb. (326 kg).
Landing speed on wheels, said *Aero Digest,* Feb. 1937, was 58 mph (93 km/h).
Romeo Vachon of Canadian Airways, Winnipeg, said that the "Twin Motored Beechcraft" needed ballast in the back of the cabin when flying with less than three passengers.

BEECHCRAFT D18S

First Flight ....April 26, 1946
Cost $125,000 (1994)
Wing Span ....47 ft. 7 in. (14 m)
Length ....34 ft. 2.75 in. (10 m)
Gross Weight ....8,725 lb. (3,926 kg)
Empty Weight ....6,230 lb. (2,804 kg)
Fuel Capacity ....235 imp. gal. (1,069 l)
Engine ....450-h.p. Pratt & Whitney Wasp Jr R-985
Cruise Speed ....130 knots
Seating 8
Payload with Full Fuel ....6,230 lb. (2,804 kg)   empty weight
                                                   1,692 lb. (761 kg)   fuel
                                                   180 lb. (81 kg)   pilot
                                                   50 lb. (23 kg)   misc.
                                                   8,152 lb. (3,668 kg)   total
Payload ....8,725 lb. (3,926 kg)
                                                   -8,152 lb.(3,668 kg)
                                                   =573 lb. (258 kg)

Beechcraft 18 seaplanes such as C-FZRI of Rusty Myers Flying Service in Fort Frances, Ontario, climb fully loaded at 125 knots and 700 ft. (210 m) per min.

In cruise, seaplane Beechcraft burn 21 imp. gal. (96 l) per hr. per engine.

In 1988, most charter operators charged $3.25 per mi.

Seaplane Beechcraft 18s must have an overhead escape hatch installed. Rough water operation, said AME Robert Kortz of Gimli, Manitoba, caused sagging engine mounts and broken cowl gills. On one occasion, both engines fell off after a hard landing.

Six 45 imp. gal. (205 l) drums of stove oil were not an unusual long distance load, one pilot recalled.

FAIRCHILD F-11-1 HUSKY

First Flight ....June 14, 1946
Cost New $36,505
Wing Span ....54 ft. 9 in. (16 m)
Length ....37 ft. 5 in. (11 m)
Gross Weight ....6,300 lb. (2,835 kg)
Empty Weight ....3,900 lb. (1755 kg)
Fuel Capacity ....96 imp. gal. (437 l)
Engine ....450-h.p. Pratt & Whitney Wasp
Cruise Speed ....123.7 mph (199 km/h)
Seating 10
Payload with Full Fuel ....3,900 lb. (1755 kg)   empty weight
                                          691 lb. (311 kg)   fuel
                                          180 lb. (81 kg)   pilot
                                          50 lb. (23 kg)   misc.
                                          4,827 lb. (2,172 kg) total
Payload ....6,300 lb. (2,835 kg)
                                          - 4,827 lb. (2,172 kg)
                                          = 1,473 lb. (663 kg)

Husky CF-BQC is believed to be the only model with manual flaps.
Alvis Leonides Huskies used three-blade de Havilland propellers.
Some publications claim original Wasp-powered Huskies had 6,800 lb.
gross weights.
The last commercial Husky CF-EIM was flown by North Coast Air
Service, Prince Rupert, British Columbia. After sinking in rough seas, it
was salvaged by British Columbia's Canadian Museum of Flight &
Transportation for restoration.

DE HAVILLAND DHC-2 BEAVER

First Flight ....August 16, 1947
Cost New $21,000
Wing Span ....48 ft. (14 m)
Length ....30 ft. (9 m)
Gross Weight ....5,090 lb. (2,291 kg) (seaplane)
Empty Weight ....3,316 lb. (1,492 kg) (seaplane)
Fuel Capacity ....79 imp. gal. (359 l)
Engine ....450 hp Pratt & Whitney Wasp Jr.
R-985 SB-3
Cruise Speed ....98 knots
Seating 7
Payload with Full Fuel ....3,316 lb. (1,492 kg)   empty weight
568.8 lb. (256 kg)   fuel
180 lb. (81 kg)   pilot
50 lb. (23 kg)   misc.
4,114.8 lb. (1,852 kg)   total
Payload ....5,090 lb. (2,291 kg)
-4,114.8 lb.(1,852 kg)
=975.2 lb. (439 kg)

On wheels, the Beaver can be landed as slow as thirty-nine knots and as a seaplane, as short as 702 ft. (211 m) in zero wind.
A Canadian aircraft maintenance engineer said de Havilland Beaver parts have become extremely expensive because spares are becoming scarce and are being hoarded.
In 1993, a Beaver sold for $240,000.
The oil tank is filled from inside the cabin. While taxiing for takeoff, one pilot noticed his passenger removing the cap. The American believed it to be an ash tray.

DE HAVILLAND DHC-3 OTTER

First Flight ....December 12, 1951
Test Pilot.....................................George Neal
Cost New ....$80,000 (wheels)
Wing Span ....58 ft. (17 m)
Length ....41 ft. 10 in. (13 m)
Gross Weight ....8,000 lb. (3,600 kg)
Empty Weight ....5,104 lb. (2,297 kg) (seaplane)
Fuel Capacity ....178 imp. gal. (810 l)
Engine ....600-h.p. Pratt & Whitney Wasp R-1340
Cruise Speed ....110 knots (seaplane)
Seating ....16 (Dept. of Transport doc. June 1, 1959)
Payload with Full Fuel ....5,104 lb. (2,297 kg)   empty weight
                         1,281.6 lb. (577 kg)   fuel
                         180 lb. (81 kg)   pilot
                         50 lb. (23 kg)   misc.
                         6,615.6 lb. (2,977 kg)   total
Payload ....8,000 lb. (3,600 kg)
                         -6,615.6 lb. (2,977 kg)
                         =1,384.4 lb. (623 kg)

Ontario's Department of Lands & Forests standardized with three-man fire attack crews plus tents, axes, hoses, etc., to 1,615 lb. (727 kg). With reduced equipment, it was common to dispatch five-man fire fighting groups.
Early gross weights of Otters were 7,200 lb. (3,240 kg).
One de Havilland Otter, CF-ODJ, is known to have had a Lear L-2 autopilot installed for aerial photography in April, 1954.

FOUND FBA-2C

First Flight ....May 9, 1962
Cost New ....$24,849 (floats & skis)
Wing Span ....36 ft. (11 m)
Length ....26 ft. 5 in. (8 m)
Gross Weight ....3,000 lb. (1,350 kg)
Empty Weight ....1,891.5 lb. (851 kg)
Fuel Capacity ....56 imp. gal. (255 l)
Engine ....Lycoming 250-h.p. 0-540-A
Cruise Speed ....115 mph (185 km/h)
Seating 5
Payload with Full Fuel:................1,891.5 lb. (851 kg)   empty weight
                                                     403.2 lb. (181 kg)   fuel
                                                     180 lb. (81 kg)   pilot
                                                     50 lb. (23 kg)   misc.
                                                     2,524.7 lb. (1,136 kg)   total
Payload: ....3,000 lb. (1,350 kg)
                                                     -2,524.7 lb. (1,136 kg)
                                                     =475.3 lb. (214 kg)

Found CF-OZV went from the industry to Centennial College in Toronto
and finally to the National Aviation Museum by 1979.
When FBA-2Cs reached Canadian operators, Cessna had already
produced and sold nearly 650 Model 180s in Canada during an eight-year
period.
An Ontario company appreciated the Found FBA-2C's 120 cu. ft. (3.6
m^3) cabin. Pilots and helpers collected empty beer cases from fishing and
hunting lodges and cashed them in.
A northern Saskatchewan Found owner "bulled" a 45 imp. gal. (205 l)
drum of fuel inside as well as ten 10 imp. gal. (46 l) gas kegs—totaling
over 1,100 lb. (495 kg).

1977 MODEL 180K SKYWAGON

First Flight ....1953 (type approval granted 1952)
Cost New ....$12,950 (1953) plus floats
Wing Span ....36 ft. (11 m)
Length ....25 ft. 7.5 in. (8 m)
Gross Weight ....2,800 lb. (1,260 kg)
Empty Weight ....1,648 lb. (742 kg)
Fuel Capacity ....80 U.S. gal. standard tanks (364 l)
Engine ....Teledyne Continental
O-470-U 230 h.p. at 2400 rpm
Cruise Speed ....142 knots
(Book wheel cruise at 75 percent power)
Seating 4
Payload with Full Fuel ....1,648 lb. (742 kg)   empty weight
480 lb. (216 kg)   full fuel
180 lb. (81 kg)   pilot
50 lb. (23 kg)   misc.
2,358 lb. (1,061 kg)   total
Payload ....2,800 lb. (1,260 kg)
-2,358 lb. (1,061 kg)
=442 lb. (199 kg)

6,193 built in Wichita, Kansas.
Cessna claimed the rear seat could be converted to a quarter-ton cargo area in "just six minutes, fifty-seven seconds."
Production terminated in 1981.

CESSNA 185

First Flight 1961
Cost New $18,950
Wing Span ....36 ft. (11 m)
Length ....25.6 ft. (8 m)
Gross Weight ....3,200 lb. (1,440 kg) (wheels)
Empty Weight ....1,520 lb. (684 kg)
Fuel Capacity ....84 U.S. gal. (382 l)
Engine ....260-h.p. Continental IO-470-F
Cruise Speed ....130 mph (209 km/h)
Seating 6
Payload with Full Fuel.................1,520 lb. (684 kg)   empty weight
                                                      504 lb. (227 kg)   fuel
                                                      180 lb. (81 kg)   pilot
                                                      50 lb. (23 kg)   misc.
                                                      2,254 lb. (1,014 kg) total
Payload ....3,200 lb. (1,440 kg)
                                                     -2,254 lb.(1,014 kg)
                                                     =946 lb. (426 kg)

3,859 built.
Larger dorsal fin than Cessna 180 to compensate for extra engine power.
Most pilots use twenty degrees flap for seaplane takeoffs.
Standard price in September, 1982: $78,450.

CESSNA 206 (WHEELS)

First Flight	1964	
Cost New	$22,950 (1966)	
Wing Span	36.7 ft. (11 m)	
Length	27.8 ft. (8 m)	
Gross Weight	3,300 lb. (1,485 kg)	
Empty Weight	1,705 lb. (767 kg)	
Fuel Capacity	65 U.S. gal. (296 l)	
Engine	285-h.p. Continental IO-520-A	
Cruise Speed at 75 percent	166 mph (267 km/h)	
Seating	6	
Payload with Full Fuel	1,705 lb. (767 kg)	empty weight
	390 lb. (176 kg)	fuel
	180 lb. (81 kg)	pilot
	50 lb. (23 kg)	misc.
	2,325 lb. (1,046 kg)	total
Payload	3,300 lb. (1,485 kg)	
	- 2,325 lb. (1,046 kg)	
	= 975 lb. (439 kg)	

2,480 built in Wichita, Kansas.
Double cargo door on right side/no door for pilot.
Electric slow running flaps.
1983 price for Cessna 310-h.p. T-Stationair 6: $101,700.

Glossary

ADF—Automatic direction finder. Low-priced electronic device used to home in on low-frequency navigation beacons.

AILERONS—control surfaces on aircraft wings. One deflects up and the other down when the pilot moves control column or stick to effect a banking attitude.

AIR LOCKS—Occasionally air becomes trapped in fuel lines through thermal expansion. Results in sputtering or complete engine failure.

AIRFOIL—A device obtaining a useful reaction from air moving over it, i.e. a wing.

ALVIS LEONIDES—Aero engine manufacturer originally headquartered in Coventry, England and founded in 1935. One model was selected to upgrade the Fairchild Husky.

AVRO—British aircraft manufacturing firm founded by A.V. Roe in 1908. In the early 1960s, Avro was merged into Hawker Siddeley.

AVRO ANSON—General purpose twin engine aircraft originally known as the Avro 652 when it flew a maiden flight at Woodford, England in 1935. After World War II, bush airlines snapped them up at surplus prices. The Canadian-built MK V model flew on skis but, its wooden airframe could not stand the strains of northern operations.

BAFFLES—When aircraft banked or skidded during turns, fuel sometimes sloshed away from the outlet valve to the engine. Consequently, the engine stopped. Also refers to metal plates installed on the front of engine to reduce cold air flow.

BAG TANKS—Many airplanes manufacturers installed rubber gasoline cells inside wings. Damage occurs when fuel handlers puncture the rubber with gasoline nozzles.

BAKELITE—Hard plastic-like material used for airplane flooring.

BALANCE—With too much weight in the rear of an aircraft, the airplane flies extremely tail heavy to the point that a pilot would be unable to control the attitude.

BALL JOINT—Ball-shaped end of a strut or rod that is allowed to pivot.

BEECH—Beech Aircraft Corporation was founded in 1932 by Walter and Olive Ann Beech, a husband-wife team. Known initially for its "Staggerwing" cabin biplanes, Beech today focuses on constructing business airplanes.

BEECHCRAFT KING AIR—Turbine-powered twin first flown on January 24, 1964, in Wichita, Kansas. Designed exclusively for business executives, they became popular as charter airplanes. Over 5,000 have been produced.

BIPLANES—Aircraft with an upper and lower pair of wings. Most have only one set of ailerons. Some biplanes are produced today for agricultural purposes or aerobatics competition.

BLOWPOTS—A portable blast burner, still used occasionally. Gasoline-fed blowpots were required winter equipment to preheat airplane engines. Left unattended, they caused many fires.

BLUEBERRY BLONDE—Slang for a person with black hair.

BMW—Founded in 1916, the Bayerische Motoren Werke A. G. originally produced six-cylinder airplane engines with oversize cylinders and high compression ratios. One model powered the Junkers Ju 52 but it could not endure Canadian cold and was replaced by a British Rolls-Royce.

BOAT—Refers to aircraft which land only on water and never have retractable wheels. Some pilots use the term "straight" boat when referring to types like the Curtiss HS-2L.

BOOST—Measure of engine power often expressed in inches of manifold pressure. Most pilots use 35-inches of boost for takeoff in the de Havilland Beaver.

BOREAL FORESTLAND—Northern forest, above the prairies and east of the Rocky Mountains to Labrador covers a quarter of Canada. Consisting mainly of balsam, spruce and jackpine, it is home to numerous Native settlements supplied almost entirely by bushplanes until the 1970s.

BOW STRUTS—Usually refers to baars or supports joining both sides of a pair of seaplane floats.

BOX SPARS—Square or rectangular-shaped poles extending from wing tip to wing tip and providing the wing's main strength. Usually hollow.

BRASS—Sheeting used on ski bottoms. Durable, it slid easily across the snow. Mechanics also make or buy a special brass screwdriver for adjusting compasses.

BULK HAULING—Occurs when a bushplane's cabin runs out of space before reaching maximum gross weight. A load of bread would "bulk out" quicker than heavy compact freight like drill rods or cement bags.

BUNGEE—Rubber shock cords used in landing gear of airplanes such as Piper PA-18 Super Cubs.

CANADIANIZE—Few airplanes were designed to handle the northland's rough climatic conditions. As a result, mechanics often improvised. Sometimes, Canadianization included removing superfluous items like window shades, toilets or heavy upholstered seats. The name of the game, said one pilot, was to carry payload; forget the comfort.

CANTILEVER—Wing without external supporting struts. Strength came from double spars, often box types, inside the structure.

CARGO DROPPING—To drop supplies, de Havilland's Beavers and Otters were manufactured with permanent circular holes in the rear. Most dropping took place with parachutes although forest-fire-fighting agencies often free-dropped items such as shovels or hose.

CESSNA—One of the world's largest manufacturers of light aircraft, based in Wichita, Kansas. Founded in 1927 by Clyde Cessna.

CESSNA 170—Four-place tailwheel airplane introduced to Canada in 1948. Price was $6,600 for a standard model. It had a six-cylinder Continental engine and carried 30 gallons of gasoline. Top speed, said *Canadian Aviation* magazine, was 140 miles per hour.

CESSNA T-50—A five-seat civil business twin-engine airplane first flown on March 26, 1939. In World War II, the RCAF ordered 826 "Crane" models powered with 245-h.p. Jacobs engines and wooden propellers. One sold as late as the 1960s for $5,000 on floats.

CHANGE-OVER—In spring, airplanes are switched from skis to seaplane floats. Before winter, floats are exchanged again for skis.

CHECKOUTS—Normally refers to in-flight and ground familiarization of a pilot with a new type of airplane.

CHEWING THEIR WAY—Propellers of early airplanes turned so slowly that individual blades could be seen at certain angles. To observers watching a lumbering type such as the Curtiss HS-2L, it appeared as if the airplane gobbled chunks of air and pushed them back to stay airborne.

CHROMATE—Chemical paintlike compound applied to metal parts to reduce corrosion. Usually green or yellow.

CHUCK—A body of water, usually calm and sheltered. Preferred by coastal pilots for landing and takeoff.

COACH-WORK—Airplane manufacturers of the 1930s compared their products to automobiles which some people still called coaches. Wood trim was common and although it may have looked fashionable, air service owners did not appreciate unnecessary weight.

COMFORT STATION—Slang term for lavatory.

COMMERCIAL LICENSEA commercial pilot license had to be obtained before anyone could earn a living flying airplanes. It was preceded by a private certificate which allowed a holder to carry passengers in airplanes of a certain weight category.

CONSTANT SPEED PROPELLER—Propeller which maintains a constant blade angle selected by the pilot. Usually hydraulically operated by oil pressure but may be electric.

CONTROL WHEEL—See control column.

CONTROL COLUMN—Most early airplanes were controlled by a stick referred to as the "joystick." To turn left or right, the pilot pushed it in the appropriate direction.

COWL—Usually the front portion of the engine covers directly behind the propeller, e.g., nose cowl.

COWLING—The forward portion of an airplane enclosing the engine.

CRANE—See Cessna T-50.

CURTISS—Founded in 1909 by Glenn Curtiss and Augustus Herring as the Curtiss-Herring Company, Curtiss was one of the oldest builders of aircraft in the United States. Its most famous airplanes included the Jenny. In 1929, Curtiss merged with the Wright Aeronautical Company to form the Curtiss-Wright Company.

CYLINDER FINS—Piston engine cylinders were built with metal cooling fins extending into the airstream.

DIRECT DRIVE—Engine starter system which immediately turns the propeller over when the pilot selects the start switch.

DOGRIB—Group of Natives whose ancestors inhabited the area between Great Bear and Great Slave Lake. The name derives from a legend describing their descent from a dog.

DOPE-COVERED—Refers to a protective sealing substance applied to the fabric-covering of an airplane.

DOUGLAS DC-3—The first DC-3 flew on December 17, 1935. By 1946, they began pouring into Canada as commercial and military transports. As bush transports, they excelled wherever airstrips could be built. Powered by two 1200-h.p. Pratt & Whitney R-1830 engines, they averaged 26,900 pounds gross takeoff weight and landed as short as 800 feet.

DRAG-INDUCING—Unstreamlined objects produced certain types of drag and slowed an airplane. Antennae, steps, struts and skis or floats took their toll on airspeed.

DRILL CORE—Mining exploration companies sample potential ore-bearing areas by extracting circular rock cores. Placed in flat wood boxes for transport.

DRIVER—Euphemistic term for bush pilots, usually in reference to hardy individuals who flew Noorduyn Norsemen with any load in any weather.

DROP THE FLAPS—Some flap types produce lift up to a specified setting beyond which they create drag. For shorter takeoffs, the de Havilland Otter use a setting marked takeoff flap. Full flap attains extremely short landing runs.

DROP SPEED—Indicated airspeed beyond which water bombing drop doors must not be opened because of excessive strain on the mechanism.

ELEVATOR—Movable airfoil attached to an airplane's tail. It produces upward or downward pitch, i.e., nose up or nose down, when the pilot uses the control column or wheel.

FABRIC-COVERED—Most early airplanes were covered with cloth fabric, usually linen or cotton, and treated with dope. In 1964, lincoln cloth from Millhaven, Ontario, became popular. Other modern synthetic fibers such as ceconite have also entered the market.

FLAPS—Extension of the wing to modify lift characteristics. During takeoff and approach to land, they provide extra lift. When selected full down, they create drag and reduce forward speed.

FLARE—Sometimes refers to magnesium units dropped by parachute during night emergencies to enable landing. Also refers to the point at which a pilot stops his glide and raises the airplane nose to slow forward speed before touching down.

FLIGHT WATCH SYSTEM—System in which ground personnel must be contacted by a pilot each time he lands. Also refers to monitoring an airplane's progress by radio to ensure someone knows the location at all times.

FLYING BOXCAR—Popular nickname for the gigantic Junkers Ju 52 flown by Canadian Airways. Its bare interior resembled the inside of a railway boxcar except for several windows and loading doors.

FOKKER—European aircraft manufacturer, founded by Anthony H. G. Fokker before World War I. Fokker produced fighters for both world wars.

FUEL SLOSH—Refers to the tendency of gasoline to move freely in a fuel tank unless slowed by baffles.

FUSELAGE—Body of an airplane minus wings and tail.

GLASSY WATER—Dangerous condition when it is impossible to judge altitude when landing on a lake during windless days. Power assisted, nose-up approaches and more distance are required.

GLIDE RATIO—Used as a measure to determine how far an airplane glides with the engine stopped. Gliders have extremely high glide ratios because of long tapered wings.

GRAB BARS—Some early airplanes did not have seat belts but only bars to hold during flight.

GROSS WEIGHT—Weight of the airplane including pilot, load, gasoline and equipment the moment before takeoff.

GROUND LOOP—Occurs on landing or takeoff when the pilot loses control and runs off the runway. More common in tailwheel landings when the tail wheel does not remain in contact with the ground and loses steering capability.

GRUMMAN—American aircraft manufacturing company founded in 1929 by Leroy Grumman in New York. The company specialized in naval fighters.

GRUMMAN (S2F) TRACKER—Developed by Grumman Aircraft Engineering Corp. in Long Island, N.Y. and first flown on December 4, 1952, this twin-engine airplane was powered by nine-cylinder Wright R-1820 engines. In 1970 and 1971, Ontario's Ministry of Natural Resources converted several to fire-bombing configuration. The Province of Saskatchewan still flies several on forest-fire-fighting duties.

GRUMMAN TBM AVENGER—Single-engine, ex-torpedo bomber first flown in August, 1941. In May, 1950, they entered service with the RCAF but were phased out ten years later. Converted to fire bombers, they became popular in British Columbia and kept water bombing Fairchild Huskies and de Havilland Beavers out of the province's forest fire activities.

H-BOAT—Nickname for the Curtiss HS-2L flying boat.

HAMILTON METALPLANE—All metal type produced by a branch of Boeing in the United States. The Ontario Provincial Air Service, the only Canadian users of this type, owned four in 1930 at a purchase price of $38,000 each. The last one went to Alaska in 1944.

HANDSTARTING—Most early airplanes did not have starters. The author, for example, learned to fly on a small two-seat tailwheel trainer called an Aeronca 7AC. It had to be started by standing in front of the engine and swinging the propeller by hand.

HEADLESS VALLEY OF THE YUKON—Valley opening at Nahanni Butte, Northwest Territories, and leading northwestward into an area of hot springs and orchids which formed the basis for legends of a lost tropical valley and gold mine. Thirty mysterious deaths have been reported and several headless bodies found.

HEAT-TREATED—Metals are heated for additional strength to specific temperatures and cooled at a predetermined rate.

HELL DAMNERS—Slang for Noorduyn Norseman, thought to have been coined by aircraft maintenance engineer Nelson Scutt of Kenora, Ontario.

HERMAN—Large type of gasoline-powered heater called the Herman Nelson. It is used extensively by air services operating in cold climates to preheat engines.

HORIZONTALLY OPPOSED—Engine type with horizontally arranged cylinders. The modern Cessna series all have horizontally opposed or "flat" engines.

HUDSON STRAIT EXPEDITION—A 1927-1928 air and sea expedition to find a northern water route for exporting Canadian grain to Europe. Six Fokker Universals and a de Havilland Moth were included and flown between the southwest side of Baffin Island and Arctic Quebec.

INERTIA STARTER—Starter in which the pilot selects a switch to spin an inertial device. At a certain tone, the unit will not spin higher and he engages a clutch to turn the propeller. Most inertia starter airplanes had their units replaced with direct drive types.

JUNKERS—German aircraft manufacturer, founded in 1895 by Hugo Junkers, which in 1915 built the world's first all-metal aircraft.

LEAR L-2—Brand of autopilot selected by the Ontario Department of Lands & Forest for photosurvey de Havilland Otter CF-ODJ.

LIBERTY ENGINE—A U.S. aircraft engine developed in 1917, said to have been designed and built in just three months following the United States' entry into World War I.

LINE CUTTERS—Men who cut presurveyed lines through bush country for roads, power lines or mine sites.

LOCKHEED VEGA—Sleek, single engine cantilever monoplane, the Vega was the type flown by Silas Alwyard Cheesman in the Antarctic in December, 1929.

MAINPLANES—Main lifting surface or wings of an airplane exclusive of struts.

MANIFOLD PRESSURE—Measure of engine power in inches of mercury. A de Havilland Beaver, for example, takes off with 35 inches of manifold pressure.

METALLIZE—Some fabric-covered airplanes such as the Noorduyn Norseman or Stinson SR-10s had wings and fuselage recovered with metal. In most cases, the weight of the metallized version proved less than fabric models.

MICROSWITCH—Small electrical switch. In some airplanes, this switch makes contact on touchdown to prevent accidental retraction of landing gear.

MIXTURE CONTROL—Cockpit control used by the pilot to adjust the ratio of gasoline to air in the carburetor for efficient fuel burning and consumption.

MOCK-UP—Before assembling a prototype airplane, most manufacturers build full-size models to test seating, doors and provide customers with a concept of the final product.

MODS—Slang abbreviation for modification to an airplane.

MONOPLANE—Airplane with one wing, i.e., one on each side of the fuselage.

MOTH, DE HAVILLAND—De Havilland Aircraft Company Ltd. was formed on September 25, 1920, in Great Britain and went on to build numerous successful designs named after animals and birds. A series of biplanes called Moths flew in Canada and a Canadian manufacturing plant was established at Downsview, Ontario.

MULESKINNERS—Originally coined to describe men who drove mule teams but adapted to include hardy individuals in charge of mechanical bulldozers.

NASA/NRC—National Aeronautics & Space Administration of the U.S.A. and Canada's National Research Council often share aeronautical information.

OBSERVER—During the Curtiss HS-2L's hey-day, these men rode the cockpit ahead of the pilots to sketch maps or record fire locations.

OLEO—Shock-absorbing device in which a substance is forced through a small orifice to reduce airframe stress.

OUTFITTERS—Specialists catering to tourist traffic who usually have camps or tourist lodges at fly-in lakes. They rarely depend on winter customers but spend off seasons traveling to sports shows and signing clients for fishing or hunting expeditions.

OUTPOST—Smaller fly-in camps, away from a tourist outfitter's main lodge. Not as luxurious but selected for hunting or fishing potential.

OVERHAUL—All airplane engines must undergo complete teardown and rebuild after a determined number of operating hours.

PACKING RING—Airplanes used felt as buffers in engine cowlings to absorb shock and provide a better seal for proper cooling.

PARACHUTE FLARES—Some airplanes carried flares which could be ejected and ignited electrically for emergency night landings. Often carried on early mailplanes.

PAYLOAD—Portion of airplane weight which earns money for the air service owner. Does not include pilot, gasoline or equipment.

PICK-UP SCOOP—See PROBE.

PIPER PA-18 SUPER CUB—First flown in November, 1949, with 95 h.p., the two-seat Super Cub progressed to 150 h.p. in 1954. Noted for exceptional STOL capabilities, Super Cubs with balloon tires were flown throughout the High Arctic.

PITCH—Movement up or down relative to the horizon and produced by easing the control column or control wheel back and forth.

PONTOON-EQUIPPED—Refers to seaplanes but is a term never used by professional pilots. Correct term is "float-equipped."

PORPOISE—Excessive fore and aft movement of an aircraft nose on landing or takeoff caused by excessive nose down attitude and control mishandling.

POWERPLANT—Airplane engine.

PRATT & WHITNEY—American builder of aircraft engines. Today part of United Technologies Corporation, Pratt & Whitney was founded in 1925 as a specialist in air-cooled radial engines.

PROBES—In water bombing airplanes, like the de Havilland DHC-3 Otter, a small rectangular square open front scoop allows water to enter containment tanks. It is lowered before or after touchdown and retracted to reduce drag for takeoff.

PROTOTYPE—Original model flown on which successive ones are patterned.

PUCK SYSTEM—Shock absorbing system in which rubber blocks are installed in landing gear to reduce stress on landing or while taxiing over rough ground.

PYRENE—Fire-extinguishing agent.

RADIAL—Engine in which cylinders are arranged in a circle around a crank shaft. The Pratt & Whitney R-985 of Beechcraft 18s and de Havilland Beavers are radials.

RADIO DESTROYER—Explosive device inside an airplane radio during wartime. It was to be used if the airplane was in danger of capture. Canadian bush operators removed them.

RAM AIR SCOOPS—Openings on the front of airplane engines. Air rammed into the scoops during flight provided engine cooling.

RED-LINED—Airplane instruments such as airspeed indicators or temperature and pressure gauges are marked with a red line to indicate maximum limits. The de Havilland Beaver airspeed indicator, for example, is red-lined at 180 mph.

RELIEF TUBE—Funnel-shaped device for use by male pilots when they could not land and needed to urinate.

ROLLOVER TANKS—Water dropping tanks attached to the top of a seaplane float. When activated, they roll inward or outward.

ROLLS-ROYCE—This European automobile maker, founded in 1906, began manufacturing aircraft engines in 1915.

RUDDER—Moveable airfoil at the rear of an airplane which causes the airplane to turn left or right when activated by pedals on the cockpit floor.

SAFETY GLASS—In some of the first airplanes, regular glass was used in windshields and windows. Dangerous to the extreme, it was replaced by safety glass which shattered into numerous pieces in the event of a mishap.

SAILING—When winds are too strong for a seaplane to turn, the pilot idles the engine, lowers flaps and raises water rudders to sail backwards. Raising or lowering ailerons helps provide direction.

SEAPLANE KITS—Airplanes such as Cessna 180s, 185s and 206s were not designed as seaplanes. Consequently, they required modification with extra strengthening and attachment blocks for float fittings.

SIDESLIP—To sideslip, a pilot banks the airplane in one direction. Before the nose turns in the direction of the lowered wing, opposite rudder is applied and the descent rate increases rapidly. The method is used in flapless airplanes.

SLOTTED WINGS—Wings with a narrow slot along the leading edge to provide smooth airflow over the lifting surface at lower speeds.

SLUSH—Regardless of outside air temperature, snow insulates the layer above the ice of a frozen lake. Once exposed, it freezes but the soft mixture of water and snow traps skiplanes and makes life miserable for winter bush pilots.

SMOLTS—Recently hatched fingerling fish mature enough to be planted.

SPIKING—Slang term for hand-starting an airplane.

SPRAY LINE—When the pilot applies power for a seaplane takeoff, the nose raises and a wave line spreads outward from the float. When this line stabilizes, usually about midfloat, the aircraft may be placed "on the step" to increase speed for liftoff.

SPREADER BARS—Aluminum bars joining the opposite floats of a seaplane.

STABILIZER—May be horizontal or vertical. The vertical fin and horizontal stabilizer allows the airplane to continue straight and stable flight.

STALL—Point at which an airplane drops below a certain airspeed and loses lift. It may occur at any weight or speed and varies with loading. To recover from a stall, the pilot lowers the nose to increase speed.

STINSON, KATHERINE (1891-1977)—Well-known exhibition flier before World War I. In 1913, she became the first woman to fly the mail. She toured extensively in England, China and Japan, giving flight exhibitions.

STOL—Short Takeoff and Landing. Airplanes like de Havilland Beavers and Otters are designed to takeoff and land in short distances. Fast cruise speeds are not a concern, only an ability to use confined spaces.

STONEBOAT—Nickname for the slow-flying de Havilland Otter. Derived from a wooden sledlike arrangement used by pioneers clearing their land of stones, it was dragged across the fields by horses.

STRESSED SKIN—Method of airplane construction in which strength comes from the covering itself. Cessnas and Fairchild Huskies, for example, used stressed skin construction.

STRUT-BRACED—Supporting method to add strength to an airplane wing or horizontal stabilizer. The Found FBA-2C lacked struts of any kind as opposed to the strut-braced Cessna series.

SUPERCHARGER—Device which forces air into an internal combustion engine to increase power. Also allows sea level power to be retained at higher altitudes.

SWELL PATTERN—Seaplane pilots, especially those flying from large bodies of water, understand that sometimes calmer patches will be found regardless of wind. "Calmer" is a relative term regarding wave height.

TAIL WAG—Sometimes to slow an airplane, pilots will deliberately sway the tail back and forth with rudder pedals. It also occurs when inexperienced pilots overcontrol during takeoff and landing.

TEFLON-LINED—Plasticlike material used to prevent wear on airplane components. Same substance found on household frying pans.

THROW-OVER—Single control wheel oriented toward the pilot's side. By pulling a pin, it can be released and swung to the right for familiarization during check-out flights.

TIN SNIPPERS—Derogatory term applied to airplane manufacturers who rarely see their products in the real working world.

TORQUE—Tendency of an airplane to rotate in the direction opposite to that of the propeller, especially on takeoff. May also be a slang term for increasing power or turning, e.g., "He put the torque to her and that airplane, she came off the water."

TRICYCLE GEAR—Instead of a tail wheel, most modern trainers have a wheel below the nose. Easier to land and control, "tri-gear," some veteran bush pilots say, has removed the requirement for skill.

TRIM TABS—Small surfaces attached to ailerons, elevators or rudders to reduce forces needed to maintain selected attitudes of flight.

TRIM—Verb referring to the use of the TRIM TABS.

TURBINIZATION—Refers to replacement of high-maintenance, weather-sensitive piston engines with turbine types which require less care and contain less moving parts.

TURN AND BANK INDICATOR—Cockpit instrument with a needle and ball. The needle depicts the direction of the lowered wing, and ball indicates slip or skid.

TURNAROUNDS—Airplanes in commercial service must be unloaded quickly and reloaded as soon as possible for another flight. No airplane earns revenue while sitting on the ground.

V-BRACES—Often found behind the windshield of airplanes converted to floats. Installed to reduce vibration and add strength.

VANADIUM—Silvery metallic element used as a toughening ingredient in steel landing gear legs.

VARIABLE PITCH—Propeller whose blade angle can be adjusted from the cockpit. Pilots select fine pitch for takeoff and a courser blade angle for cruise.

VICKERS—British manufacturer of armaments and airplanes, founded in 1911. In the early 1960s, the company was absorbed into the British Aircraft Corporation.

VICKERS VEDETTE—Canadian-built flying boat flown first at Montreal on November 3, 1934, this all-wood airplane had an empty weight of

2,140 pounds and 42-foot wingspan. One owned by the Ontario Provincial Air Service in 1936 had a 90-mph cruise speed with a 185-h.p. engine.

VORTICES—Whirling masses of turbulence caused by the displacement of air by an airplane during flight. Usually they are strongest at the wing-tips and consists of two counter-rotating cylindrical vortices.

WALK-ON LOAD—The pilots' dream. Refers to passengers able to board airplanes themselves. Nonwalk-on loads are freight to be tied down, untied and unloaded at destination.

WATER RUDDER—Metal rudder at the rear of a seaplane float. Used for steering on the water, they must be pulled up before takeoff. Pilots who forget, traditionally buy a case of beer or round of coffee at the Lakeview Restaurant in Red Lake, Ontario.

WHIRLWIND ENGINE—Air-cooled, radial engine produced by the Wright company beginning in 1925.

WHITEOUT—Winter condition when neither shadows, horizon nor clouds are discernible and any sense of depth and orientation disappears. Occurs when pilots attempt to cross a large lake on overcast days.

WING ROOT—Portion of a wing where it meets the fuselage of the airplane.

WOBBLE PUMP—Usually a hand pump found in airplanes such as de Havilland Beavers that increase fuel pressure and allow gasoline into the lines to ensure an engine start. Also refers to a device for transferring fuel from gasoline drums into airplanes.

ZERO TIME—All airplane engines have a limited number of hours before a major overhaul must be carried out. After overhaul or when new, they are said to be "zero-timed."

Bibliography

Aviation In Canada, by L. Milberry (Toronto: McGraw-Hill Ryerson Ltd., 1979).

Avro Aircraft Since 1908, by A. J. Jackson (London: Putnam Aeronautical Books, 1965).

Bush to Boardroom, by Duncan D. McLaren (Winnipeg: Watson & Dwyer Ltd. 1992).

Canada's Aviation Pioneers, by Alice G. Sutherland (Toronto: McGraw-Hill Ryerson Ltd., 1978).

Canada's Flying Heritage, by Frank H. Ellis (Toronto: University of Toronto Press, 1954).

Canada's National Aviation Museum, by K. M. Molson (Ottawa: National Aviation Museum, 1988).

Canadian Aircraft Since 1909, by K. M. Molson, H.A. Taylor (Stittsville: Canada's Wings, 1982).

Curtiss Aircraft 1907-1947, by Peter M. Bowers (London: Putnam Aeronautical Books, 1979).

De Havilland Aircraft Since 1909, by A. J. Jackson (Annapolis: Naval Institute Press, 1987).

The De Havilland Canada Story, by Fred W. Hotson (Toronto: Canav Books, 1983).

Fokker Aircraft Builders to the World, by Thijs Postma (New York: Jane's Incorporated, 1980).

Images of Flight, by William J. Wheeler (Willowdale: Hounslow Press, 1992).

125 Years of Canadian Aeronautics, by G. A. Fuller, J. A. Griffin, K. M. Molson (Willowdale: Canadian Aviation Historical Society, 1983).

Pioneering in Canadian Air Transport, by K. M. Molson (Winnipeg: James Richardson & Sons, Ltd., 1978).

The Snowbird Decades, by William P. Ferguson (Vancouver: Butterworth & Co., 1979).

US Civil Aircraft Vol 7, by Joseph P. Juptner (Fallbrook: Aero Publishers, Inc., 1978).